What Great Coaches Do *Differently*

Eleven Elements of Effective Coaching

Rob Haworth
Todd Whitaker

EYE ON EDUCATION
6 DEPOT WAYWEST, SUITE 106
LARCHMONT, NY 10538
(914) 833–0551
(914) 833–0761 fax
www.eyeoneducation.com

Library of Congress Cataloging-in-Publication Data

Haworth, Rob.
  What great coaches do differently : eleven elements of effective
coaching / Rob Haworth, Todd Whitaker.
      p. cm.
  Includes bibliographical references and index.
  ISBN 978-1-59667-150-8 (alk. paper)
  1. Coaching (Athletics) 2. Coaches (Athletics) 3. Coach-athlete
relationships. I. Whitaker, Todd, 1959- II. Title.
  GV711.H33 2010
  796.07′7--dc22

                                                        2010007633

10 9 8 7 6 5 4 3 2

Production services provided by
Rick Soldin, Book/Print Production Specialist
Jonesborough, TN — www.book-comp.com

Also Available from Todd Whitaker

What Great Principals Do *Differently:*
15 Things That Matter Most
Todd Whitaker

What Great Principals Do *Differently:* Study Guide

Leading School Change:
9 Strategies to Bring Everybody on Board
Todd Whitaker

Implementation Guide:
Leading School Change
Todd Whitaker

Motivating & Inspiring Teachers:
The Educational Leader's Guide for
Building Staff Morale, 2nd Ed.
Todd Whitaker, Beth Whitaker, and Dale Lumpa

Seven Simple Secrets:
What the Best Teachers Know and Do!
Annette Breaux and Todd Whitaker

What Great Teachers Do *Differently:*
14 Things That Matter Most
Todd Whitaker

What Great Teachers Do *Differently:* Study Guide

Great Quotes For Great Educators
Todd Whitaker and Dale Lumpa

What Great Teachers Do *Differently* **DVD**
What Great Principals Do *Differently* **DVD**
Featuring Todd Whitaker

What Great Teachers Do *Differently* **Audio CD**
What Great Principals Do *Differently* **Audio CD**
Featuring Todd Whitaker

More from Todd Whitaker

50 Ways To Improve Student Behavior:
Simple Solutions to Complex Challenges
Annette Breaux and Todd Whitaker

50 Ways To Improve Student Behavior: Study Guide

Dealing With Difficult Parents:
(And With Parents in Difficult Situations)
Todd Whitaker and Douglas Fiore

Dealing With Difficult Teachers:
Second Edition
Todd Whitaker

Teaching Matters:
Motivating and Inspiring Yourself
Todd Whitaker and Beth Whitaker

The 4 Core Factors For School Success
Todd Whitaker and Jeffrey Zoul

Six Types of Teachers:
Recruiting, Retaining & Mentoring The Best
Douglas Fiore and Todd Whitaker

**FEELING GREAT! The Educator's Guide For
Eating Better, Exercising Smarter & Feeling Your Best**
Todd Whitaker and Jason Winkle

Invite Todd Whitaker to speak to your group!
E-mail **t-whitaker@indstate.edu**
Call **(812) 237-2904**
Or visit **www.toddwhitaker.com**

What they're saying about
What Great Coaches Do *Differently*

"This book isn't just about sports. This book is about life".
—Frank Hamblen, *Assistant Coach, Los Angeles Lakers*

"Many think that coaching is only about X's and O's. While that is important, there is so much more to being a great coach. This book can serve as a guide for all coaches, both new and experienced."
—Coach Tom Beach, *Two Time Indiana High School State Basketball Champion*

"**What Great Coaches Do *Differently*** reveals the true joy of coaching, teaching, and changing the lives of young people in a positive ways. All coaches at every level should do themselves and their players a favor and read this book."
—Tim Flannery, *Assistant Director, National Federation of State High School Associations and Director, NFHS Coach Education Program*

"**What Great Coaches Do *Differently*** creatively relates the values of interscholastic athletic programs and ties those values to education. The book defines the role of the coach and how the coach best serves his or her athletes by teaching the values of participation in sport."
—Robert B. Gardner, *President, National Federation of State High School Associations*

"This is a great book for any coach who wants to positively impact athletes and leave a legacy that spans generations. It is a tool that will not only help you be a better coach, but also a better person."
—Donna Noonan, *FCA Vice President and former Golf Coach, University of South Carolina*

"This book cleverly demonstrates for coaches at all levels how to be successful both on and off the field of athletic competition."
—Jim Carr, *President and CEO, National Association of Intercollegiate Athletics*

Contents

Acknowledgments

Rob would like thank his wife Amy for her support and help with the editing. He would also like to thank Olivia and Eric, who provided inspiration throughout the writing of this book.

Special thanks to Mike Blackburn, Associate Executive Director for the National Interscholastic Athletic Administrator's Association, and to Tim Flannery, Assistant Director of the National Federation of State High Schools Association, and Director of the Coach Education Program, for assisting in identifying great coaches and athletic administrators. Finally, we want to acknowledge the great coaches we have had the opportunity to play for, coach with, and coach against.

Rob Haworth and Todd Whitaker

About the Authors

Dr. Rob Haworth is a vice president for the National Association of Intercollegiate Athletics (NAIA) and Director of the Champions of Character program. The Champions of Character program provides character education to coaches, athletes, and parents at all levels of sport participation. The goal of the program is to improve the culture of sport. Rob, who is recognized as an up-and-coming leader in the field of character-driven athletics, has made several presentations at the local, state, and national levels. He is married to Amy. They are the parents of Olivia and Eric.

Prior to joining the NAIA in July 2008, Rob spent 20 years in public education. During that time, he served as a school district superintendent, assistant superintendent, athletic director and teacher. Rob's duties also included many years as a high school baseball and basketball coach. He is a graduate of Greenville College, Illinois, where he competed in cross-country and track and field. He holds a master's degree in education from Indiana University and a doctorate in philosophy in educational leadership from Indiana State University.

Dr. Todd Whitaker has been fortunate to be able to blend his passion with his career. Recognized as a leading presenter in the field of education, his message about the importance of teaching has resonated with hundreds of thousands of educators around the world. Todd is a professor of educational leadership at Indiana State University in Terre Haute, Indiana, and he has spent his life pursuing his love of education by researching and studying effective teachers and principals.

Before moving into higher education, he was a math teacher and basketball coach in Missouri, and he still holds a school record for most wins in a season at one of the high schools where he coached. Todd then served as a principal at the middle school, junior high, and high school levels. He was also a middle school coordinator in charge of staffing, curriculum, and technology for the opening of new middle schools.

One of the nation's leading authorities on staff motivation, teacher leadership, and principal effectiveness, Todd has written 22 educational books including the national best seller, *What Great Teachers Do Differently*. Other titles include *Dealing With Difficult Teachers, Teaching Matters, Great Quotes for Great Educators, What Great Principals Do Differently, Motivating & Inspiring Teachers*, and *Dealing With Difficult Parents*.

Todd is married to Beth, also a former teacher and principal, who is a professor of elementary education at Indiana State University. They are the parents of three children, Katherine, Madeline, and Harrison.

Introduction

In any given sports league or athletic conference, coaches have access to the same clinics and the same instructional DVD's. They have approximately the same amount of practice time as well as year in and year out access to about the same levels of athletic talent. Why is it then that some coaches succeed season after season while other coaches suffer through one losing season after another?

This book is about what great coaches do that sets them apart. Clarifying what the best coaches do, then practicing it ourselves, can lead to our own success as coaches. To clarify what great coaches do means we have to differentiate their actions from ineffective coaches. If the last five state championships, coaches conducted scouting sessions of their opponents, we might conclude that scouting leads to a state championship. However, we know this not to be true, because there are many coaches who scout their opponents but never wear a championship ring. This book is not meant to be a 12-step program to better coaching. Rather, this book frames the landscape of successful athletic teams from the perspective of great coaches. On what do they focus their attention? How do they spend their time and energy? What guides their decisions? How can we gain the same advantages?

This book flows from three different perspectives. First, Dr. Todd Whitaker's research studies on effective leadership. Dr. Whitaker has participated in a number of research studies that have examined the concept of "great and differently." Second, our joint work with several schools, districts, and athletic programs. Through years of observing, visiting and interviewing principals, athletic administrators, coaches, and athletes, we have gained insight into the attitudes and behaviors that lead to success. The third perspective is very personal: We write from our own experiences as coaches, teachers, and school administrators. We have worked with many outstanding coaches. What made them great? What kept others from reaching that level?

Dr. Whitaker's work on "great and differently" began with an examination of school principals and other educators. His work was compiled in the book **What Great Principals Do** *Differently* (2002). Before long, it became evident that great principals and great teachers share many of the same qualities. It makes sense: Part of being a great principal is to be a great teacher; part of being a great teacher is to be a great leader. Dr. Haworth, as a former doctoral student of Dr. Whitaker's, examined the effects athletic participation has on moral and social character. In examining the relationship between character and athletic participation, it became evident that the coaches were the difference makers in character development. What was found was that sports do not build character—coaches do.

Which has led us to this work, **What Great Coaches Do** *Differently.* These chapters are not dedicated to offensive and defensive tactics nor are they dedicated to athletic skill and fundamental development. These chapters focus on the beliefs and behaviors, attitudes and interactions that form the athletic triangle of athlete, coach, and parent. Learning can happen in isolation; coaching happens between people. Effective coaching calls for "people skills," and the best coaches practice those skills every day.

The format of this book is straightforward. An introductory chapter provides context on the importance of learning from the most effective coaches. A concluding chapter asks us to consider our own core beliefs. And in between are the essential elements of what effective coaches do differently. You will also find Coach Fox—a coach who would love to have success but who follows the way of many ineffective coaches.

Chapter 1

Why Look at Great?

C oaches all around the globe have access to the same stuff—the same amount of practice time, the same drills, access to basically the same information. Why is it that with all the same stuff at their disposal some coaches succeed year in and year out with almost the identical talent as other coaches whose teams struggle season after season?

To answer that question, let's look at Coach Fox, who has been the varsity coach at Orange County Jr.-Sr. High school for six seasons. Over those past six seasons Coach Fox's athletes sweat it out in the hot summer months just like all the other teams in the AAC (All-American Conference) and work all season long to improve. In fact, Coach Fox's Rumbling Sloths actually spend a little longer in preparation than most teams in their conference, which includes their cross-county rivals and defending AAC champions, the Green County Eagles. Coach Fox's team suffers through the same two-a-day conditioning drills as do the Eagles and the rest of the AAC. They attend pre-season conditioning just like the Flying Eagles and the rest of the AAC. In terms of natural talent, Coach Fox's athletes have the same natural talents as other teams in his conference. The Sloths practice the same amount of time as other conference schools. Each spring Coach Fox's coaching staff loads up the school van and heads off to attend the same clinics as the other coaches in the conference. Yet Coach Fox has never competed for the conference title. Not only that, but over the past six seasons, the Sloths have failed to post a winning season.

Why is it that while Coach Fox struggles to get players to practice on time, the Green County Flying Eagles are showing up earlier to practice and staying late? Why is it that Coach Fox's athletes have their heads down after a mistake, and the Flying Eagles keep their heads up and move on to the next play? Why is that Coach Fox's athletes are concerned about playing time, but the Green County High athletes continually demonstrate a sense of loyalty to the team concept? Why is it that Coach Fox fails while the Eagles reach new heights? Maybe it's the coach!

Dr. Todd Whitaker, co-author of this book and a former basketball coach, teacher, and school administrator, has been studying "great and differently" for years. His studies have yielded many interesting insights by asking one simple question: What do the greatest do differently?

For example, if four outstanding coaches hang an inspirational quote on the locker room bulletin board—"Play Like a Champion Today!"—we might conclude that one key to effective coaching is an inspiring quote posted in the locker room. However, what if less effective coaches display the same banner? The quote itself then does not guarantee success. So what are the effective coaches doing differently than other coaches? Of course it does not mean that you should not post inspirational messages in your locker room or that you must copy everything great coaches do. But the practices of great coaches do not get in the way of their success—and others can learn from them.

A valuable component of Dr. Whitaker's work has shown that greatness is composed of a wide variety of skills. In his informal observation and interviews, he has identified differences between the more effective and the less effective professionals. We have applied the same principles to coaches. Of course, he found some identical behaviors that showed up in most every setting. For example, in examining what great teachers do differently, he found that almost every teacher—from the best to the worst—takes attendance. But as he sifted through his observations, he began to compile traits of the best teachers and the variables that set them apart from their less successful peers. For example, in an athletic setting almost every team stretches and warms up before practice. So what are the differences between what great coaches are doing and what Coach Fox and other less effective coaches are doing?

The Clinic

Would you spend money to see Coach Fox give a clinic on offensive and defensive philosophy? Of course not. You are not going to spend a dime of your coaching salary to hear Coach Fox. Then if not Coach Fox who would you spend money on to see at a coach's clinic? We're not talking about the athletic department's money; we're talking about your hard earned paycheck. We bet it would not be the coach whose team you beat easily during the regular season nor the coach who routinely has a losing season. No, you wouldn't spend either your money nor your time listening to either one of those coaches. Although you might argue that you should sit in on Coach Fox's clinic session to hear what not to do.

The truth is, as coaches, we already know plenty of what not to do. We know not to berate athletes in front of their teammates, not to try something during a game that we have not practiced during the course of the week, not to treat our star athlete differently than other members of the team (or should we)? We don't need to sit in on a coach's clinic to learn what not to do. As coaches, we face a number of choices, but eliminating what not to do does not move us forward.

So, who would you would spend your money to see? Coach Phil Jackson, Coach Pete Carroll, Coach Pat Summit, a coach that has been successful against you, or the coach who year in and year out has had success? Look at it this way— if you had your choice of listening to an outstanding coach, who had won championship after championship or Coach Fox, you would surely see the championship coach. As Coach Rob Haworth, I had this experience at a coaching clinic at the University of Tennessee in the 1990s. At the conclusion of the clinic session featuring the head men's coach from Appalachian State University, the host gave the coaches in attendance a choice. As coaches we could go and listen to the assistant men's coaches from the University of Tennessee, or we could sit and listen to an actual practice session for the Lady Vols. I actually think the men's coaching staff wanted to take a break because nobody moved. All 300 plus coaches stayed in their seats to listen and watch the all-time winningest coach in NCAA basketball history and one of the few college coaches with 1000 or more wins. It was really not even a choice for those coaches in attendance. In fact, I would bet that many of the coaches only came to the clinic to hear eight-time national champion coaching great, Pat Summit, head coach of the Tennessee Lady Vols basketball team.

The lesson is clear: Coaches who want to become better find value in examining what great coaches do rather than what other coaches do not do.

Self-Reflection

One challenge in any profession is the ability to self-reflect accurately. If you have ever been to a wedding reception and watched people dance, then you know exactly what I mean. There are some individuals at the wedding reception who move gracefully around the dance floor and then there are those who couldn't dance the hokey-pokey or the chicken dance. The only problem is that the hokey-pokey, solid gold dancer doesn't know he's bad. In any organization, those who know how they are coming across to others, that is, how their behavior is received, work more effectively than those who do not. We all struggle to achieve this self-awareness, but all too often we fall short. In the studies of educators described earlier, practically all thought they were doing a great job; but only some of them were right. Effective coaches have the ability to self-reflect.

Throughout our careers we have known several ineffective coaches who think they are great coaches. These coaches see themselves as Krzyzewski, Paterno, or La Russa when in fact they are Coach Fox. They have an image of themselves that does not match how they come across to others, and just like their fellow educators in the classroom, most are doing the best they can.

The Curse of Previous Knowledge

They are doing the best they can because it is all they know how to do. They use those methods and practices they were taught as an athlete or as an assistant coach as their guide on how to be a coach. They, like all of us, call upon previous knowledge when confronted with a new task—previous knowledge that does not always serve us as we would have hoped.

Take former educator of the year, Guy Doud (1998) for example. Guy tells of a situation in which he called upon previous knowledge only to have it end up as one of his most embarrassing moments. As the story goes, Guy was a young lad in middle school attending his first physical education class. This class required that all young middle school boys wear an athletic supporter (jock strap). Now Guy was an overweight student, who went to his first PE class having never worn a jock. As he opened up his leather gym bag with the white plastic handles attached to the side, he found his jock still in its blue and yellow box. Guy opened the box and pulled out his jock strap. Now Guy, who had never worn a jock strap before, pulled it out of its box and called upon a tried and true method that had never failed him before. That tried and true method was something he had heard ever since he was able to put his clothes on by himself—the tag goes in the back. Unfortunately for Guy, the tag for a jock strap is in the front. What was an embarrassing and frustrating moment for Guy Doud can also be a frustrating time for young coaches who have only previous knowledge to work from. Not that they are going to put their jock on backwards, but that they miss out on an opportunity to become a more effective coach.

Effective coaches understand the concept of the curse of previous knowledge and attempt to not let it hinder their performance. They understand this concept is a powerful force, as well it should be, because all of education depends upon it.

Read the following passage and while you are reading it count the number of "F's."

In his book, "Efficient Filing Systems," Peter R. Robertson of Yale University reports, "Finished files are the result of scientific study combined with the years of experience.

How many "F's" did you come across? If you found fewer than 9 "F's," count again. If you still can not find them, here is a hint: Make sure you count the "F's" in the word "of." Why were you unable to find all of them? Your mind was simply exercising muscle memory and the curse of previous knowledge. Ever since you were old enough to read you have been exercising your mind to say and think of the letter "F" in a different way. You have trained your mind so well that it does not see the "F." As your mind reads over the word "of" it does not process an "F," but rather processes a "V."

Previous knowledge could either be a blessing or a curse. It could be what is referred to as the curse of knowledge (Heath & Heath, 2007). If your mentors and previous coaches were poor, and that is all you know, then you are hampered by your coaching tree.

The Coaching Tree

A coaching tree is similar to a family tree; however, instead of showing the various descendants from your great-grandfather Adam, it shows the relationships of coaches. The most common way to make the distinction is if a coach played under or worked as an assistant for a particular head coach. If you are familiar with the trivia game "Six Degrees of Kevin Bacon," you understand the concept. This trivia game based on the assumption that an actor can be linked through his or her film roles to actor Kevin Bacon within six steps. Think of it this way—how many steps are between legendary football coach Bill Walsh and Mike Tomlin? As head coach of the San Francisco Forty-Niners, Coach Walsh employed assistant Coach Dennis Green, who would become the head coach of the Minnesota Vikings. As head coach of the Minnesota Vikings, Coach Green employed Tony Dungy as his defensive coordinator. Coach Dungy left Minnesota to coach the Tampa Bay Buccaneers and later the Indianapolis Colts. However, while at Tampa Bay, Coach Dungy hired a defensive backs coach named Mike Tomlin who would later go on to coach the 2009 Super Bowl Champion Pittsburgh Steelers. Coaching trees are found in every sport. For example, Pat Summit and Hank Iba have extensive basketball coaching trees.

The coaching tree process works out great if you start out with a great coach at the base of your coaching tree. However, most coaches are not fortunate to have a Bill Walsh at the bottom of their tree. Also the farther away you get from the patriarch of the tree, the more outcomes are affected as well. Coach Fox from Orange County High is part of a coaching tree. Probably not the Bill Walsh coaching tree, but a coaching tree all the same. He is the product of what he has been taught. If you are currently coaching, you are part of a coaching tree.

Purpose of the Book

This book is intended to help you branch out as a coach and to examine what great coaches do differently. It is not about the tactical and technical aspects of sports. You will not find tips on your offense and defense or breakdown drills in this book.

This book is about who we are as coaches; more directly it is about what we do as coaches. This book is not complicated; in fact many of you are probably doing some of these things some of the time. Yet the great coaches, the coaches of significance, are doing these things all the time. A coach of significance is a coach who positively impacts the lives of the people he or she encounters as well as enjoys success in the win-loss column.

Think of the greatest coaches in your league. Not necessarily the coach who has the most wins but the coach who enjoys the success of having made a difference in the lives of others and has consistently enjoyed the sweet taste of victory along the way. Is that a coaching tree you would like to be a part of? What if every coach in your league was like that coach? Would that be a great league? Of course it would. And if all athletic programs had coaches like the greatest coaches in your league, the athletes who walk off the field of competition will be better as a result of their experience. As you read through this book, you will find the contents to be simple in concept—but not always easy to consistently implement.

Instant Replay

Why Look at Great?

1. **What the Greatest Do Differently.** If four outstanding coaches hang an inspirational quote on the locker room bulletin board—"Play Like a Champion Today!"—we might conclude that one key to effective coaching is an inspiring quote posted in the locker room. However, what if less effective coaches display the same banner? Then the quote itself does not guarantee success. So what are the effective coaches doing differently from other coaches?

2. **The Clinic.** Who would you spend money on to see at a coaching clinic? You are not going to spend a dime of your coaching salary to hear someone that cannot help you become better. Coaches who want to become better find value in examining what great coaches do rather than what other coaches do not do.

3. **Self-Reflection.** One challenge in any profession is the ability to self-reflect accurately. In any organization those who know how they are coming across to others and how their behavior is received work more effectively than those who do not. We all struggle to achieve this self-awareness, but all too often we fall short.

4. **The Curse of Previous Knowledge.** Ineffective coaches are doing the best they can because it is all they know how to do. They use those methods and practices they were taught as an athlete or as an assistant coach as their guide to how to be a coach. That previous knowledge could be either a blessing or a curse. It could be what is referred to as "the curse of knowledge." If your mentors and previous coaches were poor and that is all you know then you are affected by the curse of previous knowledge.

5. **The Coaching Tree.** A coaching tree is similar to a family tree; however, instead of showing the various descendants from your great-grandfather Adam, it shows the relationships of coaches instead of family members. The most common way to make the distinction is if a coach played under or worked as an assistant for a particular head coach.

6. **Purpose of the Book.** This book is intended to help coaches examine what great coaches do differently. It is not about the tactical and technical aspects of sports. This book is about who we are as coaches; more directly, it is about what we do as coaches.

Chapter 2

People, Not Programs

One reason that Coach Fox may not know success is that he does not know what really matters most. What matters most to Coach Fox may be the "system." Coach Fox may spend countless hours developing complex systems built around the X's and O's of sports and the strategies needed to score and to stop the opponent from scoring. Or, it may not be the X's and O's but rather the various methods to shave a second here or add an inch there. Whatever the sport, there are countless systems associated with it, and coaches can spend countless hours developing it. Yet what do the most effective coaches do? Coach Fox's problem may come from the belief that great teams are the product of unique offensive and defensive systems. However, great coaches will tell you that winning has very little to do with what offense or defense a team runs or the quality of the training rooms, team rooms, and locker rooms they have. They will tell you that if you have a team of great athletes, then the chances of having success are dramatically increased. Great coaches understand that it is all about the people—not the program.

Jills and Joes, Not X's and O's

The improvement of a team is a simple concept. There are really four ways to improve the quality of a team:

1. Bring in different athletes
2. Improve the athletes you already have
3. Bring in a new coach
4. Improve the coach you already have

Since interscholastic and many youth sports organizations frown upon recruitment and have several rules prohibiting it, bringing in new players may not be an option. Since no one is ready to lose their job, bringing in a new coach is out of the question. That means we must improve the athletes we already have, and since we are asking our athletes to improve, it seems that we should expect the same for ourselves.

Since we must grow our athletes, we can either spend a great deal of time and energy, like Coach Fox, looking for the magic offense or an impenetrable defense that we believe can instantly lead us to the state championship, or we can spend time cultivating our relationships with the athletes we coach.

While Coach Fox is busy reviewing a DVD or attending a coaching clinic to see Championship U make it look easy, effective coaches are spending their energy with their players. Instead of looking for the magic offense, which can be executed only by the elite collegiate team and their elite athletes, effective coaches focus on what really matters—their athletes. This does not mean that a new offensive or defensive scheme will not benefit your team. Or that a new technique will not increase your chances of success. However, no one offense or defense, or no one technique, will inherently bring you greater success on the scoreboard or clock. If that were the case, it would already be a part of every coach's arsenal.

Every coach reading this book can think of some new innovation that has passed through the locker room doors marketed as an easier way to victory. Although all too often we expect that next new thing to solve our problems, win contests for us, and get our contract renewed, we need to keep in mind that programs are never the solution, and they are never the problem. Think of all the great innovations, offensive and defensive schemes, training aids, nutritional supplements, and exercise regiments your sport has experienced. There is nothing inherently wrong with any of these methods and we may have actually been able to employ one of them to achieve greater success. Even so, great coaches will say that success has much more to do with people.

The Spread Offense

Although I do not claim to be an expert on the spread offense in football, I will try to explain its origin and how it changed the landscape of American football. The spread offense is an offensive football scheme. Today it is used at every level of football. Today the scheme consists of the following: no-huddle, a quarterback in the shotgun formation, and spreading the field out by using multiple receiver sets. The object of the scheme is to open up the field by forcing the defense to spread itself thin across the field.

Today there are many forms of the spread offense system. And although we can identify many great coaches who use varying spread offense schemes, the person credited with inventing it was a great high school football coach named Tiger Ellison. Faced with his first losing season, Coach Ellison in 1950 turned to the strength of his personnel. As he tells us in his book, *Run-and-Shoot Football: Offense of the Future* (1965), Ellison was a believer in a program—the power running game. However, he soon realized that the success of his team had much more to do with people than a program. Faced with the knowledge that his personnel were not able to execute his program along with the possibility of suffering through his first losing season, Coach Ellison made a change.

Coach Ellison, who was about to lose his job, received his inspiration from a pickup football game in the school yard. What he witnessed that day inspired what would become known as the spread offense. As coaches we must understand that programs are not solutions. Just as Coach Ellison realized the power running game was not going to lead to success, we must know our people in order to determine what the right fit is.

Now, as you can imagine as this great coach was able to win, the surrounding coaches came and watched practice, attended clinics, or purchased Coach Ellison's book on what he called the run and shoot offense. Yet, where did they see this offense being run to perfection? Not with their team, but with Coach Ellison's team. When they saw Coach Ellison's team executing the spread offense to perfection, many coaches mistakenly thought that their team could use the spread. Yet what really made the run and shoot work for Coach Ellison was his players and his coaching staff.

Unlike professional and collegiate teams, high school rosters are composed of whoever walks through the door, and parents are sending us the very best that they have. They are not holding anybody back at home. And who they are sending may not be able to execute the run and shoot. So when we go to a clinic, purchase the latest DVD, or read a book, do what great coaches do and understand that success has much more to do with the Jills and Joes than it does X's and O's.

The Social Contract

To focus on the people rather than programs simply means to focus on relationships. Gregory Dale, a professor and sports psychology consultant at Duke University, suggests that the "most successful coaches are those that not only win most of the time but also are able to develop meaningful relationships with athletes they coach" (Dale, 2005). That relationship is in the form of an agreement or social contract between an athlete and a coach.

The social contract between a coach and an athlete means that the coach will coach and the athlete will learn and execute. Nothing is signed. It is simply understood. For example, at 4:00 p.m. immediately following classes, all athletes will report to the field of athletic competition and Coach Fox will show up to coach. The athletes will have their practice gear on and Coach Fox will show up with the clipboard and whistle. The differences between the effective coaches and the Coach Foxes of the world begin there. Coach Fox shows up to practice with clipboard in hand expecting to already have the respect and admiration of the athletes. The truth is many athletes will offer this respect and admiration simply because of the title "coach." However, the actions of Coach Fox will determine how long the athletes will maintain that respect.

Player–Coach Relationship

Effective coaches usually never need to restore player-coach relationships yet the great coaches are always fostering stronger relationships as if they do. They are always working their team, either during practice or behind closed doors, to ensure greater trust. They are always in someone's ear, keeping their relationships strong and in good repair.

Contrast that to coaches that never do repair. Look at their body language, tone of voice and their mannerisms, and even their physical proximity to their team during practice sessions. Less effective coaches coach from the outside-in. That is, they let their outside circumstances affect how they are going to react. If they are experiencing a bad day, then everyone around them knows it and chances are everyone is going to be affected by it. Think about how they treat their athletes—the same athletes they are asking to master a particular skill or strategy and to develop as teammates. Do these coaches need to work on building stronger relationships? The answer is obviously yes. But the problem is that these coaches, the coaches that never repair, are not aware that they need to.

We have all interacted with people who don't realize how they were being perceived. They offend and are rude not because they are trying to be but because that is who they really are. They don't see that their actions are turning people away. Quite the contrary, they see themselves as engaging, humorous, and vital to the interaction. They lack people skills. Many coaches are the same way. They don't work at building relationships because they perceive all their relationships to be strong. They don't repair relationships because they don't understand when they have been damaged. They see themselves as a good coach and having a positive impact on their athlete, but their perception and what is reality are not even close. Once they see themselves for who they really are, they can begin building stronger player-coach relationships.

Running for Mistakes

We are possibly familiar with the concept of making an athlete run for a mistake. I believe all coaches have this punishment in their coaching methods toolbox. In fact, we have seen this form of punishment handed out in many practices including our own. We do wonder, however, what cross-country and track coaches do for punishment. As one cross-country t-shirt put it, "Our sport is your sport's punishment."

A few years ago, I, Dr. Haworth, had the good fortune of working with Coach Leslie Akers, a volleyball coach at Springs Valley High School, French Lick, Indiana. As her athletic director, I had the opportunity to sit in on many of her practices. Part of my duties included evaluating her performance; however, many times I would sit in and just observe how she managed her practice. She is a fabulous coach and as the boy's basketball coach I would try to pick up a few things by watching how she handled her athletes.

During one end-of-the-season evaluation session, we began talking about this concept of making athletes run for mistakes.

Although I had seen athletes running during her practice I had failed to realize that they were running for mistakes. Why, because they were running hard, demonstrating positive body language when they ran, and did not seem to despise the fact that they were running. In fact, they were running on their own. The coach had not called them out to run; they were running simply because they realized their mistakes.

When I contrasted her practices with others I had seen, the results were not the same. Coaches were yelling across the field at their kids, athletes were loafing, mumbling under their breath about running. I can recall an incident when I was having a young man run for an inappropriate remark made during practice. Unhappy with the young man's effort, I began yelling across the gym while increasing the number of laps with every negative glance he flashed my way. I think I was at about lap 45 before I tossed him out of practice.

Clearly making an athlete run for a mistake could work because one of the most successful volleyball coaches in the state of Indiana used it. So why was it not working for other members of the coaching staff? Running for a mistake was a viable solution for reinforcing actions, but what made it successful was the relationship the coach had with the athletes. You see, Coach Akers did not see running for a mistake as necessary to correct that mistake. It was simply one tool that she used as an effective coach and she knew when and how to use it.

As coaches, we want athletes who arrive early to practice and stay late. We want athletes who will trust us and be loyal to the team. Coaches want athletes who are aggressive yet under control during competition. We want athletes who are willing to give their all—all of the time. The attractiveness of playing time will result in some of these actions. Yet, great coaches understand the social contract to mean something very different than just showing up. They understand the social contract to mean that they must earn the respect of their athletes before they will execute at the highest levels.

Instant Replay

People, Not Programs

1. **Jills and Joes, Not X's and O's.** The improvement of a team is a simple concept. There are really four ways to improve the quality of a team: Bring in different athletes, improve the athletes that you already have, bring in a new coach, or improve the coach that you already have.

2. **The Spread Offense.** The spread offense is an offensive football scheme. Today it is used at every level of football. Although we can identify many great coaches who use varying spread offense schemes, the person credited with inventing it was a great high school football coach named Tiger Ellison. Faced with his first losing season, Coach Ellison in 1950 turned to the strength of his personnel. Coach Ellison understood that success has much more to do with the Jills and Joes than it does X's and O's.

3. **Social Contract.** To focus on the people rather than program simply means to focus on relationships. That relationship is seen in the form of an agreement or social contract between an athlete and a coach. The social contract between a coach and an athlete means that the coach will coach and the athlete will learn and execute. Effective coaches understand that contract to mean more than just blowing the whistle and establishing the practice plan.

4. **Running for Mistakes.** Coaches are familiar with the concept of making an athlete run for a mistake. Running for a mistake is a viable solution for reinforcing action but what makes it successful is the relationship the coach has with the athletes. Effective coaches do not see running for a mistake as necessary to correct that mistake. It is simply one tool that is effective if you know when and how to use it.

Chapter 3

Inside Out

Everyone has high expectations for the upcoming season. Parents have high expectations for their son or daughter. Communities have high expectations for their schools. Great coaches have high expectations for their athletes and teams—as do less effective coaches. The truth is everyone has high expectations.

Coach Fox starts a season with high expectations. Coach Fox expects athletes to arrive early and stay late for practice. Coach Fox expects the team to be fully engaged during practice no matter how much standing around there is. Coach Fox expects great execution on the floor regardless of how flawed the strategy is or how weak the preparation was entering the contest.

So if everyone has high expectations, what makes the difference between successful and unsuccessful teams? What matters most on the field of athletic competition? Effective athletic administrators and those in and around successful athletic programs understand the answer to these questions; they know that the real issue is not WHAT is the difference but WHO is the difference. They understand that the difference maker is the coach.

What is it that great coaches do differently? Great coaches have high expectations for their athletes but even higher expectations for themselves. No matter the talent level, strength of schedule, or injury report, effective coaches understand that they are the difference makers.

How many of you could predict which teams in your athletic program will experience success next year? Without looking at the schedule or without knowing what athletes are returning, how many of you could predict the coaches who will have the fewest parent problems, the fewest eligibility issues, and the fewest discipline problems? If I were to ask athletic administrators this question, I bet almost every hand would go up. Why? Because they know who the difference makers are. They know that it really does not matter what athletes are on the team or what parents belong to what team. They know that the real difference maker is the coach.

I bet I could ask the athletes in the school and the old timers in the bleachers this question and they would have the same answer. Probably the only people who could not answer this question are the coaches who experience many discipline problems, parent issues, and eligibility concerns. If everyone in the community can recognize this, then why isn't anyone talking about it? I'm not talking about putting a "For Sale" sign in the coach's yard, or writing a letter to the editor or launching www.firethecoach.com. I simply mean taking the necessary steps to improve performance. Remember in the last chapter we said there were four ways to improve the performance of a team. Since we ruled out bringing in new players and a new coach that left us with only two other choices—improve the athletes and the coach we already have.

Outside-In

Who is the difference maker? Not the athletes, because they are only going to be as good as their preparation. Not the officials, because they are going to call the game fairly and accurately. Not the parents, because they have sent the coach the very best that they have. No, the difference maker is the coach and difference makers coach from the inside-out rather than the outside-in.

Coach Fox operates as an outside-in coach. Coach Fox allows feelings and emotions to control coaching decisions. To put it another way, the outside-in coach is reactive rather than proactive. We are all familiar with outside-in people. If it's raining, then they are going to have a bad day. If someone cuts them off in traffic, they get right up on their bumper to show their displeasure. Outside-in people believe they are the only ones ever affected by a price check in the Wal-Mart checkout line. Outside-in coaches are no different. They base their decisions and actions on the outward circumstances of the moment and are greatly affected by their physical environment. The crowd noise, the magnitude of the game, or an official's call will have an impact on their performance. Outside-in coaches also blame performance and outcomes on people or things. It was the official's fault, it was the weather's fault, or it was the athlete's fault. Nothing is ever the fault of the outside-in coach.

Read the paper or listen to the radio following a local athletic contest in which the coach is being interviewed. Now let's say the outside-in coach is on the radio or has given an interview following an athletic contest. Listen to what that coach has to say. If the team finishes in the win column, who gets the credit? If the team loses, who gets the blame? If it was a win, the coach gets all the credit, but if it is a loss it was the official, the fans, the players. For example, you can hear him saying, "If these kids would only do what I told them," or "I can't get in there and hit the ball for them," or our personal favorite, "It is hard to win when you are playing eight on five."

Inside-Out

Effective coaches are just the opposite. They coach from the inside-out. They are not affected by the physical environment because they use a set of core values as the basis for their decisions and their actions. The inside-out athletes are character-driven and as such have credibility. Their character allows them to coach as promised even when circumstances change.

Now let's say the inside-out coach is on the radio or has given an interview following an athletic contest. Listen to what that coach has to say. If the team finishes in the win column, who gets the credit? If the team loses, who gets the blame? If it was a win, the team gets all the credit, but if it is a loss, it was the coach's fault. Although core values may vary among inside-out coaches, Responsibility, Respect, and Sportsmanship are three inside-out values found in all effective coaches.

Responsibility

Effective coaches understand responsibility as the social force that binds them to their team. Not only are they engaged in the procedural responsibilities associated with coaching—budget, statistics, reviewing game film, going to clinics, talking to other coaches, and evaluating their processes—but they look inside themselves for answers and take responsibility for their teams' actions. The great coaches credit the opposition in defeat but clearly look to their preparation and strategy for answers.

Great coaches take responsibility for the climate and culture of their team. When we talk to great coaches about creating a climate and culture of success, whose behavior do you think they talk about? Their own, of course. They say very little about overzealous parents, ineffective athletic administrators, poor community support, or coddled athletes. Because these great coaches coach from the inside-out, they are empowered to make a difference.

Coaches who coach from the outside-in believe they have very little responsibility in creating the climate and culture of the team. We hear them talking about parents, athletic administrators, the community, the officials, and everyone else but themselves. Most coaches have had the feeling at one time or another that they are at the bull's-eye of a community's concern. Great coaches cherish being in the bull's-eye.

House for Sale

Speaking of bull's-eyes, Dr. Haworth has had the good fortune of being a public school superintendent, assistant superintendent, athletic director, teacher, baseball coach, and a boy's basketball coach all in the good state of Indiana. The one thing about Indiana is that they love their basketball. During my tenure in public education I have led school districts in building projects that affected local property taxes, I have had to cancel school because of weather-related issues, and I have assigned grades that were earned by students that kept them from graduating. Yet in all those professional tasks, I have never had anyone place a "For Sale" sign in my yard as the result of my teaching or administrative performance. However, following a disappointing loss in the Indiana boy's state basketball tourney, I returned home to find a "For Sale" sign posted in my front yard. Now if the truth be known, I felt so badly about the loss that I would have probably taken a good solid offer at the time.

The point is coaches are in the public eye. Our abilities as coaches are played out in public—unlike other professions in which performance evaluations may take place once or twice a year and in private. A coach's evaluation takes place every time his or her team competes. We constantly hear criticism being

What Great Coaches Do *Differently*

shouted by fans or being written in the local newspaper or local web page. All coaches constantly hear the criticisms, yet great coaches know how to filter the criticism and put it into context. Others, including our critics, focus on their own situations and needs. By the same token, everyone's effectiveness depends at least in part on what they expect of themselves, not of others. Great coaches expect a lot of themselves.

Equally we expect a lot from athletic participation. Not only do we expect the local team to win more than they lose, and to make a run into the championship series every other year, we also expect athletic participation to develop such things as loyalty, responsibility, respect, citizenship, and how to handle adversity and success and so on. Ask the person on the street why we have athletics in our nation's schools and they will probably tell you that sports builds character. The truth is the sports in and of themselves do not build character. Just rolling the balls out, putting on the pads, lining the field, and lacing up the shoes does not build character. There is even research that points to the fact that sports participation in fact has a negative effect on character development (Haworth, 2004; Rudd 2002).

If sports are to build character, the entire school community must take responsibility. Houses do not build character but great parents do. (Which parents take responsibility for setting expectations about their children's actions? Which parents are the quickest to blame others?) Schools do not build character but great teachers do. (Which teachers take responsibility for setting expectations about their students' actions? Which teachers are the quickest to blame others?) Sports do not build character but great coaches do. (Which coaches take responsibility for setting expectations about their athlete's actions? Which coaches are the quickest to blame others?).

Accepting responsibility is an essential difference between more effective and less effective coaches, teachers, and parents. If athletics are to build character, we must help the entire community, including coaches, take responsibility for their performance. Success in any profession starts with an individual's desire to become a difference maker. One's own self is truly the only variable that we can control. Difference makers understand this empowering approach toward teaching and coaching others. Great coaches take on this responsibility as well.

Respect

Treating someone with respect is not difficult to do. It is not difficult to treat someone in the way that you would like to be treated. However, what is difficult is doing it all the time. Everyone understands the concept of the "Golden Rule"—Treat others the way you would want to be treated. This life philosophy is found in many world religions and has stood the test of time, yet it can be difficult to treat everyone with respect every day. Coach Fox demonstrates respect most of the time. Coach Fox nine days out of ten treats others the way he would like to be treated. But what about that one day? We have all been the recipient of that one day, and many of us will probably never forget it. Effective coaches, however, find a way to demonstrate respect ten days out of ten. That includes their assistant coaches, managers, ball boys, and their best athletes as well as their worst. That includes the athletes you like and the ones you like less.

Think of the best and worst coaches you know, not from a strategy standpoint but from a total impact standpoint—how do they treat their athletes? Surely they both have athletes they like more than others. Do they treat the athletes they most like differently than the athletes they liked least? As coaches our behaviors say much more about us than our beliefs. We may believe we treat all athletes the same, but what are our actions telling others? The athletes of less effective coaches know who the coach values and who he does not. These are the same coaches who see their athletes as only a means to an end on their resume.

Inside-out coaches respect the individual, the team, and the game. They value the individual for more than their physical attributes and what an athlete can do for their winning percentage. Inside-out coaches care and have an understanding for what is going on in the lives of their athletes, managers, and assistant coaches and care about them beyond the playing field.

Respecting the Individual

These effective coaches demonstrate respect for their players by staying true to the word. The Coach Foxes tell their athletes one thing and then go and do another. Although many ineffective coaches do not intentionally lie, they are not always as forthcoming with the truth as they should be. The inside-out coaches are honest regarding a player's role on a team. They respect their athletes by acknowledging the fact that each athlete has only a few seasons and in those limited number of seasons, there are a limited number of contests, attempts, swings, plays, and minutes. As a result, they don't promise playing time to anyone and by doing so demonstrate respect for the team.

Respecting the Team

Athletic teams come in all shapes and sizes. However all teams, from the bowling team to the football team, have a unique dynamic. Teams are made up of individuals with special skills. They have a common goal. They cannot achieve that common goal without the special skills of all the members. Think of all the great championship teams in sport—even those that had magnificent individual athletes. In order to hang those championship banners, those magnificent individual athletes needed help. Bill Russell needed Bob Cousy, Jordan needed Pippen, Bradshaw needed Swan, Brady needed his offensive line, Billy Martin needed Reggie Jackson, and the 1980 USA hockey team needed each other.

Effective coaches respect that dynamic by not outwardly showing favoritism toward one athlete over another. Although everyone understands that every coach has favorites, on the teams of effective coaches, no one knows who they are. In respecting the dynamic they administer playing time on what is best for the team and that common goal. Once an athlete reaches 13 or 14 years of age, they have an understanding of where they are in relationship to their teammates. They understand those special skills they have to offer to the common goal and are usually smart enough to know when playing time matches those skills. They also understand rules and consequences and want them judiciously carried out.

Coach Fox promises everyone playing time and tends to play the athletes that can help him politically and socially. On Coach Fox's team the school board president's athlete gets more playing time than the local factory worker's athlete. On Coach Fox's team the rules are not applied consistently to all athletes.

Those that have a high degree of specialized talent have the same rules as everyone else; they just have different consequences. This happens on Coach Fox's teams. For example, Coach Fox had told everyone on the team that practice starts at 4:00 p.m. Coach Fox went on to say that they were on military time, which means that to be on time means that you are actually late and to be early means you are on time. However, Coach Fox had a very gifted athlete. When the team showed up to get taped, the gifted athlete was nowhere to be found. When the team began warming up, the gifted athlete showed up to get taped, when the team began running drills, the gifted athlete was warming up. Although he was by far the best athlete on the team, the team resented him and Coach Fox. While the other athletes, who had skills that could easily be found in most every other athlete, were running, missing parts of games, or maybe being kicked off the team for being late to practice, the gifted athlete was getting a strong talking to. The coach failed to respect the team, and the result was that the team underachieved in the game they loved.

Respecting the Game

Effective coaches respect the game and those who administer it. They understand that an athletic contest is a game that has value. The value is found in the teachable moments that exist for all who "participate" and "spectate." Of those who think that sports is just a game and has no real value, ask, "Why then is it tied to educational institutions?" The reason is simple; it has educational value. Sports may be among the most powerful human expressions in complicated and not-so-complicated ways. Sports elaborates in its ritual what it means to be human: the play, the risk, the trials, the collective impulse of games, the thrill of physicality, the necessity of strategy, defeat, victory, defeat again, pain, transcendence and, most of all, the certainty that nothing is certain—that everything can change and be changed (Early 1998). Sports have been critical to tearing down racial, gender, social, and political barriers. It has proven to be a better indicator of future academic success than a student's GPA. According to the Educational Testing Service and College Board Study, "Participation in high school athletics and activities are a much better indicator of overall college performance than other yardsticks (Iowa High School Athletic Association, 2009)." According to Douglas H. Heath's Fulfilling Lives—Paths to Maturity and Success, a 40-year survey, extra-curricular participation is a school's best predictor of an adult's success (Heath, 1991).

Effective coaches respect the game by understanding its value and by treating others in a manner they would want to be treated. They understand the role of officials, umpires, clock managers, athletic administrators, custodians, concession stand workers, bus drivers, and all who make the game happen. Coach Fox doesn't demonstrate respect for the official by berating him. Coach Fox doesn't demonstrate respect for the scorekeeper by finding fault with the clock manager. Coach Fox doesn't demonstrate respect for the custodian or the bus driver by leaving a messy locker room or bus. The effective coach respects those duties and even remembers to say thanks. They understand that the game is made up of more than just some boundaries, a ball, and a scoreboard. They understand it is made up of people doing the best they can.

Sportsmanship

A part of respecting the game is demonstrating sportsmanship. Unfortunately many coaches view sportsmanship as an outdated part of their game. Sportsmanship may seem uncool. Athletic success is based upon a number of things: effort, intensity, character, patience, talent, opponents, and the rules. Sport is based upon rules and regulations. Without the rules, there is no game. Many coaches need to understand that without sportsmanship, there is no game. How uncool is that?

Getting a coach to go along with a sportsmanship-related activity for the sake of doing it has limited value. Rather, the key is to develop and establish a program-wide sportsmanship environment that supports every coach's attempt to promote sportsmanship. Inside-out coaches not only talk about sportsmanship, they practice it and they make it cool. These effective coaches understand that sportsmanship is more than following the rules. Effective coaches know that sportsmanship is also understanding the etiquette and spirit of competition. They understand its relevance to citizenship and thus humanity. Coach Dave Rohlman of DeKalb High School in Illinois and Milwaukee Madison boys' basketball coach Aaron Womack understand the concept of sportsmanship, etiquette, and spirit of competition. Their brand of sportsmanship is what we want most from athletic participation—the will to win but only in the right way. Amid a difficult situation, these high school coaches and their teams displayed rare acts of sportsmanship and the spirit of the game.

Here is a summary, based on the story written by AP Sports columnist, Tim Dahlberg.

> The Barbs from DeKalb, Illinois, were to play their third non-conference game against Milwaukee Madison on a Saturday night in February, 2009. Madison's coach Womack was going to cancel the game, however, out of respect for his team's senior captain, Jontell Franklin, whose mom had died from cancer that afternoon. But Franklin wanted his team to play and when he arrived after the game had started, he said he wanted to play also and Coach Womack agreed.
>
> This caused some discussion among the refs and coaches. By the rules, Milwaukee would forfeit two free throws to DeKalb because Franklin wasn't on the pregame roster. For coach Womack, losing the points was far less important than letting Franklin play with his team. Rohlman, Dekalb's coach, on the other hand, didn't want to take the free throws. Just let Franklin play, he told the refs.
>
> Finally, Milwaukee's Darius McNeal stepped to the line to take the shots. Each time, McNeal released the ball to bounce softly on the floor. After a hushed moment, applause broke the silence, as competing teams and spectators honored a night of exemplary acts of sportsmanship.
>
> "I did it for the guy who lost his mom," McNeal told the Milwaukee Journal Sentinel. "It was the right thing to do." (Dalhberg, 2009)

Model It

It was the architect Frank Lloyd Write who stated, "No stream rises higher than its source." The same is true for teams and the character they display. As we interviewed many successful high school coaches and athletic administrators from around the country, they revealed the importance of modeling behaviors that they wanted their team to have. Because these nationally recognized coaches and athletic administrators wanted their athletes to demonstrate respect, responsibility, and sportsmanship, they believed that they too must demonstrate those character traits. If they wanted their teams to demonstrate respect for officials and umpires, they demonstrated the same behavior during contests. If they wanted their team to outwork all neighboring teams, they worked harder than all neighboring coaches. Effective coaches consistently model their expectations for how successful teams act.

You are the difference maker by not only what you say but also by what you do. Your players must know that you care for them more than just as athletes. Certainly, they understand that they are there to compete or play a game. But when you have them under your supervision, it's up to you to make sure that they understand that you care for them as individuals. It was college Hall of Fame Coach Alonzo Stagg who said, "I will not know for 20 years" when confronted with the question about whether his season had been successful. That is because he cared about his athletes. Effective coaches see their athletes as more than just a means to an end. Great coaches may not like all of their athletes, they may have difficulty respecting some of the decisions that their athletes make, but they do care about them just the same. If your players come to understand that you care about them, it will not be because of the things that you have said but rather the things that you have done—your actions. You can't fool your athletes. They are too sophisticated and can see through an act.

My Bad

I do not know where the phrase "My Bad" came from, but it is a term that I hear effective coaches use. It is a phrase that not only recognizes a mistake but is also an apology all wrapped up into two little words. If you are going to build stronger player coach relationships, it is a phrase you will need. What keeps coaches from saying "My Bad" or apologizing? Self-confidence or pride: Either I am afraid that my team will lose respect for me if they hear anything that remotely sounds like an apology, or I am above telling those whom I have authority over that I made a mistake.

Coaches are the difference makers and have the responsibility of leadership. Those effective coaches who care about their athletes and lead them in a way that's beneficial to them beyond the field of athletic competition usually experience success on the field as well. The ability to apologize and understanding what you are apologizing for makes all the difference in the world. Coaches can make an impact by accepting responsibility for their behavior.

Instant Replay

Inside-Out

1. **Expectations.** Everyone has high expectations for the upcoming season. Great coaches have high expectations for their athletes but even higher expectations for themselves.

2. **Outside-in.** Ineffective coaches coach from the outside-in. The outside-in coach allows feelings and emotions to control coaching decisions. They base their decisions and actions on the outward circumstances of the moment and are greatly affected by the physical environment.

3. **Inside-out.** Effective coaches coach from the inside-out. They are not affected by the physical environment because they use a set of core values as the basis for their decisions and their actions.

4. **Responsibility.** Effective coaches understand responsibility as the social force that binds them to their team. Most coaches have had the feeling, at one time or another, that they are at the bull's-eye of a community's concern. Great coaches cherish the responsibility of the bull's-eye.

5. **House for Sale.** Coaches are in the public eye. Unlike other professions in which performance evaluations may take place once or twice a year and in private, a coach's evaluation takes place every time his or her team competes. Since great coaches expect a lot of themselves, they enjoy the evaluation.

6. **Respect.** Inside-out coaches respect the individual, the team, and the game. Effective coaches demonstrate respect for their players by staying true to the word. Effective coaches respect the team dynamic by not outwardly showing favoritism toward one athlete over another. Effective coaches respect the game and those that administer it.

7. **Sportsmanship.** A part of respecting the game is demonstrating sportsmanship. Inside-out coaches not only talk about sportsmanship, they practice it.

8. **Model It.** Successful coaches and athletic administrators who want their athletes to demonstrate respect, responsibility, and sportsmanship believe they too must demonstrate those character traits.

9. **My Bad.** "My Bad" is a phrase that not only recognizes a mistake but is also an apology all wrapped up into two little words. It is a phrase you need if you are going to build stronger player–coach relationships.

Chapter 4

Coaching 101

L ike many coaches, Coach Fox understands the basic formula for coaching: Describe what it is that you want your athletes to do; demonstrate what it is that you want your athletes to do; direct your athletes toward successful completion of that task; and reinforce your athletes' attempts at what you previously described, demonstrated, and directed. Almost all coaches understand these basic principles of coaching. Great coaches take these basic principles and turn them into success stories both on and off the field, court, or pitch.

Coach Fox has a basic understanding of how to break down a skill, play, or specific strategy. What Coach Fox lacks, as do many coaches, is the ability to create a unique practice and playing environment. Effective coaches not only understand what it is they are describing and demonstrating but they also have distinct methods for directing and reinforcing their athletes' actions. Take reinforcement for example. Effective coaches know how to maximize this coaching skill. They fully understand and employ the concepts and power of positive and negative reinforcement.

Punishment

Almost all coaches understand the power of punishment. Coach Fox's number one punishment without question and probably the number one athletic punishment for all sports is running. As we have seen earlier, running can be an effective reinforcement but what about a punishment? Punishment decreases the occurrence of a behavior by introducing a negative condition (running) as a consequence of the behavior. Let's use the example of being late for practice to illustrate punishment. How do you stop an athlete from being late to practice?—make them do something they don't like to do (running) when they are late? As a coach you understand the scene: Everyone at practice is hitting, shooting, kicking, scoring, defending, throwing, or something fun, and I am over here running. How do I keep from running while everyone else is practicing?—show up on time. Coach Fox often confuses punishment with negative reinforcement, which is different.

Negative Reinforcement

Negative reinforcement increases the chance of a behavior because a negative condition is avoided as a consequence of the behavior. Many coaches run during or following practice. One common tool used by coaches to motivate their athletes is to let their athletes out of running if something positive occurs.

Coaching great Dean Smith graded his practices. Players scored points for setting good screens, drawing a charge, diving after loose balls or any other positive thing that contributed to the team's success. And what do you think those points could be used for? Points could be used for getting out of running (Smith & Bell, 2005). Learning how to praise and how to punish can be challenging. Coach Fox and many other coaches find it all too easy to spend our time looking for what is wrong, pointing out errors, and focusing on mistakes. Effective coaches, in contrast, are looking for opportunities to find their athletes doing things right. Not only that, they understand what to do when they catch an athlete doing something right and how to keep that athlete doing it right.

Ben Bissell (1992) has described five things that help make praise effective—elements that are important if attempts at praise are to have the most positive effect possible. These five characteristics define effective praise as authentic, specific, immediate, clean, and private. Let us apply these general characteristics to the specifics of motivating and praising athletes.

Authentic Praise

During Coach Fox's practices everything is great: great throw, great run, great leap, great save, great, great, great. What do you think the word "great" means to his team? Is this authentic praise? Authentic means that we are praising athletes for something genuine, recognizing them for something that is true. We can never grow weary of recognizing something of authentic value.

Sometimes coaches state that they do not praise more because excessive praise will lose its credibility or become less believable. The way to prevent meaningless praise is to make sure that praise is always authentic. Authentic praise does not mean that the accomplishment being praised is earth-shattering or magnificent. Rather, the only requirement is that we, as coaches, are intentionally recognizing people doing specific things right. Each instance is an opportunity to give authentic praise.

Specific Praise

When Coach Fox tells Pat "great game," what does Pat walk away with? Did Coach Fox mean great offense, great defense, great hustle, great teamwork, or all of the above? Effective praise is specific. The behavior we acknowledge often becomes the behavior that will be continued. If we can recognize athletes' positive efforts with specific recognition, then we can help them see specific areas of value. For example, acknowledging that a football player continued playing hard until he heard the whistle reinforces this athlete's aggressive playing style. Specific praise allows you to reinforce someone in an authentic manner. If you use specific praise, you can recognize everyone in your organization. Even athletes who are struggling can be praised. You do not have to be dishonest and say an athlete is great or that their performance was outstanding if they were not. Instead, you can identify those areas that do have merit and acknowledge them through praise.

Immediate Praise

Coach Fox's Rumbling Sloths just finished a two-hour practice. As Pat is walking into the locker room, Coach Fox says, "I really appreciated what you did tonight at the start of practice." Not only does Pat not know what Coach Fox is talking about (be specific), Pat does not know when it occurred! The third requirement for praise to work as a reinforcer is to be immediate. This means recognizing positive efforts and contributions in a timely manner. Providing authentic and specific feedback in close proximity to when it occurs is an important element in making reinforcement effective. If you are a coach who does station work during your practices or breaks your team down into positions and skills, then one tactic that allows you to give efficient feedback is a walk by. Take your clipboard and walk by your stations or your position players' practice session and take notes. When an athlete rotates out of a drill, call them over and tell them what you liked, and also write down the good things you see your assistants doing. They will enjoy a little praise as well because as you know the paycheck is not their only motivator.

Effective coaches understand that positive reinforcement is a valuable tool for change. They use it by working hard to find something positive in every practice situation and as often as possible.

Clean Praise

Coach Fox calls Pat over after practice and says, "Pat, you did a really great job tonight at the start of practice, but I wish you could have given me a little more effort in a couple of those drills midway through practice." The fourth guideline for praise is that it be clean. This is often a very challenging expectation, especially for coaches. Clean means a couple of different things.

First, praise is not clean if you are issuing it in order to get your athlete to do something in the future. In other words, it is important to compliment someone because it is authentic, not just because you are hoping that they will do something different, and unrelated, tomorrow. Take care to remind yourself of this regularly; otherwise, you will be tempted to discontinue praising because you feel it "did not work." For example, during a practice Coach Fox might praise a selfish athlete for an unselfish act; later on in practice the athlete is acting moody and less responsive. Do not feel that these two events are linked. Oftentimes we take the manner of less positive athletes personally. Though our goal is to get them to be more positive, we need to be aware that often their mood has much more to do with them and the way they feel about themselves than it does with you and how they are regarding you.

The second aspect of clean praise is a very challenging one for coaches. If praise and reinforcement are to be clean, it cannot include the word "but." If we are trying to compliment someone and we say, "I liked how well you went after that ball, but I also noticed you still don't want to play team defense," the individual we hoped to praise will very likely remember only the part after the "but," which was a criticism. If we are really intending to praise someone, then it is important that we separate these two comments. The statement, "I like how well you went after that ball" could have been an authentic, specific, immediate, positive, and reinforcing event for the athlete. Such a statement helps to clarify and reinforce your expectations about how athletes hustle during your practice. This "clean" statement makes it much more likely that the athlete will consciously seek to hustle after every ball in the future.

The other part of the comment, "I also noticed you still don't want to play team defense," should be given at another time and in another way. Tying the two together reduces or even eliminates the value of the praise. Building morale requires a consistent focus on looking for positive things. Any time the opportunity presents itself, acknowledging the good appropriately can continue to cultivate a positive mindset among others.

Praise in Private

After practice Pat is headed out the door with three teammates. Just as Pat reaches the door, Coach Fox yells from across the practice field, "Great job tonight, Pat. I am really proud of you." Once Pat steps out those doors, what do you think Pat's teammates will do or say? The fifth descriptor of praise is private. Dr. Bissell (2009) believes that almost always praise needs to be given in private. I agree with this and would also say that, if in doubt, you are always safe to praise someone in private.

One reason is to protect the feelings of our productive best players. Also, praising less productive athletes can be a demotivator for the rest of the team. If I (as an athlete) see an athlete whom I view as less hardworking (than myself) get public recognition, I may lower my effort level to regain the balance between my efforts and my rewards. However, there are still times when it is beneficial to use public praise to influence others and build morale. Let's examine some situations.

Public versus Private Praising

Understanding the difference in impact between recognizing someone's efforts publicly and acknowledging them privately is very important. To be effective, a coach must know when to praise publicly and when to praise privately.

If we never recognize accomplishments publicly, we may lose many teachable moments. Let me give an example: My two best athletes, who are also my hardest workers on the team, are staying after practice to work on a particular skill I have asked them to do. I did not ask them to stay after practice—they just are. The superstars were self-motivated to improve their performance. They did not need a coach to bring them to this point. But when I gave those athletes public recognition prior to the start of practice the next day, how many more athletes soon found time to stay after practice a little longer and work on their game? Eventually, I had to start running our players off the playing field so that the next team could get on the field. Without this avenue of public praise, the impact would have been much more limited.

Keep in mind that your best players thrive on autonomy and recognition, although this recognition does not necessarily mean only public acknowledgments. When considering the public praising of team members, remember that one of the most important facets of being the best player is being respected by others. So be aware of the amount of public recognition you give your superstars. If the other team members become resentful, superstars are no longer superstars, and this dramatically limits their ability to positively influence the team.

An easy test of whether it is okay to praise in public is the question: Is the praised behavior something anyone could have done? Publicly recognizing an athlete for staying after practices and working a little longer is something any athlete could have done. As others choose to stay after practice, the coach has many other chances to recognize staff members—many other appropriate opportunities for positive reinforcement in an authentic, specific, immediate, clean, and public manner.

Think about this way. Recognizing students publicly when they achieve a 3.5 grade point average may seem reinforcing, but many of these students would rather receive private recognition; it may not be "cool" to have high grades. It is the same in the athletic classroom. Realistically, we often have many students in our schools who could have achieved this lofty GPA. Having a private ceremony for these "honor roll" students, or sending their parents a letter, would probably accomplish the same thing without possibly building resentment among their peers. The same is true for teams.

Administering Public Praise

Another way to get the benefit of public praise without building animosity is by anonymously acknowledging a contribution using generalized public praise. This can allow for reinforcement and provide the desired "teachable moment" without as much potential for resentment. Publicly thanking "those of you who are staying after practice in order to take your game to the next level" is a way to help people who have done this feel appreciated. At the same time, this can help establish an expectation for everyone to behave in this manner. You could also individually walk over after practice and thank those that are staying after practice. However, this private acknowledgment alone will not likely get others to join them in this supervisory task.

A similar situation involves getting athletes to work on the fundamentals of their game. As coaches, we may issue reminders, which can go from friendly encouragement to heavy-handed directives. However, using generalized public praise can allow us to reinforce the behavior of those who have met or exceeded the standard, while at the same time reminding others to "get with the program." Instead of saying for the fifth time, "I think some of you could benefit by brushing up on your fundamentals immediately following practice," an approach that would be just as effective and yet more reinforcing could be to say, "I appreciate those of you who are staying and working on your skills when practice ends. That extra work will really improve your individual skills as well as benefit the team. Thanks for your efforts." This serves as a reminder to everyone and as a "thank you" to a few. Using the generalized public praise approach can also protect anyone who was a "rate buster" on the grade-sheet deadline.

Though the balance between publicly recognizing people for their efforts and potentially alienating them from their peers may be delicate, there are still many occasions when making praise public is important. Equally as difficult is knowing when to criticize, use punishment, or negative reinforcement. Being aware of how it will affect your individuals as well as your team is a skill that great coaches have. Developing a variety of methods of reinforcement provides you the opportunity to choose which type is most appropriate in a particular circumstance.

Instant Replay

Coaching 101

1. **The Basics.** Many coaches understand the basic formula for coaching: describe what it is that you want your athletes to do; demonstrate what it is that you want your athletes to do; direct your athletes toward successful completion of that task and reinforce your athletes' attempts at what you previously described, demonstrated, and directed. Effective coaches not only understand what it is they are describing and demonstrating but they also have distinct methods for directing and reinforcing their athletes' actions.

2. **Punishment.** Almost all coaches understand the power of punishment. Punishment decreases the occurrence of a behavior by introducing a negative condition (running) as a consequence of the behavior.

3. **Negative Reinforcement.** Negative reinforcement in creases the chance of a behavior because a negative condition is avoided as a consequence of the behavior. Many coaches run during or following practice. One common tool used by coaches to motivate their athletes is to let their athletes out of running if something positive occurs.

4. **Authentic Praise.** Authentic means that we are praising athletes for something genuine, recognizing them for something that is true.

What Great Coaches Do *Differently*

5. **Specific Praise.** Effective praise is specific. The behavior we acknowledge often becomes the behavior that will be continued.

6. **Immediate Praise.** Praise needs to be immediate. This means recognizing positive efforts and contributions in a timely manner.

7. **Clean Praise.** Praise needs to be clean. Clean means a couple of different things: First, praise is not clean if you are issuing it in order to get your athlete to do something in the future. Second, clean praise cannot include the word "but."

8. **Praise in Private.** Praise needs to be given in private for two reasons: The first is to protect the feelings of our productive, best players, and the second is that comparing others, praising less productive athletes, can be a de-motivator for the rest of the team.

9. **Public versus Private Praising.** Understanding the difference in impact between recognizing someone's efforts publicly and acknowledging them privately is very important. To be effective, a coach must know when to praise publicly and when to praise privately.

10. **Administering Public Praise.** A way to get the benefit of public praise without building animosity is by anonymously acknowledging a contribution using generalized public praise. This can allow for reinforcement and provide the desired "teachable moment" without as much potential for resentment.

Chapter 5

Your Best Athlete

Who are the best athletes? Coach Fox believes that the best athletes are those who can jump the highest, run the fastest, or throw the hardest. The best athletes on Coach Fox's team are the leaders in all the statistical categories. They hold the most records and have the most varsity letters. Effective coaches have a different view. Effective coaches believe that the best athletes are those things and much more.

As Rob Haworth, the athletic director and basketball coach of Springs Valley high school in French Lick, Indiana, I had the privilege of meeting Coach Bill Harris. Several years before I arrived at Springs Valley, Coach Harris had built and maintained a highly successful high school football team. During my first season as Springs Valley's high school basketball coach, I was struggling with many off the court issues from a few of my players. I will never forget the advice he provided: "I would rather have a team with average talent, great work habits, and that is dedicated to each other, than a team of talented athletes who have no sense of responsibility to their team, school, or community." The best athletes do not only exhibit greater physical skills than their teammates but also demonstrate greater character than their teammates. They are your hardest workers on the team, the most persistent, and the most responsible members of the team. They demonstrate effort, intensity, and heart as well as selflessness and compassion to their teammates. They have a tendency to always know where they are and what is going on around them. Do you know who your best athletes are? Effective coaches not only know who their best athletes are but also allow them to dominate their approach to decision making.

Decision-Making Skills

How do you suppose Coach Fox makes a decision? Well, if Coach Fox is an outside-in coach, his decision may depend upon the weather or the morning traffic into work. Great coaches, on the other hand, make decisions following three simple guidelines regardless of the physical environment:

1. What is the purpose?
2. Will this actually accomplish the purpose?
3. What will my best athletes think?

The first rule is very straightforward and is probably a question that all coaches ask themselves. Effective coaches ask the same question but do not let themselves become sidetracked. We are constantly evaluating why we do what we do. We go to the clinics and purchase DVDs because we are constantly evaluating why we do what we do and try to improve upon it. However many coaches get sidetracked. They frame their exploration the wrong way. Instead of asking, *What is the purpose?*, they settle for, *What is the reason?*

Examine every drill that you run in your practices. What is the reason you run those particular drills? Coach Fox would answer, "Because my high school did it that way" or "My college coach ran that drill." Does that make it a good drill for you? Another answer may be that we have always run that drill and it has become a tradition. Yet another reason may be that I attended a clinic and I saw a famous coach teach this drill. But if we ask, What is the purpose?, we may end up with a more productive drill and one that fits our team's situation.

In baseball how many teams are still conducting batting practice by having one athlete bat and the remainder of the team shagging balls? We hope not many, yet we believe there are still some coaches out there doing it that way. Why did coaches thirty years ago conduct practice in such a way? The answer is easy. It is what they knew, and it was convenient for them. How many drills do you run because of those reasons? Great coaches ask, *What is the purpose?*

Peeling a Banana

Which end do you peel a banana from? Do you start at the bottom or the top? As a matter of fact which is the top and the bottom end of a banana? Let's assume for argument's sake that the bottom end is the stem end. If you are like most people you peel your banana from that end. Why? I'll bet your answer is more about a reason than a purpose.

Most banana peelers begin at the stem end because that is the way they were instructed to peel a banana. However what is the purpose of peeling a banana? For most of us the purpose of peeling a banana is to eat it. Then why don't you peel the banana from the top end? By peeling the banana from the top end you create more opportunities for making your purpose more enjoyable. For instance, it is easier to peel a banana from the top (non-stem end) than it is from the bottom. You eliminate many of the stringy things that run along the side of the banana and you create a handle to hold your banana. If you don't believe me, try it the next time you eat a banana.

As you begin to create your next practice plan, ask the purpose of each drill that you are going to run. You just might come to the conclusion that there is more than one way to peel a banana.

Shoplifters Will Be Prosecuted

Have you been shopping and noticed a sign for shoplifters? A sign that reads:

> # Shoplifters
> # Will Be Prosecuted

Surely that sign is not for us. Did the store owner post that sign for me or for the shoplifter? The sign may come in a number of variations: We are watching you and on the sign is the silhouette of a camera or a pair of large eyeballs. Or there is even a sign that requires a law degree to interpret:

> ### Shoplifting is a "Class B" Felony.
> **For the Arrest and Conviction of a Shoplifter the penalty can include but is not limited to up to 20 years in prison and a fine of $15,000.00**

Do those signs do any good? Do they ever accomplish their purpose? Imagine browsing through a store. Every time you turn a corner, you encounter another sign:

Shoplifters Will Be Prosecuted!

We Are Watching You!

For the Arrest and Conviction of a Shoplifter...

Do you ever find yourself walking around a store on the verge of getting ready to steal and see that sign and think to yourself, "I almost forgot that shoplifting was against the law?" The answer is no.

How do those types of signs make you feel? Do you feel more comfortable or less comfortable when you see those shoplifting signs? Too many aggressive anti-shoplifting signs may make the honest shoppers so uncomfortable that they change their behavior and shop somewhere else. Meanwhile, the hard-core shoplifters disregard the signs—or even take them as a challenge.

What has happened here? The store owners have a purpose in mind, but they haven't thought through the question, Will this actually accomplish the purpose? The store owners have focused on the shoplifters and ignored their "best people"—their customers. Wouldn't they be better off in the long run with a store full of customers?

Coaches, do we act in the same manner? If we are going to hang a sign in our locker-room, we might ask ourselves, What is its purpose? and How does it make my best athletes feel? Think about your locker room bulletin board, your team web page, or your comments to your team during your warm-up or cool-down sessions, or any time that you have your whole team together. All too often Coach Fox is focused on the least effective people, issuing broad directives because of one or two athletes. If you are harping on missing a block, a rebound, or a sign to your entire team, when in fact your best athlete made every block, grabbed every rebound that came toward him or her, and never missed a sign during the entire game, what do you think is running through this player's mind? At best, we make our top performers feel guilty. Running through their mind is every situation in which they made or had a chance to block, rebound, or catch a sign, and they are thinking of the one they missed. At worst, we insult them. They think, "Why are you talking to me about this? Why don't you talk to them?" And they are right.

What Will My Best Athletes Think?

Many of us appoint captains before the start of the season. Effective coaches appoint their best athletes as captains and allow them to be leaders. Many times we select captains and don't think about their purpose. Many times their job descriptions consist of calling heads or tails, getting the pregame instructions from the officials, or leading stretching exercises during the warm-ups. Effective coaches use captains for a variety of tasks, one of which is bouncing ideas off them regarding decisions that affect the team.

When making decisions or attempting to bring about any change, effective coaches ask themselves one central question: *What will the best athletes think?* This does not mean that our best athletes are running the team or that coaching should be a touchy-feely group experience. It also doesn't mean that we are not going to consider views from anyone else; but many effective coaches consider what the best athletes will think.

They Will Be Fine

Many coaches focus on either their below average or average athletes because they hold to a belief that their best athletes will be fine. The truth is they will be fine. Just like the best students learn regardless of the quality of instruction in the classroom, the best athletes will be fine regardless of the quality of coaching—but if your best athletes are only fine, your team has little to no chance of being great.

Surely, these talented, hardworking, respectful athletes will continue to be a positive influence on the rest of the team without much support from their coach. Effective coaches don't take that chance. They understand that the team needs the dedication of the most valuable players. They need their athletic ability, mental approach, work ethic, and leadership to influence their teammates.

When managing a team, an easy standard to recall is to treat every athlete with the best athlete in mind. Our best athletes want lack of effort to be addressed, but never in a humiliating way. Our best athletes want us to deal with sloppy execution, but they want us to do it respectfully.

Pets Allowed

Effective coaches are great teachers. In fact I believe they are one in the same. The only difference is the size and shape of their classrooms. Effective teachers treat everyone with respect, every day. Even the best teachers may not like all their students—but they act as if they do. Great coaches care for all their students. Legendary football coach Eddie Robinson said this of coaching: Coaching is a profession of love. You can't coach people unless you love them. Let me be quick to point out that effective coaches have favorites. By the nature of their personalities, coaches enjoy some athletes more than others. But effective coaches mask this feeling. In an effective coach's practice setting, no one knows who the favorite is. No athlete wants to be the coach's pet. It is fine to consider what the best athletes will think and even discuss with them decisions that will impact the entire team, but the coach must be careful that the relationship is not perceived as favoritism. If the team perceives the relationship as anything but a coach–captain relationship, they will lose respect for both you and your best athletes.

This concept of centering on the best people may seem different, yet it is one of the crucial differences between effective coaches and the rest. Maintaining the qualities of your best athletes while cultivating those same qualities in others is an essential role for a coach. Think about it. If all of your athletes were like your best athletes, what type of team would you have?

Instant Replay

Best Athlete

1. **Best Athlete.** Who are the best athletes? The best athletes do not only exhibit greater physical skills than their teammates but also demonstrate greater character than their teammates.

2. **Decision Making Skills.** Great coaches make decisions following three simple guidelines: What is the purpose? Will this actually accomplish the purpose? What will my best athletes think?

3. **Peeling a Banana.** From which end do you peel a banana? Try peeling it from the non-stem end, and you just might come to the conclusion that there is more than one way to peel a banana.

4. **Shoplifters Will Be Prosecuted.** Have you been shopping and noticed a sign for shoplifters? A sign that reads: SHOPLIFTERS WILL BE PROSECUTED! Surely that sign is not for us. What has happened here? The store owners have a purpose in mind, but they haven't thought through the question, Will this accomplish the purpose? The store owners have focused on the shoplifters and ignored their "best people."

5. **What Will My Best Athletes Think?** When making decisions or attempting to bring about any change, effective coaches ask themselves one central question: What will the best athletes think?

6. **They Will Be Fine.** Many coaches focus on either their below average or average athletes because they hold to a belief that their best athletes will be fine. If your best athletes are only fine, your team has little to no chance of being great.

7. **Pets Allowed.** All coaches have favorite athletes whom they enjoy more than others. Effective coaches make everyone feel like they are the favorite.

Chapter 6

Expectations

Early we stated that everyone has high exceptions, including Coach Fox, and that effective coaches have high expectations of themselves. What was not noted was that effective coaches understand the importance of managing the expectations of those around them. They understand that the difference between a successful and unsuccessful season may have just as much to do with managing expectations as it does with athletic ability and execution.

Parents

A CNN report (Hilgers, 2006) estimates 41 million youth sports participants across the United States. That number has risen dramatically over the past two decades. All over the country young people are on football fields, soccer pitches, and basketball courts. With 41 million youth sports participants that makes roughly 82 million parents; 82 million parents that are intimately involved as fans, coaches, officials, league organizers, and team parents. The days of sandlot sporting events are over. No more do the neighborhood kids get together, organize themselves, officiate themselves, and play. Unfortunately "ghost men" on first and second are just that—ghost men. Those imaginary base runners that were needed when there were not enough players have been long forgotten by today's parent-organized, corporate-sponsored sporting events (Hilgers, 2006).

Think about the parent who spends $100 for a pair of shoes, $50 for practice gear, $250 for camp fees, $500 for summer league travel, and $50 an hour for a personal skill coach. Now multiply those numbers times the number of years their athlete is involved in organized sports. What do you think their expectations are going to be regarding playing time? What do you think their expectations will be regarding winning and losing? What do you think their expectations will be regarding possible scholarship dollars or having a professional career?

Maybe that is why a recent study published by *Sports Illustrated For Kids* found that out of the more than 3,000 young athletes, 74 percent said they had seen out-of-control adults at their games. According to Survey USA, 21 percent of parents polled in the Indianapolis area said they had witnessed a physical fight between adults at youth sporting events. The problem of out-of-control adults has gotten so bad that the Connecticut legislature approved a law that makes it a felony to assault an official at a youth sports event. Whether it is for the scholarship or misplaced childhood dreams, the expectations of parents is changing. They see themselves as being on the team and part of the action rather than being a spectator (Hilgers, 2006).

The Athletic Triangle

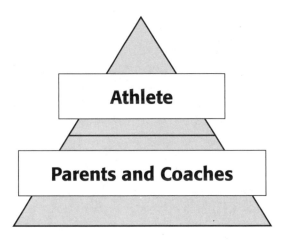

All coaches, including Coach Fox, understand that the world of amateur school sports is undergoing many changes. All coaches understand that the financial cost to participate is greater now than ever before and that the competition levels have increased since our playing days. All coaches see longer seasons and athletes with greater skill sets than in the past. Yet what ineffective coaches fail to do is see how these changes affect the expectations of their athletes and their parents. Effective coaches understand not only their role in the athletic triangle but the role of parents as well. The athletic triangle is composed of athletes, parents, and coaches. The athletic triangle stands with parents and coaches at its base supporting the hopes and dreams of the athlete. Parents have a role to play in their sons' or daughters' athletic experience. While Coach Fox is worrying about what every parent is thinking, the effective coaches already know. Every parent has high expectations for their athletic child.

Professionalization of Youth Sports

According to Dr. Dan Gould, Director of the Michigan State University Institute for the Study of Youth Sport, "We see a lot of kids, even young kids, doing it just for the scholarship now (as cited in Hilgers, 2006)." In today's sporting culture, parents are willing to hire trainers and skill-specific coaches. That does not include the dollars spent on high profile traveling teams. Why take out a second mortgage on the home? It all lies in the hope that doing so will increase the chances to be seen and improve the chances for a scholarship or a professional contract. Dr. Gould has labeled this approach as the "professionalization of youth sports." The professionalization of youth sports lends itself to "premature specialization" where a parent pressures a child into focusing all their skills on one sport. Burnout and sports injuries are all too often the result of parental pressure (Hilgers, 2006). Over zealous parents all too often fail to realize the odds. Parents fail to realize, for example, that only one in 35 high school senior basketball players makes a college basketball team and fewer than that on full ride scholarships. We hope they realize that the chances of being drafted and taking their son's game to the NBA are less than 2 percent for all college male senior basketball players. Read that again—2 percent of all COLLEGE male senior basketball players. These same types of statistics hold true in other sports as well.

What Are The Odds?

Effective coaches are not dream killers. Great coaches understand and manage the expectations of parents regarding playing and the perception that signing a professional contract or at least obtaining a college scholarship is not easy. Unlike Coach

Fox, who enters these conversations unprepared, the effective coach understands the importance of tone, tact, and tenderness. While Coach Fox is telling a parent that they have a better chance of being struck by lightning than winning a college scholarship, effective coaches are rehearsing the dialogue they intend to use over in their minds or with assistant coaches. Effective coaches understand the importance of building expectations that stretch the athlete to greater heights but are also built upon reality. Examine the following sports (NCAA, 2009) to see how many high school athletes are being drafted:

Baseball

- 1 out of 200 high school seniors will be drafted by a major league team.
- Less than 11 out of 100 NCAA players will be drafted by a major league baseball team.

Football

- 9 out of 10,000 high school senior boys playing football will be drafted into the National Football League.
- 1 out of 50 NCAA senior football players will be drafted into the National Football League.

Basketball

- 1 out of 35 high school senior boy basketball players will go on to play for an NCAA institution.
- About three out of 10,000 senior boy basketball players will be drafted by the National Basketball Association.

Soccer

- 1 in 1,250 senior interscholastic soccer players will be drafted by a Major League Soccer team
- 1 out of 50 senior NCAA soccer players will be drafted by a Major League Soccer team.

Effective coaches understand and can communicate how many athletes participate in their sport at the high school level. They know approximately how many scholarships are available, how many athletes will get part of those scholarships, and how many of those scholarships are full scholarships and how many are partial scholarships. Effective coaches can tell a parent what it costs to attend a public and a private college or university and approximately how much scholarship money is available to an athlete. Answer the following questions and then find your sport on the tables (pages 66–67) of scholarships from *The New York Times* article "Scholarships: Slicing the Pie," (Scholarships, 2008).

The College Scholarship

1. How many high school students participate in the sport I coach?
2. How many scholarships are awarded annually in the sport I coach?
3. How many students are receiving financial assistants from those scholarships?
4. Approximately what percent of those scholarships are awarded as full ride scholarships?
5. What is the yearly value of that scholarship?

Effective coaches understand the wide ranges of parent involvement in athletics. Some parents will not even bother showing up for a game. Others will take out a second mortgage on their home to ensure that their son or daughter gets a chance to participate. Effective coaches know many parents attend games for one reason: their most precious thing. Though it may be tough to look upon some of your athletes as "precious," they are to their parents and effective coaches know that they are.

Athlete

Coach Fox conducts practice all week long using every player on the roster to conduct a successful practice. During the next game, two thirds of those athletes don't get into the game.

Male Scholarships

	NUMBER OF H.S. BOYS PARTICIPATING	NUMBER AWARDED	STUDENTS RECEIVING*	SCHOLARSHIPS TOTAL AMOUNT GIVEN (IN MILLIONS)	AVG. % OF FULL SCHOLARSHIP	YEARLY VALUE PER RECIPIENT
ICE HOCKEY	32,166	1,089	1,369	$ 29.8	80%	$21,755
BASKETBALL	541,130	5,949	7,545	126.0	79	16,698
GYMNASTIC	3,495	94	186	2.5	51	13,351
FOOTBALL	1,025,762	19,549	28,299	367.3	69	12,980
FENCING	777	48	127	1.4	38	10,814
SKIING	11,854	69	143	1.4	49	9,783
TENNIS	158,796	1,257	2,927	26.5	43	9,050
LACROSSE	35,266	551	1,723	14.9	32	8,670
SOCCER	330,044	2,357	6,047	51.6	39	8,533
SWIMMING/DIVING	86,640	1,080	2,806	23.3	38	8,294
WATER POLO	13,871	83	282	2.2	30	7,756
WRESTLING	239,105	789	2,160	14.5	37	6,703
TRACK AND FIELD/ CROSS COUNTRY	713,305	3,112	8,414	54.6	37	6,491
VOLLEYBALL	35,915	129	416	2.6	31	6,360
GOLF	165,857	1,310	3,662	23.2	36	6,338
BASEBALL	451,701	3,983	12,272	71.3	32	5,806
RIFLERY	2,274	15	75	.3	21	3,608
BOWLING	10,110	—	—	—	—	—
FIELD HOCKEY	213	—	—	—	—	—
ROWING	2,186	—	—	—	—	—
SOFTBALL	1,484	—	—	—	—	—

* There are more students receiving athletic aid than there are scholarships available because many of the scholarships are divided among several students.

Female Scholarships

Note: N.C.A.A. and high school data encompass freshmen to seniors. N.C.A.A. data is for 2003–4, the most recent academic year that the information was gathered based on N.C.A.A. estimates from an internal study. High school participation figures are from 1999-2000, representing the academic year by which most college students receiving athletic aid in 2003-4 were playing high school sports.

Sources: National Collegiate Athletic Association; National Federation of State High School Associations

	NUMBER OF H.S. GIRLS PARTICIPATING	NUMBER AWARDED	STUDENTS RECEIVING*	SCHOLARSHIPS TOTAL AMOUNT GIVEN (IN MILLIONS)	AVG. % OF FULL SCHOLARSHIP	YEARLY VALUE PER RECIPIENT
ICE HOCKEY	4,245	423	529	$ 10.9	80%	$20,540
GYMNASTIC	21,620	411	512	8.4	80	16,478
BASKETBALL	451,600	6,217	8,000	123.7	78	15,459
VOLLEYBALL	382,755	4,352	6,614	84.2	66	12,726
TENNIS	159,740	2,293	3,506	44.3	65	12,629
FENCING	641	81	176	2.1	46	12,040
FIELD HOCKEY	58,372	699	1,680	17.6	42	10,464
SKIING	9,307	95	192	1.9	50	10,022
GOLF	54,720	1,224	2,302	22.6	53	9,801
ROWING	2,359	958	2,295	22.3	42	9,723
SWIMMING/DIVING	138,475	1,935	4,247	41.2	46	9,702
LACROSSE	26,677	630	1,756	17.0	36	9,685
SOCCER	270,273	3,964	9,310	78.2	43	9,404
SOFTBALL	365,008	3,637	7,877	65.0	46	8,255
TRACK AND FIELD/ CROSS COUNTRY	602,930	4,506	9,888	80.1	46	8,105
WATER POLO	11,356	153	445	3.5	34	7,793
RIFLERY	775	61	171	1.1	36	6,292
BOWLING	9,303	97	263	1.3	37	4,899
BASEBALL	1,354	—	—	—	—	—
FOOTBALL	573	—	—	—	—	—
WRESTLING	2,474	—	—	—	—	—

Effective coaches understand the level and purpose of athletic competition. At the varsity level, for example, they understand that there is an expectation of putting excellence on the field in order to win the game. Effective coaches understand that athletes want a chance to contribute to the team. Standing on the sideline or sitting on the bench can be tough for a number of reasons. If athletes do not see they are valued, they will lose interest or worse see themselves as a stumbling block to the goals of their friends and teammates. Remember our definition of team. Teams are made up of individuals with special skills. They have a common goal. They cannot achieve that common goal without the special skills of all the members. Effective coaches define roles for athletes and ask them to take those roles and become a teammate. That role can include a lot of playing time or very little.

Athletes can become jealous of their teammates and resentful toward their coach. If athletes are left to draw their own conclusions about their role on the team, it can become a difficult situation. When this occurs, what is left is a group of individuals that competes against each other rather than the opponent.

To make matters worse, when an athlete is called upon to expand his or her current role on the team, an athlete could feel the pressure of mistakes. For example, if an athlete, whose normal role is that of reserve (bench warmer), is asked to actually play, he or she may not take the necessary risks needed to demonstrate the skills they do have. They are afraid of making a mistake. Thus the athlete is right back where he or she started—on the bench.

What expectations do your athletes bring with them? After all, there is an opportunity cost associated with being an athlete. Athletes are sacrificing time and energy when they choose to participate in athletics. They could be spending their practice time with friends, family, or doing homework. They could be making a few extra dollars at a job in order to put gas in their car. What do they want in exchange for their dedication to practice? Do they want to be the star of the team? Do they want to play more? What do you think their expectations are for the upcoming season? Although coaches cannot promise delivery of those expectations, effective coaches at least know the answers to these questions.

Managing Expectations

While Coach Fox never manages expectations, effective coaches begin managing expectations before the season even starts. Many coaches trust the time-honored tradition of holding a pre-season meeting and having parents sign the parent–athlete handbook. The truly effective coaches are doing more. They understand that when parents and athletes hear or see something in a group setting they have a tendency to deflect comments; they rationalize that the coach must be addressing someone else. As a result, effective coaches, especially those involved in revenue-generating team sports, conduct individual parent meetings. The coach, parent, and their child attend this meeting.

Pre-Season Meeting

The individual meetings not only reinforce what was said at the group meeting, they allow everyone the opportunity to discuss expectations. Effective coaches want to know what their athlete's and parent's expectations are so that they can manage those expectations.

Effective coaches begin these meetings by asking the athlete what his or her expectations are for the upcoming season, prompting answers regarding such things as an athlete's expected role on the team and what would have to occur for the season to be called a success. The coaches ask what they want from their playing experience. Think of this meeting as the equivalent of the parent–teacher meeting conducted every year at the local school.

At the large group parent meeting, you can discuss eligibility, basic rules, the purpose of sports, the differences between interscholastic sports programs and club sports, and the communication chain. The focus of the individual meeting, on the other hand, is the athlete's role on the team. Effective coaches communicate what they believe to be the athlete's strengths and areas of improvement.

Effective coaches have the ability to articulate the philosophy behind the various levels of play. For example, at the middle school, the philosophy may be skill development, and as a result, everyone gets in the game and at a time that allows the athletes to demonstrate the skills they are trying to master. At the varsity level, the philosophy is much different and demonstrates a commitment to excellence: the best from each school ends up competing. We play those student-athletes who give us the best opportunity to demonstrate excellence in skill, hustle, responsibility, respect, and sportsmanship.

At the individual parent meeting, great coaches have the ability to discuss the various roles found on a team. Without stating absolutes, effective coaches discuss roles as a potential starter, a player who will see action on a regular basis, an emerging athlete, and a needed reserve. Although the category in which an athlete falls is unclear at the time of the meeting, effective coaches communicate an athlete's role as the season progresses.

Just as effective teachers have the ability to discuss how grades are assigned, a coach should be able to clarify how the various roles are assigned. Imagine discussing your son or daughter's grade in geometry and the teacher is unable to tell you how she assigns grades. How comfortable would you be with that teacher's ability? The same holds true for coaches. You are the professional in this situation. You will be assessing the needs of the individual and of the team. And as a result you will need to know how you assign roles. What things are you looking for in a potential starter for a position or event? What unique abilities will separate potential starters from emerging athletes?

Regardless of the role and how it is evaluated, the coach uses the meeting to let the athletes know that they are needed. No, they may not be the star of the team but they do have a role. If athletes begin owning that role and understanding their importance to the team, teams can begin competing against opponents and not themselves.

You will notice that the parent's expectations were not requested during the meeting. Effective coaches already know one thing to be true. Whatever the athlete's expectations are, the parents' will be greater going into that meeting. The goal is for the parent to hear their athlete's expectations and how you are going to manage those expectations in relationship to your number one concern—your team.

What Great Coaches Do *Differently*

Athlete In-Season Meeting

Effective coaches conduct individual athlete meetings through-out the sports season. Although these meetings are not long, most of them are planned. They usually take place at certain benchmarks throughout the season such as at the end of the nonconference schedule at the halfway point in the season.

As mentioned earlier, coaches have a responsibility to serve their athletes. How can a coach serve an athlete if they do not know what is going on in their lives on a more personal level? The athlete in-season meeting allows the coach to stay in touch with what that individual is experiencing on and off the field. The topics that are covered during this meeting are many: Self-evaluation—how do you think you're doing? Team evaluation—how do you think the team is developing this season? Academic evaluation—how are things going in U.S. History? Personal evaluation—how are you holding up after your dad's surgery?

The individual meetings offer an opportunity to give private, specific praise: "I appreciate your effort during the defensive drills," or "I like how you are setting the defense up at our offensive drills." The individual in-season athlete meeting also provides an opportunity to define, describe, and demonstrate athletic principles that the coach wishes to see from the athlete.

Post-Season Meeting

As they did for the pre-season meeting, the coach, parent, and their child attend the post-season meeting. The focus of this meeting is off-season expectations. Effective coaches use this meeting to allow the athlete to reflect on the past season; however, the meeting's strongest focus is about moving forward. Articulating his or her coaching philosophy regarding off-season expectations, the coach explains the off-season work-out schedule, how to contact the coach during the off-season, thoughts about camps and playing with other teams during the off-season, and expectations regarding progress in individual skill development. Effective coaches keep the meeting focused upon the future.

Instant Replay

Expectations

1. **Parents.** There are approximately 82 million parents of youth sports athletes today. Their involvement in youth sports has resulted in an expectation that they should not only be spectators but should also be part of the game itself.

2. **The Athletic Triangle.** A visual representation of athlete, coach and parent relationship, the athletic triangle stands with athletes at its pinnacle and parents and coaches at its base supporting the hopes and dreams of the athlete.

3. **The Professionalization of Youth Sports.** Parents encourage early childhood sports specialization based on the hope that the athlete's chances of winning a college scholarship or signing a sports contract are enhanced.

4. **What Are the Odds?** Effective coaches understand the odds of obtaining a college scholarship or signing a professional contract. They also understand the importance of building expectations that stretch the athlete to greater heights but are also built upon reality.

5. **Athletes.** Athletes have varying expectations about their athletic participation, whereas all athletes want a chance to contribute to the team. Effective coaches understand this expectation and therefore assign a role to everyone on the team.

6. **Managing Expectations.** Effective coaches begin managing expectations before the season even starts with parent pre-season team and individual meetings. They continue managing expectations with follow-up, athlete in-season meetings, and conclude with parent–athlete post-season meetings.

Chapter 7

Playing Time

Every coach has faced the accusation of not being fair. Effective coaches, ineffective coaches, and even Coach Fox have faced the accusation of not being fair when it comes to assigning playing time. Confronted by this age-old argument from parents, Coach Fox responds by saying, "Life is not fair" or "When they name you coach, you can decide who gets to play." Effective coaches respond first by being fair. Effective coaches are fair, but they don't necessarily treat everyone the same.

How can you be fair and not treat everyone the same? Answer this question. Is it fair to treat unequals equally? Coach Fox had a rule. He put the rule in after several of his worst players kept showing up late for a mandatory study hall session that occurred every Tuesday and Thursday morning before the start of school. The consequence of coming late was sitting out the next contest the exact number of minutes that you were late. The rule had very little impact on its intended target. Most of the athletes for which the rule was written were not playing much anyway. Then came that one day where the best athlete, the athlete who was never late and always made good grades, walked in the study hall session 15 minutes late.

What was fair? If the best athlete did not sit out 15 minutes was that fair? If the best athlete did sit out 15 minutes was that fair? Coach Fox was stuck. In order to be fair to the athletes who missed out on the playing time, which they did not have to begin with, the best athlete was going to sit the first 15 minutes of the next contest.

The effective coach would not have created that situation. Effective coaches have fewer rules than ineffective coaches. Coach Bruce Brown, the long time coach and motivational speaker, suggests that teams have only one rule, "Don't let your teammates down" (Brown, 2008). What does that rule not cover? Effective coaches understand the need for being fair and realize that the easiest way to demonstrate fairness is to have few published rules and even fewer published consequences.

Playing Time

Let's talk probably the single greatest issue in team sports that no one wants to talk about—playing time. Those who don't get any of it want some and those who have some want more of it. Those coaches that deal with parents understand exactly what I am talking about. It is the one issue that will take a mild-mannered parent and turn him or her into a nut case. Why? Parents are passionate about their children. They want what is fair and do not like to see them hurt.

Effective coaches know how to deal with the fair issue when it comes to playing time. They demonstrate to parents how being fair in all circumstances could benefit their son or daughter as circumstances change. Fiore (1999) demonstrated this concept in a potential response that an effective coach might give to the parent of a basketball player:

> Right now Pat is the ninth best player on the team and the third best guard. I am playing Pat about 2 minutes a game based on Pat's ability and being the ninth best player and the third best guard. As you probably know, typically I play our second best guard about 8 minutes a game. However, if Pat continues to work and practice hard, Pat may at some point in the future be the second best, or even possibly the best guard on the team. Of course that will depend up on Pat and Pat's teammates.
>
> What would not be fair is if at that point Pat did not get to play as much as the top guards do right now. And I would expect you to be upset with me if Pat becomes the second best guard on the team and didn't get to play about 8 minutes a game. However, it would not be fair if I did play Pat more now as third best guard because that would limit the time Pat might receive in the future if Pat improves.

Ineffective, outside-in coaches can't get to that point. They see the question as a challenge to their leadership. What they forget is that athlete is the most precious thing in the world to his or her parent.

Most Precious Thing

We hope that parents are the protectors of their most precious possessions. When their young athlete was a newborn, parents could move with the speed of an Olympic sprinter into the baby's room to check to make sure their most precious possession was okay. Then as that child grew older the parent served as their child's very own gymnastic spotter on every piece of playground equipment. The child would be helped up the steps of the slide, released, and then, as if the parent had been using technology found only on the Star Ship Enterprise, beamed down to the bottom of the slide just in time to snag their child from certain injury if allowed to hit the ground. Why? That child is their most precious possession. When parents put their child on the bus for the first time, they watched their child get on the bus and, with the skill of Spielberg, filmed them doing so. The parents then immediately jumped into the car, drove to the school breaking every town or city traffic ordinance in order to continue with part two of their film project: The walk into school. Why? That child is their most precious possession.

Effective coaches understand this and help parents understand their role in their child's athletic life. While respecting the role parents play, effective coaches carefully request that parents turn their athlete's athletic involvement over to them and the team. That can be difficult for parents to do because of the tough lessons associated with athletics, but that is exactly why parents should.

Great coaches understand that parents do not turn their children over to the local movie theater. At the local movie theater you do not see a five-year-old boy being dropped off at the newest PG-13 Batman movie. Parents do not let their ten-year-old girl visit any Internet site she wishes. You do not hear parents saying, "I think I will turn my daughter over to the World Wide Web." Why?—"The risk."

Effective coaches communicate with parents that the risk is worth the teachable moments provided by sports. Why? Because it is a game and it's their game. It's a game that, when it is done right, has wonderful things to offer beyond the scoreboard. Parents can risk having athletes shoot the game-winning free throw. Parents can risk having athletes make a throw that will either win or lose the game. Parents can risk having athletes score the winning goal. Parents can risk it because of the value it has. The teachable moment that occurs when the free throw is made or missed. The teachable moment that exists when a throw is attempted which will cause one team to win and the other team to lose. Parents can risk it because what can be gained far outweighs what can be lost.

By turning their child over to the coach and the team, the parent is telling their athlete all the successes and failures are theirs. There are not too many places in life that a parent can tell their child this. The difficult part of this is letting children work out solutions themselves. Many times, parents want to be the problem solvers because they find it painful to watch their children find their own solutions. Why? That child is their most precious possession. Athletics is a great place for young people to take risks and fail. Athletic participation creates a safe location for character to be taught and to prove itself.

I'm Sorry That Happened

There is a tool that effective coaches use that can slow down a charging parent. It is a tool that any coach, even Coach Fox, can use no matter what the details and it is a tool that builds respect. What is this magical tool? The ability to say, "I am sorry that happened." No matter the details of the situation, a coach can tell the parent that they are sorry that happened, and the truth is they are.

No coach wants a player to sit the entire contest. Yet, putting certain athletes in certain contests may take away from the team's overriding commitment to excellence. Are you sorry that Jill or Johnny didn't get into the game? Yes. Would you do it again? Yes.

By saying "I am sorry that happened" you are not saying that it's your fault or that it will not happen again. You are also not placing or assigning blame. You are just sorry that it happened. The more aggressive the parent is, the sorrier I am it happened! Inside I am saying, "I am sorry it happened, otherwise I wouldn't be here with you!" Of course we would never share our private thoughts with these parents and we would always maintain a professional attitude. Nevertheless, the simple statement "I am sorry that happened" is a powerful defusing technique.

By saying "I am sorry that happened," I am also preparing my parents for the tough conversation. Effective coaches have a version of the tough conversation that they use at the pre-season meeting with parents and for one-on-one individual parent meetings. The tough conversation may go something like this:

> Thanks for coming in today. I understand that you are upset about your son/daughter's role on the team. I would first like to explain my coaching philosophy as it applies to playing time and then I would like to listen to what you have to say. First, I would like to say that I am sorry that this is happening and I understand a parent's passion for their children. I also understand that just as a classroom teacher evaluates a student and assigns a grade, the coach evaluates an athlete. The evaluation involves several things: skill level, athleticism, execution, and following team rules, just to name a few. Your son/daughter has many of these skills, yet as I evaluate the entire team, I must assign playing time based upon the needs of the team. Of course, it is sometimes difficult to balance the feelings of the individual versus the needs of the team, yet I try to focus on the needs of the team.
>
> The truth is how I see those needs may be far different from how you see them. Yet I will say this— I am always evaluating and apply a great deal of integrity to my process. I am sure you would want a coach who would play those athletes who gave the team the best chance of winning. Though we may not agree who those athletes are, I will assure you that that is who I am trying to put into the competition.
>
> Thank you for listening to me. Now I will listen to what you have to say.

The truth is, "I am sorry this happened," is not only an effective tool when dealing with playing time. This phrase can be used any time someone is experiencing a difficult situation. An athlete's parent becomes ill, "I am sorry that's happening." An athlete becomes injured, "I am sorry that happened." A player fails a math class and loses his or her eligibility, "I am sorry that happened." Again, I was not that math teacher and I did not create the eligibility rules, I am just sorry that happened.

All coaches can see the value in being able to say, "I am sorry that happened." Effective coaches not only develop and practice this skill, but teach athletes and assistant coaches the skill. If teams learn to use it regularly, they will have a lot less repairing in the future. In particular, if our most difficult athletes can master this skill, what a service to them—and to our team.

So, we might start by suggesting that in difficult circumstances that an athlete or an assistant coach be able to say, "Hey, look, I am sorry that happened." If they are resistant, ask them if they have ever been pulled over by a police officer for a traffic violation.

The Highway Patrol

As a coach, you have several opportunities to teach this skill and other team-building skills to your athletes. Almost all team sports athletes can relate to the following example:

Chuck lives in a small town. Chuck drives a cherry red Corvette convertible. One evening while coming home from work, Chuck gets pulled over by a local police officer for going 45 miles per hour in a 35-mile-per-hour speed zone. As the officer approaches, Chuck roles down the window and starts ranting about all the cars that have been passing him like he was standing still. Chuck throws in a couple of expletives and a dirty look as he reaches for his insurance information. What are the odds that Chuck is going to get a ticket? What are the chances that the officer will remember Chuck and his car? Has driving through his small town become easier or more difficult?

Now what would have happened if Chuck had rolled down his window, placed his hand on the steering wheel, and began by saying, "Officer, I am sorry that happened." What are the odds that Chuck gets a ticket now? What are the chances that the officer will remember Chuck and his car? Has driving through his small town become easier or more difficult? Chances are Chuck may still receive a ticket; however, he has not made it more difficult to drive through his small town.

Athletes in team sports see this scenario played out every time they take the field of competition. Every time an official or an umpire makes a call this scenario is played out. No, there are no monetary fines associated for holding in a high school football game but there are fines (10 yards). A coach's or an athlete's response to that call can even make the fine worse (additional yardage or ejection).

This is not to say that every time an infraction is called your athletes run up to the official and say "I am sorry I traveled," or "I am sorry I handballed." Yet every time the whistle blows or an umpire makes a call, your athletes do have a decision to make. They must decide how they are going to react to the call. Will they react like Chuck and make things worse for themselves and their team?

Just as we teach, describe, demonstrate, direct, and reinforce any skill, we must also teach this relationship skill. If we want our athletes to walk away from every call, we must not only model this ourselves but also teach our athletes how to react. Telling someone to do something without teaching them how makes no sense at all. So teach them what to say and how to react. Why must we describe, demonstrate, and direct how to interact with an official? Because they may not have acquired those skills on their own or at home. Chuck may be, in fact, some athlete's dad.

When coaches take the opportunity to build stronger relationships with those around them and to teach the behaviors associated with successful teams, their job becomes easier. Not only that, no matter what profession our athletes enter, they will need to deal with a supervisor; and the way they respond could determine whether they succeed in that job. Some athletes already have this skill. They understand that handing the ball back to the official rather than flipping the ball down and letting it roll away from the official might impact the contest. There are athletes who understand how to improve a struggling teammate's performance with a simple look, word, or gesture. Effective coaches reinforce these behaviors; they also take advantage of teachable moments to help athletes build these skills.

Talking About Playing Time

Playing time discussions require effective coaches to be calm, cool, and collected all at the same time. They understand that these are critical conversations and therefore must hold back one inherent trait in order to engage in them—the need to win. As coaches we love to win, yet wanting to win sits atop the list of critical conversation killers. As coaches, heaven only knows, that we come by this passion naturally enough. This desire to win is built into our very fiber. Add to this the fact that playing time discussions are usually spontaneous and more often than not come after a loss. And since you're caught by surprise, you're forced to conduct an extraordinary complex human interaction in real time.

In his book, *Crucial Conversations*, Kerry Paterson (2002) explains that we are designed wrong to handle this type of conversation. When we are hit with a playing time discussion on our way to the locker-room following a loss, nature kicks in. Our emotions don't exactly prepare us coaches to have a nice chat immediately following a loss, especially when being told how terrible we are. No, that is when nature begins to kick in and genetics tells us to either fight or run.

When you combine the need to win with someone questioning your professional judgment in ways that might make a convict blush, adrenaline gets pumped into your bloodstream. You don't choose to do this. Your adrenal glands do it, and then you have to live with it. Paterson goes on to tell us that the brain then diverts blood from activities it deems nonessential to high priority tasks such as hitting or throwing a fit. So now, right when you need your reasoning skill, all you are left with is your fight or flight reaction.

The Goldilocks Test

Effective coaches enter playing time discussions remembering Goldilocks and the three bears. That's right, Goldilocks. You know the story. Goldilocks goes into the woods and visits the home of Papa Bear, Momma Bear, and Baby Bear. After trying out the sitting and dining arrangements, she finds her way to the bedroom where one bed is too hard, one bed is too soft, and one bed is just right.

When confronting parents with playing time issues, make sure that you are neither too hard nor too soft but that you are "just right." We will call this the Goldilocks Test. "How dare you approach me following the game..." is too hard. Or, "It's probably my fault for not telling you this but..." is too soft. "This is not a good time to deal with this issue—here is my card. Call me tomorrow" is just right.

When the blood starts to flow from your brain to your hands and feet and when you start to lose your peripheral vision—emember Goldilocks.

Instant Replay

Playing Time

1. **What's Fair?** Every coach has faced the accusation of not being fair. Effective coaches respond first by being fair. Effective coaches are fair, but they don't necessarily treat everyone the same.

2. **Playing Time.** It is probably the single greatest issue in team sports that no one wants to talk about. Effective coaches demonstrate to parents how being fair in all circumstances could benefit their son or daughter as circumstances change.

3. **Most Precious Thing.** It is hoped that parents are the protectors of their most precious possessions. Effective coaches understand this and help parents understand their role in their child's athletic life. While respecting the role parent's play, effective coaches carefully request that parents turn their athlete's athletic involvement over to them and the team.

4. **I'm Sorry That Happened.** An effective tool that coaches use to slow down a charging parent is the ability to say, "I am sorry that happened." No matter the details of the situation, a coach can tell the parent that they are sorry that happened and the truth is they are.

5. **The Highway Patrol.** Teaching athletes to demonstrate the same respect for officials that they would a highway patrol officer can benefit the team.

6. **Talking About Playing Time.** Playing time discussions require effective coaches to be calm, cool, and collected at the same time they are managing the inherent need to win.

7. **The Goldilocks Test.** When coaches are confronted by parents with playing time issues, effective coaches make sure that their response is neither too hard nor too soft, but just right.

Chapter 8

Who Is the Most Comfortable?

All coaches face the challenge of balancing rules and guidelines with those times when we need to make exceptions. This is especially true when it comes to behavior and execution expectations for athletes. We can be concise, be clear, and communicate, but situations still arise when tough decisions are much more in shades of gray than we wish.

Likewise, all coaches establish internal ground rules that reflect our core belief systems; even though it seems that at least some of the time other influences tread on them. Effective coaches have an internal standard that supports effective practices: When making decisions, ask *who is most comfortable?* Then, m*ake every decision based upon your best athletes.*

Treat Everyone As If They Are Good

There is a gentleman who makes a good living buying apartment buildings, fixing them up, and renting them out. When asked about his ability to control the types of tenants he wanted, his response struck a cord: "If there are tenants I would rather not have, I just remodel their apartment. They're not used to living in a nice place, so they either start behaving as if they deserve to stay there or they become so uncomfortable that they move out."

The same phenomenon occurs on athletic teams: We can remodel the climate and culture of a team in such a way that athletes become uncomfortable and change their previous habits. As coaches we want our best athletes to be comfortable and our worst athletes to become uncomfortable and to change in a positive direction. Consider the following example:

As you are walking past the locker room you hear Debbie Divider harping about not getting enough playing time, which makes your best athletes, those who are playing, uncomfortable. Regardless, all athletes who are not playing much are actually enjoying it. You now have a choice: You could pull a Coach Fox and lose it, storming in the locker room red faced and begin ripping Debbie about being selfish and not a team player. Or you could respond as an effective coach would by quietly walking in the locker room and saying, "I know everyone wants to play, I would be disappointed if you did not. Debbie, I will be here tomorrow after practice to hear more about what you were talking about if you care to pursue it." What just happened? Debbie has just lost her audience. Those athletes who want more playing time don't want to be seen as selfish and Debbie will have to stay late tomorrow, without an audience, if she wants to keep griping. In which situation are the best athletes more comfortable? Obviously, they are more comfortable in the latter.

Uncomfortable Parents

Coaches can apply this same principle to parents. If you coach at the youth sport or high school level, then I'm sure you've had to wait for a parent to arrive long after everyone else has been picked up. Coaches understand the liability issue of leaving an athlete unsupervised and as a result, may call 15 different locations trying to find a parent, grandparent or at least a first or second cousin to come and pick this athlete up and take them home. The next day, what do you do?

Coach Fox sends the following letter home:

Dear Parents,

You **MUST** pick your athlete up **immediately** following practice or contest. The **coaching staff** has been waiting for up to an **hour** after practice or a contest waiting for parents to arrive. **Please be considerate of our time.**

Now ask yourself: Out of the entire team, how many parents was that note actually written for? One or two? Do we really believe that the bold print will strike fear in the hearts of those one or two? What are the chances that those two will even read the note? If they do read it, do they now feel more comfortable about being late because they now think that everyone is picking their athlete up late after practice. What are your best parents now thinking? "Last week I was three minutes late picking up Johnny. I hope that coach doesn't think that will happen again. I hope that he does not hold this against Johnny and cut his playing time."

Even worse than this, as the coach, what do you think will happen the next time your practice spills over the allotted two hours you've scheduled? Now that the letter has been sent, the coach better not let practice run one minute over its scheduled time. Why? Please be considerate of OUR time.

The decision to send a note home makes those parents who are picking their athletes up on time feel uncomfortable. So what does the effective coach do? A better approach would be to call the small number of negligent parents, making them feel uncomfortable.

As a rule, I've learned that notes sent home really don't do that much good. But if you feel that some kind of general reminder is necessary, focus on your best parents, and treat everyone as if they were good. An effective coach would not only send a note home but would probably also e-mail a note that might read something like this:

Dear Parents,

Thank you for your support in picking up your athlete immediately following practices and contests. This enables the coaching staff to begin working promptly on tomorrow's practice schedule. Thank you for your continued support.

I still doubt that this note reaches its intended audience but if it does, it will be just as effective as the earlier example. The difference is that this note reinforces the behavior you are looking for, making the best parents more comfortable and those showing up late uncomfortable.

Uncomfortable Athletes

How do you react to the following? During a drill your laziest and often injured athlete seems to be taking the day off and not working as hard as you know he or she can. You are frustrated that this athlete is not working hard. How does Coach Fox respond? "What's wrong today?" or "What is your excuse this time?," he asks.

The next day you run the exact same drill. This time for some reason your best athlete seems to be taking the day off and not working as hard as you know he or she can. Do you respond the same way or do you react differently to your best athlete? Maybe you do not say anything and think he or she deserves to be given a pass, after all, you understand the ability to ignore and see what needs to be seen. We believe effort is not one of those things you can ignore. Believe me, the rest of the team knows how hard he or she is working and they know you know as well. So, maybe Coach Fox responds with, "Are you feeling okay?" or "How's that ankle feeling?" Who's your pet now?

The truth is you want both athletes to be working as hard as they can each and every day. Is there a way to react to both athletes regardless of their reputation? Yes, there is. An effective coach would simply ask, "Hey, what are you feeling in there today?" Doesn't that get the same information from both athletes? Doesn't it let both athletes know that you are aware of their performance? No one seems insulted, no one's effort is questioned in public, and no one is perceived as being the coach's pet.

Remember the store with the "No Shoplifting" sign? How does that same owner treat customers? Does the owner walk behind customers, faking interest elsewhere, and just as you pick something up, asks in an accusatory tone, "What are you doing over there?" How does that make you feel? It would make me feel uncomfortable. Now what if the smiling store owner said, "May I help you?" Now how do you feel? Comfortable. Neither approach may stop a shoplifter, but at least someone that might actually spend some money is still in the store. The only difference is we have treated everyone as if they were good. The store owner has created a culture that allows for his best customers, the paying ones, to feel at home. Effective coaches create a culture in which their best people feel comfortable and others aspire to change.

Uncomfortable Feelings Make People Change One Way or Another

If a coach argues with a belligerent parent, who feels uncomfortable? Not the parent; hostile parents love to argue. It's their niche. That's one good reason never to argue with difficult people—they have a lot more practice at it! However, another reason is that part of our job as coaches is to teach people appropriate ways to behave, not help them refine the inappropriate skills they already have.

No, it's the coach who argues with a parent who feels uncomfortable and is likely to avoid the parent. The parent actually feels empowered—free to go tell everyone how the coach acted, what was said, and how the argument ended. The parent will come back ready for battle the next time.

Remember the first example of the pick-up note sent home to parents. This approach does make some people feel uncomfortable, the ones who themselves to a higher standard. The same holds true for your best athletes. General broad reaching statements about performance or the lack thereof makes your best people feel affronted and behave differently, and they will be less enthusiastic about what the team is trying to accomplish.

If applied consistently, the question "Who is most comfortable and who is least comfortable?" can bring clarity to our decision making. We are not painting on a blank canvas; we will make the least effective people uncomfortable, and at the very least, our decisions will not make our best people uncomfortable. Effective coaches find that this ground rule—make the people who do the right thing feel comfortable—works for them, too. They feel more comfortable with their decision making!

Comfortable Coaches

In a previous chapter we mentioned the individual meetings at the conclusion of the season. This meeting is just as much about your performance as it is your athletes'. Effective coaches want their performance evaluated. There is a catch, however.

Some organizations allow for their athletes, and even their parents, to confidentially evaluate the coach at the end of the season. Effective coaches can be uncomfortable with this situation. The goal of the evaluation is to see areas where improvement can take place. As you can imagine, this can be a controversial process. You see many athletes, just like many coaches, make decisions based upon what is best for them. Just as true is the fact that the best athletes, just like the best coaches, make decisions based on what is best for the team.

If we seek input from our most capable athletes and colleagues, we are much more likely to make the right choices, but there is the catch. The anonymous evaluation does not let the coach know what his best athletes and best parents actually think. What if the athletic administrator was evaluated in the same way? Do you think they would want to know what their best coaches thought about their performance as opposed to their worst? Sure they would. Effective coaches also understand that it is more important to be aware of what our best athletes' views are. Effective coaches continually ask themselves who is most comfortable and who is least comfortable with each decision they make. When we face a challenging decision, we'll feel less alone if we ask ourselves, "What will the best athlete think?"

Instant Replay

Who Is the Most Comfortable?

1. **Treat Everyone As If They Are Good.** Effective coaches create a climate and culture for their teams. In doing so they want their best athletes to be comfortable so that they will continue what they are doing. They want their worst athletes to become uncomfortable and to change in a positive direction.

2. **Uncomfortable Parents.** Coaches want their best parents to feel comfortable and worst parents to feel uncomfortable. Effective coaches consider this principle when communicating and interacting with parents.

3. **Uncomfortable Athletes.** Effective coaches do not insult, do not question effort in public, and do not demonstrate favoritism. They simply make the best athletes feel comfortable and their worst athletes feel uncomfortable.

4. **Uncomfortable Feelings Make People Change One Way or Another.** If a coach argues with a belligerent parent, who feels uncomfortable? Not the parent; hostile parents love to argue. It's their niche. That's one good reason never to argue with difficult people—they have a lot more practice at it! Another reason is that part of our job as coaches is to teach people appropriate ways to behave, not help them refine the inappropriate skills they already have.

5. **Comfortable Coaches.** The best coaches, just like the best athletes, make decisions based on what is best for the team. Effective coaches, when being evaluated, want to know what their best athletes and their best parents think of their performance.

Chapter 9

Planning

Many coaches can teach the skills needed in their sport while others are fantastic at understanding and developing strategy. Yet neither coach will have success if they fail to plan. Great coaches have a plan. They understand that their team and athletes' success depends upon this plan. Great coaches have a plan and purpose for everything they do. If things don't turn out they way they envisioned, they have a plan of how they are going to reflect on performance.

In contrast, less effective coaches seem to move through their season without a clue. In some ways, it almost seems that they don't want to have a plan; they don't want to take responsibility for what happens. If things don't work out as well as they had hoped, they look for something or someone else to blame.

The effective coach is always aware that the "devil is in the details." Think about your details: finance, logistics, personnel, rules, eligibility, expectations, just to name a few. Effective coaches may not like to manage all these things—but they do. They realize the truth behind the truism, "Failure to plan is planning to fail." Many coaches understand the need to plan. Great coaches also plan but what great coaches do is break the planning down into pre-season, season, and post-season duties.

Pre-Season

During the pre-season, effective coaches have already put their staff together. That includes assistant coaches, managers, and team captains. During this time they are already engaging their staff in matters relating to team rules, finance, legal responsibility, and philosophy. Effective coaches have already established a season calendar that identifies staff, team, and parent and individual meetings. During all of the planning phases, one thing that effective coaches do is delegate. They delegate tasks to their staff based upon the strengths and weaknesses of each coach. Effective coaches also delegate when they have developed a high level of trust in the abilities of those assisting with their program. So during the pre-season, for example, effective coaches can delegate others to collect player information, establish important contact information, collect physical examination approval and parent's approval sheets, distribute equipment, secure team funds, establish the team contact information sheet, create team meeting agendas, plan special events, and establish a scouting calendar, just to name a few.

Rules versus Expectation

Coaches love rules. Everybody loves rules—except those who have to follow them and those who have to enforce them. The best advice I ever received was, "You do not have to prove who is in charge. Everybody knows who is in charge. And, the more you try to prove it, the more they try to prove you wrong."

When establishing rules or expectations during the pre-season, there are a few things that great coaches do differently. Great coaches have only necessary rules, which they have examined through the lens of reason and purpose. It is difficult for athletes to remember many rules. Great coaches understand that too many rules will cause athletes to rebel if for no other reason than there are too many rules.

Effective coaches establish only rules that are realistic, which are rules athletes have the ability to follow. A rule such as "No talking on the bus ride home when you lose," will be very difficult for athletes to follow. Why establish a rule you know any of your athletes will break or that really has no purpose?

The purpose of rules is to add to the athlete's experience. So if you think you must have rules establish only those that challenge athletes to do the right thing rather than a list of things not to do. A rule that states. "Don't leave your towels on the floor" tells the athlete nothing about what they should do with their towels after a shower. Effective coaches, in contrast, would use the rule, "Place all dirty towels in the dirty towel container" because it tells the athlete what to do with the towel. The truly great coach won't post any such rule and confront those one or two athletes that continue to not put their dirty towels away.

Instead of having iron clad rules, another possible approach may be to establish expectations. These may seem like splitting hairs, but there is a core difference. That is that rules usually are directly attached to consequences and expectations are not. The fear of the unknown is much more significant than the fear of the known. We mentioned Coach Bruce Brown's belief—"Don't let your teammate down." Is this a rule or an expectation? It is very simple. If someone asked Coach Brown, "What are you going to do if someone does let a teammate down," his response would probably be, "I don't know." The reason that would be his response is because it is the truth. Obviously it depends on what it was that happened.

When we attempt to have a rule such as, "Don't leave your towels on the floor or you will have to do 25 pushups!" two things happen. One is that since it is a rule, you as the coach now have to enforce it! And, if you laid on the consequence in advance, you have to do so equally. Now, if I have one player who consistently is disrespectful, disruptive, and pushes the limits and he or she appears to intentionally throw a towel on the floor, I may actually feel limited to just being able to have the athlete do 25 pushups when in actuality the athlete should be well beyond that. The other challenge is what if the most respectful and respective player on the team unknowingly leaves a towel on the floor? You know what happens? I just boxed myself in a corner. The least cooperative player got the same consequence for intentionally doing something for the 30th time as my team captain who apologized when seeing the manager picking up the towel! However, if we have expectations such as "Leave every room better than it was when you entered it," we have left ourselves much more leeway to do the right thing. Plus, by drawing hard lines such as "Don't leave your towels on the floor!" The players we most want to control can fight back by leaving only a shampoo bottle on the floor! Since no rule covered that, we may feel a lack of options on our end.

Whether you choose to call them rules or expectations is not the real issue. What is essential is that we approach them in the appropriate manner. Great coaches know the difference and apply it to every situation.

Earlier it was noted that effective coaches use drills that are purpose-driven rather than reason-driven. The same holds true for rules. Athletes should know the purpose of the rule. Effective coaches understand that they can control an athlete's behavior by establishing rules but the real goal is to develop athletes, not rules. Athletes should not follow rules because they have to or because they will be rewarded or punished. Rather, they will want to follow rules because they understand that the purpose of the rule benefits them.

If you have a rule, at some point or another, you are going to need to enforce it. Effective coaches are consistent in rule enforcement. The consequence of breaking a rule should be known up front and should be equally applied. In fact, this should be the number one rule in establishing rules. It will not help that athlete who breaks the rule because they will still be arguing about its fairness but what they can't argue is that they did not know it or that it is applied differently for the team's star.

Coaching guru Bruce Brown states that the best rule for any athlete is "Don't let your teammate down." What does that not cover?—eligibility, attendance, effort, preparation—it covers it all. What a great rule to establish, and it eliminates many others that are often not needed.

Season

Effective coaches carry out their pre-season plans during the course of the season. For example, they distribute the team rules and needed equipment, carry out the scouting schedule, conduct team and individual meetings, and put their coaching philosophy in action. Many coaches are preparing practice plans; great coaches take great pains in establishing purpose to those plans. In contrast, less effective coaches put their practice plans together on the fly. They are creating them between classes, recycling last week's, or not creating a practice plan at all. Effective coaches are following their season plan but are making changes based upon what they are seeing. They are seeking the input from their assistants and the best athletes and are creating plans that have a purpose. In fact, an effective coach's season plan contains the time needed to plan.

All coaches spend time during the season working on the technical aspects of their sports, but what about their tactical skills? Probably more often than not tactical errors lose as many athletic contests as do technical errors. As a result effective coaches spend just as much time developing the tactical aspects of the sport as they do the technical aspects; in fact, they combine the two. As we noted in Chapter 4, many coaches can describe, demonstrate, and direct athletes, and the truly great coaches know how to use reinforcement to bring out the very best. When they are engaged in describing, demonstrating, and directing, they are aware of doing so in the context of the contest. As they demonstrate a tactical approach to their sport, effective coaches present the technical aspects needed to carry it off. Regardless of the success demonstrated by Ralph Macchio in the "Karate Kid," for the most part, the Mr. Miyagi method does little to motivate athletes. You know the Mr. Miyagi method, wax on, wax off, sand the floor and paint the fence so that you can call upon these skills when facing a group of 1980's bullies who choose to fight you one at a time rather than just ganging up on you.

Although that method worked well in the movie, teaching a skill outside of the context in which it will be used does little to motivate athletes to learn or refine their skills. Repetitive drills conducted outside the scope of what they will use does little to encourage learning. On the other hand, activities that help athletes connect techniques to strategy are well received and encourage learning. Effective coaches allow their athletes to see what skills are needed to execute what tactics.

Effective coaches are taking this practice a step further by making tasks competitive as well as instructive. It was Aristotle who said, "We are what we repeatedly do. Excellence then is not an act but a habit." According to four-time national champion lacrosse coach Missy Foote (2009), whose practice consists of nothing but competitive situations, "If you practice to win, it will translate into playing to win," and that will be achieved if, "you allow the game to also be the teacher." This does not mean that you simply roll the balls out and start playing. According to Foote, to run an effective competitive practice the following conditions must be met:

1. Technique and skill cannot be compromised
2. The game must also be a teacher
3. Short duration, high tempo
4. The game must have meaning

There are other in-season aspects of the coach's job dealing with equipment, travel, practice calendar, maintaining the budget but maybe one thing most common among effective coaches is how they manage their time.

Multitasking

Effective coaches prioritize. They focus on a single task instead of trying to multitask. They understand that multitasking is another way of saying you are going to complete several tasks, none of which are going to be very good. Yuhong Jiang, Ph.D., assistant professor of psychology at Harvard University (Jiang, Saxe, & Kanwisher, 2004), points out that the brain isn't built to concentrate on two things at once. It works more slowly if it tries to.

Effective coaches focus on those things that need to get done and separate out everything else. Separating what's important from what's not important is prioritizing. Ineffective coaches fail to put the big tasks first. They either believe they have unlimited time, thinking that they will have more time tomorrow to get something done, or they underestimate how much time they really do have. They have no ability to estimate how long a task will take.

Post-Season

When the games come to an end, many coaches realize that the role of the coach does not. They begin totaling up statistics for end of the season awards, attend to record keeping, conduct end-of-the-year evaluations with their staff, and conduct end-of-season team meetings along with other managerial tasks. Effective coaches are doing more. They conduct individual meetings with their parents and athletes. And great coaches change their focus. During the entire pre-season and season they have focused on the needs of the team first and the individual second. Once the season comes to an end, effective coaches change their focus from the team to individual athletes.

This practice allows the coach to continue to build the player–coach relationship. For example, if an athlete is graduating off the team, the effective coaches will assist the athletes in locating other opportunities to participate. The coach of the local high school team helps the graduating seniors obtain opportunities to play at the collegiate level. The coach of the 10-and-under league will help the 10-year-old athletes to find the appropriate league in which they can continue playing. These same coaches are also locating or hosting individual skill camps that their athletes can attend. Just as effective coaches allow their athletes to evaluate them, players should also be evaluated and given specific areas to work on during the post-season.

Instant Replay

Planning

1. **Pre-Season.** During the pre-season effective coaches identify and begin training staff in a number of tasks on and off the field. This time is also used to delegate tasks and establish a season calendar for skill and tactical implementation, parent and athlete meetings, games, practices, and special events.

2. **Rules.** Effective coaches obey this one rule in establishing rules—don't have too many rules.

3. **Season.** Effective coaches carry out their pre-season plans during the course of the season and coach from the inside-out. Probably more often than not tactical errors lose as many athletic contests as do technical errors. As a result, effective coaches spend just as much time developing the tactical aspects of the sport as they do the technical aspects.

4. **Multitasking.** Effective coaches prioritize. They focus on a single task instead of trying to multitask. They understand that that multitasking is another way of saying I'm going to complete several tasks, none of which are going to be very good.

5. **Post-Season.** When the games come to an end, many effective coaches realize that the role of coach does not. During the entire pre-season and season they have focused on the needs of the team first and the individual second. Once the season comes to an end effective coaches change their focus from the team to individual athletes.

Chapter 10

Over-Coaching

Ｎll coaches try to prepare their teams for the various situations they will face in a contest. As a goal this concept is easy to strive for but difficult to achieve. As coaches we all want our athletes to be prepared for the upcoming contest. Yet how do you prepare for every situation your athletes will face?

Effective coaches understand that they are coaching people, not machines. Machines for the most part do exactly as programmed. Yet what happens to a computer's hard drive when it has used up all of its space? It slows down. The same thing is true for your athletes. Coach John Wooden noted that over-coaching is a bigger problem than undercoaching in today's game. As coaches we are constantly evaluating performance and figuring out our response. Effective coaches know what should be seen and apply a remedy that is found in what they are already doing. Ineffective coaches are adding on a whole other layer of offense or defense.

Think of all the new social information gathering and spreading technology that is available to our athletes today: texting, twittering, blogging, Facebook, MySpace, just to name a few. I can't begin to understand all the new social networking avenues that are available, let alone try to keep up with them.

Now think about throwing a new offense or defense at your athletes every other week, or ten tips on techniques during a two-hour practice session. It's no wonder that so many athletes have trouble improving the quality of the performance—they have too much to think about. How many different strategies, tips, or techniques can you teach someone before they eventually begin to slow down? We want our athletes to constantly be improving and honing their skills and execution, but at what point are we over-coaching?

Elbow here, feet here, head down, get your head up, follow through, bend your knees, get up on the balls of your feet, extend your leg, see your man and the ball, stay with your man, tuck your chin, don't tuck your chin, relax, let's get fired up, blah, blah, blah...are you becoming the adult voice in a Peanuts cartoon?

There are many dangers of over-coaching, but perhaps the most harmful is dispelling the self-confidence of a player. A leadership quote that has always resonated with me is, "Confidence is the most valuable gift we can give." If a player or person is always worried about being second-guessed or feels that the supervisor–coach whom they are working to please is questioning their every move, their ability to operate on all cylinders is greatly damaged. Though we often hear of the importance of momentum, playing sports is more about the importance of confidence. It is a fine balance though. By building and reinforcing skills in players, we build confidence. It is essential to find that balance with each of our athletes.

Effective coaches, since they have put together a season calendar, understand that they have a time and a place for teaching strategy. In breaking down a problem, they know what needs to be seen at a particular point in the season. Coach Fox passes on the entire coach's play book all at one time, which affects an athlete's performance ability. If the coach continually offers up one coaching strategy after another, the athlete soon becomes confused. Effective coaches know what to ignore and find simple tips when they see something that needs to be addressed. They know how to coach without overloading the system.

Coach Fox makes the common mistake of adjusting too much and as result makes the skill or contest more difficult than it has to be, in short, over-coaching. Coach Fox fails to see what needs to be seen and ignores nothing. All too often over-coaching leads to indecision on the part of the athletes. They simply fail to execute because their mind is filled with twenty different strategies. Effective coaches have developed the proper balance between over- and undercoaching their teams.

As a coach, how would your team perform if you weren't there? If your team could function without your presence, you have probably done a good job in your preparation. Yet, as a young coach, I thought I needed to have an offense and defense for every situation. The result was that although my teams could run just about any offense or defense known to basketball, we were never very efficient at running any of them. I had failed to understand the importance finding simplicity and depth.

KISS

The concept of keeping it simple is often seen in the acronym KISS for "Keep It Simple, Stupid" or "Keep It Short and Simple." KISS states that simplicity should be a key goal and that complexity should be avoided. By keeping it simple, effective coaches are not dummying down, rather they are taking a single concept and understanding as thoroughly as possible.

Great coaches understand the importance of depth while less effective coaches live for delivering on breadth. Depth is difficult for young coaches to grasp. They have been raised in the age of instant coverage, instant gratification, instant fame and, therefore, believe great teams can be changed with an instant fix. Great coaches ask the question, What do my athletes need from me today? While less effective coaches say, "This is what I need to cover today."

All coaches want their athletes to execute at the highest levels possible yet only the great coaches provide the instruction and opportunity for this to occur. The execution of a golf swing, a back stroke, a free throw, or any sport-specific skill takes time to develop. Great coaches understand that one time, short-term efforts or fixes do not provide lasting changes, but sustained focused efforts over a long period of time can bring long-term success. What effective coaches do differently is try to keep it simple by adding depth. Look at some of the great coaches of all time—when we think of their teams we don't think of multiple offenses or defenses, we think of a distinct game plan.

- ◆ John Wooden – High Post Offense
- ◆ Vince Lombardi – The Packer Sweep
- ◆ Phil Jackson – Triangle Offense
- ◆ Bill Walsh – West Coast Offense
- ◆ Bob Knight – Motion Offense
- ◆ Bear Bryant – The Wishbone
- ◆ Casey Stengel – Platooning

Adding depth requires a coach to understand a sport-specific skill and strategy at their fundamental levels. That is where effective coaches live—the fundamentals. Coaching 101 is describing, demonstrating, directing, and reinforcement and repeating these over and over again. Those teams that understand the basic fundamentals of their sports and can execute them under pressure are the teams who win repeatedly. Through simplicity and depth, effective coaches seek not just practice but perfect practice of the fundamentals, while not letting perfection stand in the way of progress.

The Power to Ignore

Coach Fox sees everything. An athlete is joking around with a teammate before practice—Coach Fox sees it. An athlete is 30 seconds late for practice—Coach Fox sees it. An athlete almost executes a difficult maneuver making only one mistake—Coach Fox sees and calls the athlete our for the mistake. But great coaches have the ability to see the things that need to be seen. Put simply, they have the power to ignore. This skill reflects their mastery of the situations that arise during the course of a season. Whether at practice, during a game, or off the field, they have the ability to look at a situation and respond appropriately. As coaches we could potentially stop every repetition in every drill. Great coaches know when to stop that drill and why it should be stopped. They understand their power to choose to stop practice when a mistake occurs or to choose to let the action continue.

In a study examining differences between more effective and less effective school leaders, Doug Fiore (1999) determined that one significant variation is that the very best leaders ignore minor errors. The same could be said of effective coaches. Think back to the truly great coaches you have encountered along the way. Although they were probably very detail oriented, I'll bet they allowed room for mistakes. If coaches harp on every minor mistake, the team will begin shying away from contact with the coach or worse—they will play with the fear of making a mistake. Effective coaches understand that this applies not only to their athletes but to their assistants as well.

Dirty Laundry

Coach Fox's junior varsity coach, Coach Cub, just completed a very successful first season. Coach Cub's team finished their season with an outstanding winning percentage and had won the conference. When Coach Cub met with Coach Fox for the end of season evaluation, however, it came as a surprise that he had been written up failing to do laundry. That's right—dirty laundry. Apparently the towels in the laundry room were not being kept clean (a duty that fell to the junior varsity squad). Now we all know that keeping up with the managerial duties is important to a coaching staff, but can you imagine how Coach Cub felt after that meeting? All this great stuff was happening inside this program and the varsity coach focuses on the towels. All season long Coach Cub had done everything he could to please the varsity coach and support the entire program. Not only were Coach Fox's actions hurtful, but they also took away the incentive for the junior varsity coach to put greater effort into his coaching.

Coach Fox could have chosen to see what needed to be seen and ignored the rest. If Coach Fox had done so, the relationship between the two would have been fine and the entire Rumbling Sloths program would have benefited. Instead, Coach Fox focused on something trivial, permanently affecting their relationship and the program.

As coaches, we are often our worst critics. Although we think criticism does not affect us, at some point it does. If we hear "no" too often, we begin to start tuning out those around us. Your athletes feel the same way. If we want a young athlete to become more aggressive on defense, we may have to tolerate a few officials' whistles along the way so he or she will be willing to break new ground and understand what being more aggressive feels like. If we continually point out mistakes and not give any credit to the fact the athlete is trying to execute what we have asked, he or she will eventually quit trying to become more aggressive. This is especially true of our best athletes.

Handling Your Best Athlete

Your best athletes, just like you, are often their own worst critics. You don't have to point out a mistake because your best athlete already knows when a mistake has been made. This is one reason why they are your best athletes.

When your best athletes have their shortcomings pointed out by someone else, they can emotionally deflate. Why? They hate to let others down. They expect so much of themselves and their ability to carry the team that when they hear any criticism, no matter how minor, it becomes a personal attack on everything they have committed to as an athlete. If, as coaches, our nitpicking doesn't stop or at least slow down, they may begin to take fewer risks.

I recall one such athlete. From an early age this athlete worked harder than all the rest. Not only did he have natural athletic ability, but he would always be the first one to practice and last one to leave. Later on in his career, he would help lead his team deep into the state championship tournament. Early on, however, he had nearly shut down as an athlete. Living in a small town, this athlete could not go anywhere without someone discussing his performance. Some in the community realized it was a high school sporting event and were nothing but encouraging. There were others in the community, however, who lived and died by what the high school team did on Friday night. The comments made by these people where less than encouraging. "Why didn't you see this?" "Why did you do that?" "Freshmen shouldn't play on the varsity!" It got to the point where the athlete began shutting down. You see he was already beating himself up about what he saw and what he didn't, about what he did and didn't do, and was very sensitive to the fact that he was a freshman playing on the varsity. He didn't need those things pointed out to him. The coach was able to assist the athlete in such away that he was able to keep moving forward and eventually take the team to new heights.

Your best athletes, no matter how hard you push them, are much harder on themselves. They will not settle for less than their best; they don't want to be told that their performance was great when it wasn't; nor do they want or need every mistake they make pointed out to them. Great coaches have the ability to keep their best athletes moving forward by seeing those things that need to be seen and ignoring the rest. Coaching is a fast-paced and delicate balancing act; the great coach has mastered this essential skill.

Instant Replay

Over-Coaching

1. **Over-Coaching.** All coaches try to prepare their teams for the various situations they will face in a contest. As a goal, this concept is easy to strive for, but difficult to achieve. As coaches we all want our athletes to be prepared for the upcoming contest. Yet, how do you prepare for every situation your athletes will face?

2. **KISS.** The concept of keeping it simple is often seen in the acronym KISS for "Keep it Simple, Stupid" or "Keep it Short and Simple." KISS states that simplicity should be a key goal and that complexity should be avoided.

3. **The Power to Ignore.** Great coaches have the ability to see the things that need to be seen, and the power to ignore the rest. As coaches we could potentially stop every repetition in every drill, but effective coaches do not let perfect stand in the way of progress.

4. **Dirty Laundry.** Effective coaches understand what is important and focus their efforts on those things that lead to success.

5. **Handling Your Best Athlete.** Your best athletes, just like you, are often their own worst critics. You don't have to point out a mistake to your best athlete because he or she already knows a mistake was made.

Chapter 11

Winning

E ffective coaches produce winners. They produce athletes and teams that are successful in the win and loss column. But how much time do they spend talking about winning? Do they make it a focal point of their team's culture and motivation?

Finding the Scoreboard

This is an issue that becomes a topic of debate. At one extreme is the "Lombardi Rule," which states that, "Winning isn't everything, it is the only thing," similar to the more current mantra of "We play to win the game" supported by NFL coach Herm Edwards. At the other extreme is the belief that winning is unimportant and too much focus is placed on it. The truth is, for those who wish to hide the scoreboard, they can't. At every athletic contest there is a scoreboard, stop-watch, or judge somewhere in that venue. Those measuring devices may not be visible in Pee Wee or other youth sports leagues, but believe me, they are there. Ask any six-year-old t-ball player who the winner is in a league that does not use scoreboards, and they can tell you who won.

No matter what your beliefs are regarding winning, we all must deal with its reality. Effective coaches at all levels know how to do this. Effective coaches shift the focus. Even legendary coach Vince Lombardi clarified the maxim "Winning is everything" by stating he had been misquoted. What he intended to say was "Winning isn't everything. The will to win is the only thing." Effective coaches shift the focus away from the importance of winning and to the behaviors associated with winning. We could sit around for hours debating whether or not we should keep score or the importance of athletics in an educational setting, but in the end we will only be talking about beliefs. Regardless of those beliefs, we can all work toward consensus on the consistent behaviors that are essential to winning.

Winning Behaviors

If we brought together athletes, coaches, parents, and athletic administrators and asked them the following question: "What does a scoreboard measure?," I bet we would be surprised to see all of the areas in which we agree. Key to that agreement is that fact that the scoreboard not only measures my team's performance, but the other team's performance as well. On a scoreboard there is my score and my opponent's score. No matter how much I commit to stopping my opponent, their commitment is also a factor that is displayed on the scoreboard. Because I cannot totally disregard the fact that the opponent contributes to the scoreboard, I cannot solely base my performance on it.

Now what if I asked this question instead? "What are the behaviors associated with winning?" I believe we would again be surprised by how much agreement there would be. Now then if we asked those same people the question, "Should sports participation develop those behaviors?," I again believe we would be surprised as to how much agreement there would be, and that is what effective coaches focus on. So whether we want to keep score or not, let's focus on the behaviors associated with winning, and in doing so everybody wins.

Society wants winners. More important, they want winners now and as a result many coaches look to the scoreboard as the finish line. The key for effective coaches is shifting from those commonly held beliefs about scoreboard success to behaviors associated with winning. Effective coaches find success in the behaviors or skills associated with winning as opposed to finding success on the scoreboard. Teams that demonstrate the behaviors and skills needed for success can ultimately become winners on the scoreboard as their technical and tactical skills of their sport develop. I once heard legendary coach Pat Summit tell her team the following after a defeat:

> I'm going to be real brief so you all get your heads up
> and let's talk about this. I want eye contact, so let's sit
> up and move on. I was really proud of your effort, your
> intensity, and your heart tonight. I'm telling you that
> means more to me right now than winning or losing
> for this team. I want you to remember this—you did
> not lose here tonight because of heart. You did not lose

here because of effort. You lost because of execution and the beauty of that is that it is November. We've got a lot of time to get better and if I was in here today and you were not upset about this, then I would be upset. Because I want to coach a team, I want our staff to work with a team that hates to lose, and that is willing to play hard every game—EVERY GAME and today you played hard.

What determines an effective coach's approach to the sport they have decided to coach? The athletes they have to coach and the skills sets they need to be successful—not the scoreboard. Effective coaches see themselves beside their athletes, helping them develop the behaviors associated with winning. What are those behaviors? Although I believe no one complete list can be found an examination of great might provide us with a good start. In 1934 a first-year English teacher and coach at Kentucky's Dayton High School defined it like this:

> Success is peace of mind which is a direct result of self-satisfaction in knowing you made the effort to become the best or which you are capable. (Wooden & Jamison, 2005)

That first-year English teacher was John Wooden. Coach John Wooden would later write this to his UCLA Bruins regarding the behaviors associated with success:

> Others may have far more ability than you have, they may be larger, faster, quicker, able to jump better, etc., but no one should be your superior in team spirit, loyalty, enthusiasm, cooperation, determination, industriousness, fight, and character. Acquire and keep these traits and success should follow. (Wooden & Jamison, 2005)

A further listing of winning behaviors can be found in examining coach Wooden's Pyramid of Success, which served him well on the way to winning ten national championships (Wooden & Jamison, 2005) . Effective coaches all have their own list; however, most would agree on the following behaviors.

Effort

Coach Wooden (2005) called it "industriousness" and it is a cornerstone of the Pyramid of Success. Most coaches refer to it as "effort." Effort is old-fashioned hard work. While many coaches equate movement to work, effective coaches understand there is a difference. Effort is more than just showing up—it is the engaging of our physical and mental energy to produce. It requires exertion. It's getting up early and staying late. It is found in planning, preparation, practice, and performance. Although we see a sporting culture always looking for shortcuts to success, effective coaches realize that there are no shortcuts. Winning on a consistent basis can be found only in hard, productive work.

Intensity

Winning requires not only effort but intensity. It is not only how hard you are willing to work but how hard you are willing to work at working. Intensity is the force that allows for us to give 100 percent 100 percent of the time. Although many coaches link intensity to motivation, effective coaches see it as a constant force that can consistently be applied. As a young junior varsity basketball coach, I thought it was important to inspire my team before they took the floor. As a result I would work very hard at trying to get my team "fired up" before they took the floor for warm-ups. My teams looked great in warm-ups; we looked ready for action. The only problem was the real action was going to take place 20 minutes after the warm-up period had started. This was pointed out to me by the varsity coach when he reminded me that you don't get any points for looking good in the warm-ups.

Great coaches don't try to win the warm-ups; they try to win throughout the course of the season by getting better each time out. They understand that effective intensity, rather than burning extremely hot for a few short minutes and then burning out, burns hot over the course of many weeks. As Coach Summit put it earlier, it's only November. Coach Summit, like all effective coaches, realizes that intensity is the ability to sustain effort over a period of time. The greater the intensity, the greater the ability to sustain the effort.

Heart

Great coaches understand the importance of developing the heart or what might be called character. A winning behavior that effective coaches try to instill in their athletes is a strong character, but what is the definition of character? Many think of character from a morality standpoint. They ask the questions of what's fair, what's just, what's noble. Others consider character from a social standpoint. They ask the question of who is willing to sacrifice for the good of the group. As we read and watch news reports regarding character in sports, we see both the moral and social definitions being used depending upon the slant of the story. Despite the difficulty in defining character, effective coaches combine the moral and social definitions of character to develop a list of qualities that have been historically linked to the word "character." An effective coach's definition of character is one who is "loyal, cooperative, persevering, self-sacrificing, courageous, honest, responsible, fair and respectful" (Haworth, 2004; Rudd & Stoll, 2004).

Patience

Winning takes time, which means it takes patience. Maybe that is why patience is seen at the top of Coach Wooden's Pyramid of Success. Patience, or the ability to endure in the face of adversity, is a key to success. Just as good teams require effort, intensity, and heart, they also need time. Most things of value take time to develop and successful teams and athletes are no exception. Don't get me wrong; impatience is not necessarily a bad thing as it does fulfill a role in coaching. Impatience in the end moves us to action and beyond where we currently are (Wooden & Jamison, 2005).

Many coaches, however, are too impatient. They fail to see that you can't plant the seed and harvest the crop all in the same day. Effective coaches understand that it takes time to grow a team. Remember, most of us must take who lives in our district and walks through our door. However, even those coaches who have the ability to go out and acquire the athletes they want still take time for those teams to develop.

The Coach's Legacy

As coaches we all want to be remembered and many of us want to make a difference, but how do the effective ones actually do it? Coach Fox would measure legacy by the number of championship banners hanging from the rafters or by the number of wins compared to the number of losses. Effective coaches don't set out to be legacy builders, but that is what they become. Don't get me wrong—effective coaches are hanging banners and many have more wins than losses, but the major difference between them and less effective coaches can be found in three legacy building blocks.

We should remind ourselves that this book is not about coaches who are in it for the money and who also have the ability to bring in blue chip recruits or employ their talent. We are talking about those coaches that take the talent that walks through their door and turns it into something special on a consistent basis. These coaches see their vocation differently than their less effective peers. Effective coaches expand upon what is traditionally considered success to include not only scoreboard results but also personal fulfillment and succession. All coaches understand the importance of scoreboard results and the win versus loss column. This concrete measure of success, however, is only one building block of a legacy. Think about the man who had a lifelong goal of climbing a mountain. The man, after several months of planning and conditioning, climbed the mountain only to realize that there was no where else for him to go. Just as important to scoreboard success is a building block more difficult to define—fulfillment.

Great coaches don't think of the number of lives they are going to impact over the course of their career. For example, you don't see effective coaches in pregame warm-ups thinking of the legacy they hope to leave behind nor do you find great coaches in the huddle drawing up their legacy during a timeout. What you do find are coaches who care about their athletes. Effective coaches see fulfillment as part of the process of coaching, not a byproduct of it. All coaches embrace the fact that winning can bring temporary highs and losing emotionally draining lows because we all understand that it is a contest. Fulfillment comes through the behaviors or processes of winning, which for effective coaches means happiness and meaning. Yet effective coaches derive happiness and meaning much differently than their less effective peers. Do effective coaches enjoy the wins?—Yes. Are they emotionally drained by a loss?—Yes. Yet they still enjoy coaching and teaching young people. Happiness and meaning are derived from their interaction with their athletes. Those effective coaches who are now retired will tell you that they miss the practices more than they miss the actual contests. They will tell you they miss the interaction. Effective coaches give of themselves in such a way that their athletes know that they care about them on and off the field. That is where happiness and meaning are found, not only in the score, but in their ability to leave a little bit of themselves in the lives of their athletes.

Succession is another building block of a legacy. In earlier chapters, we describe modeling as a basic tenant of coaching. However, the truly great coaches can step away from modeling the appropriate skill and tactics and allow their athletes to own that skill. That is succession. I would expect that many of you reading this book can think of a coach who had a profound impact on you— the type of coach that you would do anything for. As Rob Haworth, the high school track athlete, I was privileged to have two such coaches: Coach Darrell Newkirk and Coach Roy Kline. It has been over 25 years since I stepped out on a track under their leadership, but many of the things we experienced together are very much a part of who I am as an educator. That is succession.

Why would I write fond words of two guys that required me to log mile after mile on the hilly roadways of southern Indiana? Why would I care about two guys who became visibly upset with me when I failed to hit my interval times exactly as planned on a hot and humid Indiana summer day? Why are those high school coaches a part of who I am as an educator? Because their process for success expanded upon what was traditionally thought of as important to include the building of relationships. When I was a high school athlete, the thought never crossed my mind that these two men actually got paid for coaching, if you can call $1,200 dollars getting paid. If their goal was to just win, they could have selected a handful of athletes and won just as many conference championships. However, my high school, which had a male enrollment of less than 250, had over 40 athletes on the boy's track team. Yes, the two of them enjoyed championships and more wins than losses, but they valued each and everyone on that team. In as much as this is true for me, I would dare say the same thing holds true for the hundreds of young men and women these two men coached. The byproduct of building a locally successful track and field team is a legacy built upon valuing others and having others pass it on.

Developing as a Coach

Every coach's experience is different because every team is different. But regardless of the makeup of their teams, great coaches have much in common. In this book, we have highlighted eleven elements of effective coaching. We have drawn on several experiences and observations regarding effective and less effective coaches. In the end, the difference lies in the core of beliefs that guide their work. Here, we have shared the core of what matters to us as educators.

We hold fast to certain essential beliefs. We are convinced that the coach is the filter for whatever happens on a team. We believe the quality of the coaching determines the quality of the athletic program. We recognize that in any athletic department, conference, or league, some programs are more successful than others—but we are sure that success comes from people, not programs.

Being a coach is an amazing profession. It is challenging, dynamic, energizing, and draining, but most of all it is rewarding. Our impact extends far beyond anything we can imagine. We know that our athletes talk about us; so do our colleagues, and so do people throughout our communities. We can decide what we want those conversations to be like. Every coach feels the pressure of outside influences. Almost everyone in the community has a vested interest in athletics from the Pee Wee levels to the professional ranks—and anyone who ever participated in athletics can claim to be an expert. This is not criticism, just a fact of human nature. However, as coaches we must adhere to our core values. No matter what others want us to do, we must focus on what is right for our athletes.

Coaching can be a lonely profession. Though we spend a great deal of time with our athletes, their perspective on the day is not the same as ours. Though we work in a community of coaches, our decisions are our own. Without a core of firmly held beliefs, it's difficult to steer a steady course. With this core, we feel secure and confident. And most importantly, so will our students.

This book does not present a cookie-cutter approach to coaching or a doorway to success. Instead, it shows the framework that sustains the work of all great coaches. Think of it as a blueprint. The coaches are the architects. The practices and the contests are the foundation on which to build. The athletes move into the building and fill it with life and meaning.

Every coach has an impact. Great coaches make a difference.

Instant Replay

Winning

1. **Finding the Scoreboard.** At one extreme is the belief that winning is everything and at the other is that too much emphasis is placed upon winning. The truth is, for those who wish to hide the scoreboard, they can't. At every athletic contest there is a scoreboard, stop-watch, or judge somewhere in that venue.

2. **Winning Behaviors.** There are a certain number of behaviors that can be associated with winning. Effective coaches find success in the behaviors or skills associated with winning as opposed to finding success on the scoreboard.

3. **Effort.** Effort is old-fashioned hard work. Effort is more than just showing up: It is the engaging of our physical and mental energy to produce. It requires exertion.

4. **Intensity.** Intensity is the force that allows us to give 100 percent 100 percent of the time. Although many coaches link intensity to motivation, effective coaches see it as a constant force that can consistently be applied.

5. **Heart.** Great coaches understand the importance of developing the heart or what might be called character. Despite the difficulty in defining character, an effective coach's definition of character is found in one who is loyal, cooperative, persevering, self-sacrificing, courageous, honest, responsible, fair, and respectful.

6. **Patience.** Most things of value take time to develop and successful teams and athletes are no exception. Effective coaches understand that it takes time to grow a team.

7. **Developing as a Coach.** Being a coach is an amazing profession. It is challenging, dynamic, energizing, and draining, but most of all it is rewarding. Remember every coach has an impact, but it is the great coaches who make a difference.

References

Bissell, B. (1992, July). *The paradoxical leader.* Paper presented at the meeting of the Missouri Leadership Academy, Columbia, MO.

Brown, B. (2008, June). *Athletes of Character.* Paper presented at the meeting of Champions of Character Conference, Georgetown University, KY.

Dahlberg, T. (2009, Feb. 18). Retrieved from http://www.kokomotribune.com/sportscolumns/local_story_049232057.html

Dale G. (2005). Successful coaching: Gaining and maintaining credibility. *Olympic Coach 17*(4), 11–13.

Doud, G. (1998). Keynote speaker at the Dubois County Teacher's Conference, Vincennes University Jasper Center, Jasper, IN.

Early, G. (1998). Sports: A view from left field. *The Nation.* Retrieved May 22, 2003, from http:ferris.edu www/isar/archives/early/homepage.htm

Ellison, T. (1965). *Run-and-Shoot Football: Offense of the Future.* West Nyack, NY: Parker and Co.

Fiore, D. (1999). The relationship between principal effectiveness and school culture in elementary schools.

Foote, M. (n.d.).*Competitive Games to Use in Practice.* Retrieved April 22, 2009, from http://www.uslacrosse.org/events/pdf/foote.pdf

Haworth, R. (2004). *Are there differences in moral and social character between high school athletes and non-athletes?* (Doctoral dissertation.) Indiana State University, Terre Haute.

Heath, Douglas. (1991). *Fulfilling Lives: Paths to Maturity and Success.* San Francisco: Jossey-Bass Inc.

Heath, C., & Heath, D. (2007). *Made to Stick: Why Some Ideas Survive and Others Die*. New York: Random House.

Hilgers, L. (2006). *Youth sports drawing more than ever.* Retrieved April 17, 2009, from http://www.cnn.com/2006/US/07/03/rise.kids.sports/index.html

Iowa High School Athletic Association. (2009). *A case for high school athletics.* Retrieved May 3, 2009, from http://www.iahsaa.org/hsactiv.htm

Jiang, Y., Saxe, R., & Kanwisher, N. (2004, June 8). We Weren't Made to Multitask. *Psychological Science.* To read the article, visit www.psychologicalscience.org/media

National Collegiate Athletic Association. (2009). *Estimated Probability of Competing in Athletics Beyond the High School Interscholastic Level.* Retrieved April 23, 2009, from http://www.ncaa.org/wps/ncaa?key=/ncaa/ncaa/academics+and+athletes/education+and+research/probability+of+competing/methodology+-+prob+of+competing

Paterson, K. (2002). *Crucial Conversations: Tools for Talking When Stakes are High*. New York: McGraw-Hill.

Rudd, A. (2002). *What type of character do athletes posses? An empirical examination of college athletes versus college non-athletes with the RSBH Value Judgment Inventory.* Manuscript submitted for publication.

Rudd, A., & Stoll, S. (2004). What type of character do athletes possess? An empirical examination of college athletes versus college non-athletes with the RSBH Value. *The Sport Journal, 7*(2), 1–10.

Scholarships: Slicing the Pie. (2008, March 10). *The New York Times.* Retrieved April 22, 2009, from http://www.nytimes.com/imagepages/2008/03/10/sports/20080310_SCHOLAR_GRAPHIC2.html

Smith, D., & Bell , G. (2005). *The Carolina Way: Leadership Lessons from a Life in Coaching*. New York: Penguin Group.

Summit, P. *Coaching is.* Retrieved May 22, 2009, from www.charactercombine.com/videoandlinks.html

Whitaker, T. (1999). *Dealing with difficult parents (and with parents in difficult situations)*. Larchmont, NY: Eye on Education.

Whitaker, T. (2004). *What great teachers do differently: 14 things that matter most*. Larchmont, NY: Eye on Education.

Wooden, J., & Jamison, S. (2005). *Wooden on leadership*. New York: McGraw-Hill.

We also recommend . . .

Dealing with Difficult Parents
(And with Parents in Difficult Situations)
Todd Whitaker & Douglas J. Fiore

"This book is an easy read with common sense appeal. The authors are not afraid to share their own vulnerability and often demonstrate a sense of humor."

> *Gale Hulme, Program Director*
> Georgia's Leadership Institute
> for School Improvement

This book helps teachers, principals, and other educators develop skills in working with the most difficult parents in the most challenging situations.

It shows you how to:

◆ avoid the "trigger" words that serve only to make bad situations worse.

◆ use the right words and phrases to help you develop more positive relationships with parents.

◆ deal with parents who accuse you of not being fair.

◆ build positive relationships with even the most challenging parents.

2001, 175 pp. paperback 1-930556-09-8 $29.95 plus shipping and handling

Bring Todd Whitaker to Your School!
Todd Whitaker...on DVD!

"It is amazing how much substance is packed into this presentation...our attention never wanders. This DVD holds up a mirror so we can look at ourselves and our classroom practices through a new set of eyes."

Rick Wormeli
Best-selling Author and Consultant

What Great Teachers Do *Differently* **DVD**

This $499 package includes—

- ◆ 11 programs totaling over two hours
- ◆ Facilitator's Guide
- ◆ Also included is a copy of the best-selling book
  What Great Teachers Do *Differently*:
  14 Things That Matter Most

2007, 1-59667-053-3 $499 plus $13 for shipping and handling.

What Great Principals Do *Differently* **DVD**

This $499 package includes—

- ◆ 6 programs on one DVD totaling over two hours
- ◆ Facilitator's Guide
- ◆ Also included is a copy of the best-selling book
  What Great Principals Do *Differently*:
  15 Things That Matter Most

2007, 1-59667-052-5 $499 plus $13 for shipping and handling.

Use these DVDs in teacher workshops, study groups, or with school improvement teams.

Free Preview Clips at www.eyeoneducation.com

Ten Commandments Of Faith And Fitness

A Practical Guide
For Health And Wellness

Henry G. Brinton
Vikram Khanna

CSS Publishing Company, Inc., Lima, Ohio

TEN COMMANDMENTS OF FAITH AND FITNESS

Copyright © 2008 by
CSS Publishing Company, Inc.
Lima, Ohio

Scripture quotations are from the New Revised Standard Version of the Bible, copyright 1989 by the Division of Christian Education of the National Council of the Churches of Christ in the USA. Used by permission.

Library of Congress Cataloging-in-Publication Data

Brinton, Henry G., 1960-
    Ten commandments of faith and fitness : a practical guide for health and wellness / Henry Brinton, Vikram Khanna.
        p. cm.
    Includes bibliographical references.
    ISBN 0-7880-2463-9 (perfect bound : alk. paper)
    1. Physical fitness—Religious aspects—Christianity. 2. Spirituality. I. Khanna, Vikram. II. Title.

BV4598.B75 2008
248.4—dc22

                                                                    2007039770

For more information about CSS Publishing Company resources, visit our website at www.csspub.com or email us at csr@csspub.com or call (800) 241-4056.

Cover design by Barbara Spencer
ISBN-13: 978-0-7880-2463-4
ISBN-10: 0-7880-2463-9
                                              PRINTED IN USA

To the memory of my mother, Gyan, whose quiet dignity, faith in God, devotion to family, and belief in the transformative power of hard work provided me with my life's greatest lessons.
— Vikram Khanna

In memory of my father, Henry, who taught me the value of faithfulness and of perseverance, which have served me well in the long run.
— Henry Brinton

Disclaimer

The information in this book is general educational material about exercise and nutrition, which may or may not be suitable to your specific needs. Get medical clearance from your doctor before beginning, resuming, or changing an exercise program. Ask a qualified exercise specialist for help with planning your exercise program and a registered dietician for assistance with nutrition to ensure that your efforts are safe and appropriate for your needs. All physical activity entails some risk of injury or illness. Neither CSS Publishing Company nor the authors bear any responsibility for injuries or illnesses that result from your use of the information presented here and nothing in this text shall be construed as personalized exercise or nutrition advice.

Our Invitation

An invitation to our readers and potential readers. Although we write from a Christian perspective, and this point of view is evident throughout this book, there is a great deal of scientific information in these pages that will prove useful to people of any religious tradition, as well as to people of uncertain faith or no faith at all. We believe that everyone can benefit from the health-giving advice that we have drawn from the exercise science and nutrition literature documented herein.

Erratum: There is a publisher's error on page 55. The correct web address for Crosstrainer fitness software is **www.crosstrainer.ca.**

Table Of Contents

The Life-Enhancing Benefits Of Commandments

Commandments are controversial.

In the lobby of the courthouse in Pulaski County, Kentucky, the Ten Commandments were once posted for all to see. In 2001, a US district judge ordered that the display be removed, a decision that was upheld by a federal appeals court in 2003. The appeals panel held that courthouse postings of the Ten Commandments violated the First Amendment of the Constitution, which forbids Congress from making any law "respecting an establishment of religion."

Down came the commandments, by order of the court.

A number of Kentuckians rose up to fight this ruling and took their arguments all the way to the Supreme Court. In 2005, the court ruled that such a display of the Ten Commandments was unconstitutional because it promoted a religious message. But other postings of the Commandments were deemed by the Supreme Court to be constitutional, as long as they stood as a tribute to our nation's legal and religious history.

Religious message, no. Religious history, yes. No wonder people are confused about the Ten Commandments!

Aside from constitutional issues, the commandments pose a problem for us because they contain a list of rather daunting "thou-shalt-nots." But it is important for us to realize that these ten rulings from the Lord are not meant to drag us down with a negative message. In fact, they are intended to be life-enhancing, and to give us a very positive framework for the living of our days. The first four commandments provide us with guidance for our relationship with God, and the last six explain what it means to have a healthy relationship with each other (Exodus 20:1-20).

The Ten Commandments break nicely into two parts, fitting onto the two tablets of stone that God used to deliver the commandments to Moses. In his theological masterpiece, the *Institutes of the Christian Religion*, Protestant reformer John Calvin wrote that "God has so divided his law into two parts, which contain the whole of righteousness, as to assign the first part of those duties of religion which particularly concern the worship of his majesty; the second, to the duties of love that have to do with men."

Worship of God's majesty. That's part one. And love of one another. That's part two. They are equally life-enhancing, equally innovative, equally well-crafted. No doubt Jesus had this two-part approach in mind when he said that the greatest commandment called us both to "love the Lord your God" and to "love your neighbor as yourself" (Matthew 22:36-40).

Let's not get ahead of ourselves. Looking at the Ten Commandments, we see that the first part contains the divine directives that instruct us to have no other gods except the Lord, to avoid idolatry, to refrain from misusing the name of God, and to remember the sabbath day and keep it holy. These are simple and straightforward, forming a clear picture of what it means to be in a right relationship with the Lord, including "the worship of his majesty."

Are they negative? Not at all. They can certainly be a challenge for us, especially when we find ourselves tempted to bow down to the idols of Wall Street and Hollywood and Madison Avenue. They can be countercultural, particularly when we struggle to maintain a sabbath day in a fast-paced, over-programmed, and ever-accelerating twenty-first-century culture.

But remember: God's commandments are designed to help us, not to hurt us. We tap into a source of energy and security when we worship God, rather than the powers of this world. And we lead a much healthier life when we take the time to rest and play, instead of working around the clock, seven days a week. The worship of God's majesty is a positive, not a negative. It makes us stronger, not weaker.

The very same can be said for the second part of the Ten Commandments, despite the repeated "thou-shalt-nots" that it contains. There is an enormous amount of guidance and direction to be gained from these final six commandments, despite our natural tendency to rebel against any limitations on our human freedom.

8

You may have heard the story of what happened when Moses came down from Mount Sinai after a long day of negotiating with God. He looked very tired, but the Israelites were anxious to hear what he had to say.

Moses said, "I have some good news and some bad news ... The good news is that I got him down to only Ten Commandments ... The bad news is that he wouldn't budge on the adultery issue."

Whether the flashing red stoplight appears in front of adultery or stealing or covetousness, we don't like to hit the brakes and hear "thou-shalt-not." But these commandments are not all about the negatives — they also provide a positive framework for the living of a good life in relationship to our neighbors. When we honor our parents, prohibit murder, resist adultery, turn from stealing, speak with truthfulness, and refrain from envy, then we find ourselves much better able to love our neighbors as ourselves. The keeping of these commandments moves us into relationships that not only reflect the will of God, but also provide us with much happier and healthier lives.

Sure, we may joke about "the adultery issue," but we know the real destructiveness of adultery to marriages, families, and communities. We may think that a little stealing is no big deal, but then we pay inflated prices to cover the cost of theft in stores across the nation. We may believe that "thou shalt not covet" is an old-fashioned notion, but then we realize that we're being eaten up by the envy we feel when we watch shows about the fabulous lives of various celebrity superstars.

People talk about "breaking" the Ten Commandments, but that's not exactly right. We cannot actually break anything as solid as the law of God, even when we engage in some serious sinfulness. Instead, it's more accurate to say that we break ourselves *against* the Ten Commandments. Think of the commandments as big slabs of stone that we smash ourselves into — we crash into these rocks and we hurt ourselves through acts of adultery or stealing or envy.

When we collide with the commandments, it's only we humans that get hurt.

To avoid this kind of agony, it's important that we put the Ten Commandments back where they belong — in the very middle of

9

our personal lives. It's critical to realize that the commandments are a reliable guideline for moral choices, and an excellent framework for daily words and deeds. It's time to reclaim the very positive view of God's law that was once common in the Christian community. Martin Luther saw that the law has a social use because it exercises a restraining influence on society. He also realized that it has a teaching use since it points out sin and reminds us of our need for Jesus Christ. It may be that John Calvin had the best insight of all: He saw that the law has a guiding use, since it acts as a rule of life for us.

The Ten Commandments are a framework for worshiping God and loving one another. When you read the New Testament and come across the great commandment of Jesus to love God and love neighbor, it is important to visualize the two tablets of the Ten Commandments and to post them prominently in your heart and mind. On one tablet you have the first four commandments concerning your relationship with God. And on the other you have the last six commandments concerning your relationship with neighbor.

On one side is God. On the other side is neighbor. Both are important. Both are God's will. Both are found throughout the Bible, Old Testament and New. Both are close to the heart of Jesus.

Because we, the authors of this book, have such a positive view of the Ten Commandments in the Bible, we have decided to call this program *Ten Commandments Of Faith And Fitness*. Like the Bible's ten rulings from the Lord, the commandments in this book are not meant to drag you down with a negative message. They are intended to be life-enhancing, and to give a very positive framework for faith and fitness. These commandments are designed to help you, not hurt you, and to enable you to tap into hidden sources of energy and strength. You might even notice some close connections between God's Commandments and ours: Both lists include an order to rest, because we know that we lead much healthier lives when we take the time to rest, instead of working and exercising incessantly.

But who are we to write this book? Allow us to introduce ourselves. Henry Brinton is senior pastor of Fairfax Presbyterian

10

Church in Fairfax, Virginia, and a staff writer for the *Homiletics* preaching journal. He is also a frequent contributor to *USA TO-DAY* and *The Washington Post*, as well as the author of the book, *Balancing Acts: Obligation, Liberation, and Contemporary Christian Conflicts* (Lima, Ohio: CSS Publishing Company, Inc., 2006). He is a popular retreat and conference speaker on topics ranging from healing to social justice, and from Christian vocation to faith and fitness. Henry received his B.A. from Duke University and M.Div. from Yale Divinity School. A long-distance runner, he has completed one marathon a year since he turned forty in the year 2000. He is married to Nancy Freeborne, a physician assistant, and together they have two teenage children, Sarah and Sam.

Vikram Khanna, M.H.S., P.A., is an exercise coach, health educator, and CEO of Galileo Health Partners, LLC of Ellicott City, Maryland. Vik works with both individual consumers and businesses to teach evidence-based principles of exercise and nutrition that can help people reduce their risk of serious chronic illnesses, such as heart disease and obesity. Vik is an active and involved parishioner at St. John's Episcopal Church in Ellicott City, Maryland, one of several Washington DC-area parishes where he implemented innovative Fitness Ministries. Vik is an Exercise Specialist®, certified by the American College of Sports Medicine; he also has a B.S. (cum laude) in physical education from SUNY Cortland (1979), is a physician assistant (B.S., with honors, Hahnemann University, 1982), and he earned his Master of Health Science from the Johns Hopkins University School of Hygiene and Public Health in 1984. A lifelong weight lifter, Vik is also an avid cyclist and runner. He is married to Teri Deutsch, an economist, and they have one son, Jaxon.

We believe that the ten commandments of faith and fitness, like the Ten Commandments of God, are designed to lead you to a much happier and healthier life. They are not full of punitive "thou-shalt-nots," but instead are organized around very positive "thou shalts." They are meant to give you direction in your own journey toward physical and spiritual health, and to offer you day-to-day guidance as you engage in your own program of exercise and reflection. Moreover, our commandments aim to help you cut through the often-confusing messages about diet and exercise that dominate our culture. Instead of quick fixes, we offer clarity and direction derived from the best information and guidance that today's exercise and nutrition sciences can offer.

God will not punish you if you disobey our ten commandments. You'll only hurt yourself. Remember, you don't tend to break commandments, you break yourself *against* them.

So let's enter into a process of understanding and applying these commandments to our lives. You may find yourself moving quickly through this program, completing the exercises for all ten commandments in ten weeks. You may find that you need ten months to get through all the challenges that lie before you. Or, it may be that this book becomes your roadmap for the next ten years of faith and fitness, one that you use again and again. However you put these commandments to work in your life, we hope that you find them to be truly life-enhancing, and a real asset to your physical and spiritual health.

God gives commandments to help us, not hurt us. To build us up, not break us down. It is in this same spirit that we offer you these "Ten Commandments of Faith and Fitness":

Commandment One — *Thou shalt be knowledgeable*
Commandment Two — *Thou shalt be self-aware*
Commandment Three — *Thou shalt endure*
Commandment Four — *Thou shalt be strong*
Commandment Five — *Thou shalt eat from the garden ... (of Eden, that is)*
Commandment Six — *Thou shalt raise the bar*
Commandment Seven — *Thou shalt periodize*
Commandment Eight — *Thou shalt rest*
Commandment Nine — *Thou shalt reflect*
Commandment Ten — *Thou shalt remember*

With the help of the God who gave Moses the Ten Commandments, may our journey toward spiritual and physical fitness begin!

Commandment One

Thou Shalt
Be Knowledgeable

Know What Fitness Is, And How It Relates
To The Christian Faith

As with any new endeavor in life, we believe that your mission of faith and fitness should begin with introspection and reflection. Think about why you value your faith, and why you seek physical fitness and wholeness through diet and exercise. Reflect on the important factors in both pursuits that can motivate and inspire you to find greater health and a deeper spiritual grounding.

Faith and fitness share important common elements. First, both require believers to adhere to a certain core set of principles. In faith, those are: reverence for God's creation, compassion, sacrifice, kindness, humility, perseverance, and strength in adversity. There are parallel sets of principles that help guide people along the path to fitness. These are avoiding fads and having a willingness to learn, change, and sacrifice — some of these feel onerous in the short term but are likely to help create long-term change.

Second, faith compels believers to act upon their beliefs even in difficult circumstances. Doing what's right (even when it is not convenient or beneficial to you personally) and thinking of others first is an essential part of the teachings of Jesus. The parallel beliefs related to fitness require that you stick to what you know is correct, even in the face of slick marketing campaigns that want to seduce you into buying products or services with the promises of quick results. Faith and fitness take time, energy, effort, and a commitment to continual learning.

Faith and fitness both yield short- and long-term consequences. In the short term, both pursuits offer us the opportunity to renew ourselves with a commitment to something greater than ourselves. In the longer term, faith offers us the prospect of abundant life and salvation, while living a fit life helps ensure that we are able not only to meet the demands of our own lives with greater energy and joy, but also that we have the physical vitality and strength to reach out to others to bring them into the circle. Nothing could possibly be more compelling than using your own strength and energy to help those around you.

We ask that you start to think about the roles that both exercise and diet play in your life. Do you exercise regularly? If yes, how frequently and how intensely? If you do not exercise, why not? What do you think are your biggest obstacles to having a success- ful, ongoing exercise program? Is your schedule a problem? If you believe that you do not have time to exercise, we believe that you have misstated the point — in reality, you don't have time *not* to exercise. With every workout that you forego, you rob yourself, your family, your church, and your community of quality of life — and, more likely than not, you take time off your longevity.

In the same way, we want you to ask yourself if you eat in a way that will maximize your health and vitality and allow you to maintain a healthy body weight, which, in turn, reduces your risk of many chronic ailments such as diabetes, elevated cholesterol, and heart disease. Do you eat a sound diet? What do you think are your biggest barriers to eating a balanced diet, one rich in fruits, vegetables, whole grains, heart-healthy fats, and lean protein? Are you blocked by time, knowledge, or personal taste? These are the kinds of questions that we will ask — and that we will ask you to inquire of yourself — throughout these Ten Commandments of Faith and Fitness.

As we go forward, we will ask you to take certain "action steps" at the end of each chapter and to write down your responses to a number of challenges. Writing things down is a powerful process. It not only presses you to express yourself honestly (after all, you are only kidding yourself if you fail to do so), but it also is the first step in conducting critical self-assessment and analysis, which are essential to long-term success in both faith and fitness.

For example, the first thing that we want you to do is to take a good look at your schedule. Whether you keep it with computer software, on paper, or on a wall calendar, your ability to prioritize activities and apportion your time will play a critical role in your exercise program. If you are new to regular exercise, we would like you to start with this simple step: to prepare for your first exercise sessions, we want you to make exercise appointments with yourself for three periods of exercise that will each last about 10 to 30 minutes. (The more fit and experienced you are, the longer and more frequently you can work out, but for most novices and sedentary people, 10 to 30 minutes is a good place to start.)

There are several important reasons to make these exercise appointments with yourself. First, you need to elevate the conceptual importance of exercise in your life. Just as you would not fail to note a meeting with your boss or an event at your child's school or at church, neither should you let your exercise times go unrecorded. Second, we want you to appreciate one of the magical elements of exercise, which is that it is remarkably flexible. While we advocate having a continuous block of 30 minutes of time, the reality is that you can chop up your workout time into smaller increments.[1] So, if you have a full day that does not offer a 30-minute window, do not despair ... look for three 10-minute blocks, or two 15-minute segments.

What matters is reaching your total of 30 minutes of exercise for the day and building from there. Starting small is not only okay, for many people it is the best way to acclimate to the time, organizational, and physiologic demands of exercise. Finally, once these exercise appointments are in your calendar, they are visible, clear reminders of your obligations. Then, when complications do arise, as they inevitably will, your "exercise appointment" becomes a meeting that you need to reschedule, rather than remaining an invisible commitment that is easy to overlook. At the end of your first month, go back and look at how many of the exercise appointments you kept with yourself and which ones you did not keep. Try to understand why, so that you can begin to understand and identify obstacles and develop strategies to surmount them in the months that follow. Your retrospective review of your success at keeping exercise appointments may also teach you a good bit about your own time management and prioritization skills.

Making exercise appointments with yourself is also the first step in what will become a long-term record-keeping process. We believe strongly in the process of keeping an ongoing exercise and diet diary, which we will explain in greater detail shortly; suffice to say here that there is evidence that people who keep track of how they are doing have the greatest chances for long-term success.[2] The process of writing things down may also help you stay focused on the things that are most important in this process: having goals, identifying and solving problems, and tracking your progress.

Know The Value Of Persistence

In his book, *The Challenging Child*, child psychiatrist, Stanley Greenspan, identifies five "difficult" types of children. One is the defiant child — a boy or girl who is unusually stubborn, negative, and controlling, but at the same time, the owner of such positive traits as energy and persistence. If you have such a child in your house, you know how maddening and yet how oddly admirable such behavior can be.

Many defiant children are unusually clever, writes Greenspan, able to figure out ways to defeat your most sophisticated arguments. They can also be extraordinarily well-organized and methodical, as well as deliberate and purposeful. "The key challenge for parents and teachers is helping the defiant youngster use these various assets in a constructive way so that, as he gets older, he can use his talents for such pursuits as science, mathematics, philosophy, law, or any other field where persistence and organization are an asset."[3]

Persistence and organization are qualities that are equally important in the world of fitness and faith. Without perseverance, we cannot grow stronger in either body or spirit.

In Luke 18:1-8, Jesus tells the story of an adult who may well have been "a difficult child" in her youth — a widow who refuses to give up. She approaches a judge again and again, asking him to grant her justice against her opponent. The judge refuses at first but finally decides to give her what she wants, because he fears that she will wear him out with her persistence. Jesus makes the point that God, like the judge, will "grant justice to his chosen ones who cry to him day and night," and he encourages his followers to be like the widow, praying persistently and faithfully. Two lessons emerge from this story of a difficult child.

First, persistent prayer is the way to pray. Jesus does not want us to be casual about prayer, but serious, intentional, determined, and disciplined. Julian of Norwich says prayer is an activity which involves desiring, begging, imploring ... and finally seeing God, face to face. While it is doubtful that Jesus wants us to pester God, he most certainly wants us to be diligent in our lifting of requests to the Lord. It is in our prayers that we grow closer to the One who is the source of every good and perfect gift.

There is nothing wrong with being dependent on God and full of desire for the gifts of God that give us abundant life. "We are made for God," writes Archbishop Desmond Tutu, "we yearn to be filled with the fullness of God, and so we come asking the One who is always eager to give. We place ourselves in his hands as suppliants, in the attitude of those who know they have nothing that they have not received, before the One who is ever the gracious one ready to give beyond our asking and our deserving. We are like a parched land thirsty for the gift of rain — yearning, beseeching, waiting and asking, yet assured that we will be heard and that we will be given. Jesus taught his disciples to pray, 'Give us this day our daily bread.' "[4] If we are persistent in prayer, we will see God more clearly and will receive the gifts that are part of abundant life.

The second lesson is that persistent prayer is faith-inspired prayer. A difficult child will only make demands on a parent who loves her and who will provide for her. She knows that if she asks her father for bread, he will not give her a stone; if she asks for a fish, he will not give her a snake (Matthew 7:9-10). In the same way, those who pray persistently to God are people who have faith that God will answer them. They trust that the Lord will help them quickly, granting them justice and mercy, fullness of life, and everlasting salvation.

Perhaps more than anything else, such difficult children long for God's love and God's presence. They yearn to behold the Lord, to see him face to face. The God you call upon will finally come, promises Frederick Buechner, "and even if he does not bring you

17

the answer you want, he will bring you himself. Maybe, at the secret heart of all our prayers, that is what we are really praying for."[5] Persistent prayer is a sign of intense desire for God's presence, God's power, and God's peace. It is a quality of Christians who are determined to strengthen and deepen their relationship with the Lord who has created them to live a life of health and wholeness, purpose and peace.

Persistence is a challenge, in both our exercise programs and in the practice of prayer. The Bible tells us that God grants justice to his chosen ones "who cry to him day and night," and Jesus commends the faith of people who pray always and do not lose heart (Luke 18:1, 7). Perseverance is a positive quality in the life of faith, helping us to maintain a lively, ongoing relationship with our Lord, as well as in the pursuit of fitness, enabling us to increase our strength and vitality over the course of a long-term program of exercise.

From a fitness perspective, perhaps no other quality will serve you as well as persistence. As you will learn throughout the course of this book — we are extremely persistent in sending this message — exercise is something that you must do repeatedly, and for as far into the future as your mind's eye can see. You cannot expect to take a single breath and live a normal lifespan, nor should you expect to undertake one run or walk, or complete one weightlifting session, and expect fitness permanence. The effects of exercise dissipate when you stop and you can actually revert to being quite unfit in a matter of months. Thus, your diligence and persistence are as important to the success of your participation in the fitness portion of our approach as they are to success in the faith portion. Neither God nor we will give up on you, nor should you give up on yourself. Regardless of your present state of health, there is both room and opportunity for change and improvement. Change may take time and present notable challenges, but the opportunities are nearly endless for those who persist in their strategic pursuit of exercise and good diet as the centerpieces of physical health and well-being.

Know The Importance Of Change

If people picked baby names on the basis of historical importance, the world today would be full of Orvilles and Wilburs.

But it's not.

Still, few people have changed the course of history more than the Wright Brothers of Dayton, Ohio. A little over 100 years ago, these bicycle-making brothers achieved the goal of powered human flight, piloting the very first airplane that could be controlled in the air. In the process, they developed steering techniques that are still being used in twenty-first-century airplanes, spacecraft, submarines, and robots.

Orville and Wilbur were world-changers, and they changed the world for the better.

On December 17, 1903, Orville took off from the Outer Banks of North Carolina, near Kitty Hawk, and flew the gasoline-powered Wright Flyer for 12 seconds. That same day, Wilbur piloted the plane for 59 seconds, covering a grand total of 852 feet.

What a shock this was to people who never expected humans to fly. It revolutionized travel and transport and gave people a whole new perspective on the world.

An even greater world-changer was Jesus Christ, who called people to follow him on a path of faith and love, purpose and peace. He showed people a whole new way of life, one that radically transformed them — a way of life based on faith in him and on love for one another. "For God so loved the world that he gave his only Son," says Jesus, "so that everyone who believes in him may not perish but may have eternal life" (John 3:16). Later Jesus said to his disciples, "I give you a new commandment, that you love one another. Just as I have loved you, you also should love one another" (John 13:34). Faith in Jesus and love for one another — these discoveries revolutionized religion and gave people a whole new perspective on the world.

Jesus believed that we could change, and he calls us into personal transformation. He wants us to soar with him in a life of purpose and peace, and to experience health and wholeness in body, mind, and spirit. It doesn't matter who we are, or what we've done. It doesn't matter where we are starting the process, or what kind of barriers we have to overcome. It doesn't matter if we are young or old, male or female, fat or thin, weak or strong. With a decision to believe in Jesus and love one another, we can start a process of transformation that will change us into the people God wants us to be. With the mighty wind of Christ's Spirit beneath our wings, we can ascend to a whole new level of living, one in which we experience the truly abundant life that God desires for us.

Change is always possible. That truth was made clear by the flight of the Wright Brothers and by the ministry of Jesus Christ. Improvement is always an option, because our Lord is always working to help us soar to new levels in our physical, mental, emotional, and spiritual fitness.

This was a shock to people who never expected humans to fly ... or to change in any significant way. But transformation is a clear promise of Jesus, because he has come not to condemn the world, but to change it.

We do not adhere to the old adage that "people never change." In fact, we find that phrase a disingenuous dodge; people change all the time, especially when they are empowered with good, credible information that is persistently reinforced, and an alignment of internal and external forces to motivate and support them. For example, one of Vik's clients is a business executive who has had what anyone would consider a very successful career. However, at age 45, very overweight and inactive, he looked around and saw an adolescent daughter whose college graduation and wedding he would very much like to attend one day. He wondered whether that was feasible if he did not *change* his exercise and diet habits. So the process began for him; for another client, it was the realization that a growing waistline, rising blood pressure, and cholesterol levels were a recipe for a medical disaster, not a happy retirement. That internal realization began the process of *change* for him.

Albert Einstein is reputed to have once said, "Without changing our patterns of thought, we will not be able to solve the problems we created with our current patterns of thought." We don't know whether Einstein exercised regularly or not, but we certainly think that his comment crystallizes a useful way of looking at diet and exercise as both the end products of change and critical components of the change process.

Personal change — even when it portends a useful end — naturally unnerves people because it requires exploration of unfamiliar emotional, physical, and psychological terrain and a certain amount of uncertainty. As Einstein intimates, however, thinking differently about problems is essential to the process of solving them. No matter whether your past exercise or eating habits have been unbeneficial or your current ones unhelpful, you have the capacity for adaptation, which means that you have the power to change *and* improve. And, when you change by solving problems with new thought processes, you improve your own life as well as the lives of those around you.

Know The Importance Of Accountability

Persistence, change, and accountability — all three are foundational elements in an understanding of spiritual and physical fitness. One of the interesting things about the concept of accountability is that our approach to a task — our diligence and devotion to it — often derives from how we feel about the person to whom we are accountable. People we respect, love, and admire are much more likely to get our best effort from us, even for menial tasks, than are people we simply do not like serving. While fear is a powerful motivator, it is a negative one, and one that we believe is very secondary to success in this program.

Thus, we want you to look around your life and identify a friend, spouse, or coworker to whom you are willing to make yourself accountable and ask them to be your Covenant Partner. Your Covenant Partner should be someone with whom you can communicate, whom you trust and can confide in, and, most importantly, someone who will invest himself or herself in your success, as God invests himself in each of us, and we invest ourselves in God. We know from the Bible that a covenant is a promise-based relationship, one in which God makes a promise to us, and we make a promise to God. When Moses delivers the Ten Commandments to the Israelites, for example, he says, "Hear, O Israel, the statutes and ordinances that I am addressing to you today; you shall learn them and observe them diligently. The Lord our God made a covenant with us" (Deuteronomy 5:1-2). Your Covenant Partner should be invested in your success with this same level of seriousness and diligence. At the end of this chapter is a sample covenant that you can use with your partner.

This person does not need to work out with you, but certainly can, if the two of you choose to do so. Rather, your Covenant Partner is your sounding board. In a sense, he or she serves the purpose of being your "exercise echo," reminding you of your goals, commitments, and desires for this program. Their role will be to review your goals with you, understand your present strength and fitness data, and help you build and assess your faith and fitness plan going forward. It is also your Covenant Partner's role to cajole, convince, and cheerlead your efforts.

The most delicate role that this person will play is as your critic. He or she has to be willing to call you out on things that you do not do, and you need to be willing to hear their criticism. We believe strongly that the criticism should be constructive, positive, and, ultimately, aimed at identifying and overcoming specific obstacles. We see no use for anger, humiliation, or pointless upbraiding. If your Covenant Partner cannot abide this most important guideline, then we ask that you turn to another person to work with you.

For some people, it may help to have as their Covenant Partner a person who is already quite physically fit and who has mastered making exercise an integral part of life. Not only is this person likely to be able to impart a number of useful ideas for problem solving (because he or she has already faced and surmounted them), but he/she will also be a great current role model. One of the best ways to build any skill set is to work and communicate with people who are better than you are today.

We do not advocate that you and your Covenant Partner operate on any particular schedule or timetable. Rather, what matters is that the two of you understand each other's roles and expectations. If you want your Covenant Partner to call you to task when you miss a workout or overeat, then you will need to develop a communication system that meets this need. In this day of email, paging, cell phones, and text messaging, rapid and consistent communication is certainly achievable.

Alternatively, you and your Covenant Partner could just meet periodically to go over progress, brainstorm solutions to particular problems, and even pray together for God's continued strength in your journey. If you call upon someone who wants to walk this entire path of faith and fitness with you, that is all the better.

It is clear to us that the life of faith — like the life of fitness — is much better experienced as a team sport than as an individual activity. It is much easier to develop Christian virtues such as compassion, kindness, humility, meekness, patience, forbearance, forgiveness, love, harmony, peace, unity, thankfulness, wisdom, and praise if we work on these skills together — instead of in isolation. We need a Covenant Partner for our spiritual well-being, as well as for our physical well-being.

A modern philosopher, Thomas Hibbs, likens the acquisition of virtue to athletic training: Both require repetition and hard work, and both are most easily learned by following examples. While books and classes and sermons can be helpful, virtue is still best learned by practice, not through abstract thought. For example, if you want to learn to shoot hoops, playing basketball beats reading a book about basketball.

Developing Christian virtues, then, requires practice and the help of others. This means that you have to call on a community of accountability and support, a healthy and unified body like the church. When our children go to Christian education classes, they absorb from their teachers virtues of compassion, kindness, humility, meekness, patience, forbearance, forgiveness, love, harmony, peace, unity, thankfulness, wisdom, and praise. When you go to worship on Sunday morning, you learn from the biblical role models that are lifted up in scripture readings and sermons — role models that can teach you how to play the Christian "game" with integrity.

It is helpful to remember, however, that these qualities are not so much taught as they are "caught," in settings such as families and churches — small communities that contain both teachers and learners who help each other strive for excellence. In a community of faith, we are in the best possible position to practice the lifesaving virtues that our Lord wants to give us. We are also in a place where vital relationships with God can deepen — relationships that contain a sense of personal accountability to the Lord. Since our approach to a task — our diligence and devotion to it — derives from how we feel about the person to whom we are accountable, then our performance of Christian tasks is naturally going to be enhanced by a healthy relationship with God.

Whether we are focusing on physical or spiritual wellness, accountability to a divine and human Covenant Partner is going to be a critical factor in our success.

Know The Fitness Trinity

All great structures, people, and ventures rest upon an unshakable foundation. Houses and buildings rest upon foundations of concrete and steel, and great people have at their core the intangible qualities of character, intelligence, compassion, and moral values. As Christians, we have as our foundation the belief that God sent his only Son to share our human nature, to live as one of us, and to die for our sins, thus providing us with the prospect of everlasting life.

A life of faith and fitness is no different from any other worthwhile pursuit in that it must rest upon an immutable set of principles, which provide a solid base for other activities and pursuits. For exercise and nutrition, we believe that there is a compelling concept that you should use as the foundation for what you are doing, which we call The Fitness Trinity:

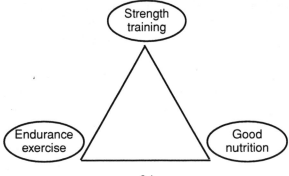

For lifelong health and well-being, we believe firmly that this trinity provides a foundation that every person can build upon, regardless of current health status or goals. We believe this for several essential reasons:

- *Strength training* — No form of exercise is more essential to strong, healthy muscles and bones than learning how to strength train properly. Strong muscles are particularly important as we age, because they help reduce the risk of disability — especially from falls — and enable us to live independently. Although strength training is feasible, in limited ways, with tools such as exercise bands and tubing, we will focus our discussion on weight lifting with either machines or free weights (dumbbells and barbells). Everyone can learn to lift weights, from the young to the old, and benefit from developing healthy muscles and preserving your bones as you age. It is a myth that weight lifting will make you muscle-bound. Healthy, strong muscles are an intrinsic good, and strength training is a lifetime fitness skill that you *must* learn and master. Chiefly, as you age, strength training will help you preserve muscular strength and power, as well as bone strength. This will help you retain your mobility, physical dexterity, and balance — important physical characteristics that we all need to protect and cultivate as we get older. In turn, this will help increase the likelihood that you can live independently for as long as possible, by reducing the risk of falls and giving you the muscular engine that you need to fruitfully engage in what exercise scientists call "activities of daily living (ADL)," such as taking care of your home, doing chores for yourself, playing sports, or simply crossing a street quickly and safely.

- *Endurance exercise* — This term encompasses walking, running, cycling, or any other activity that requires the repetitive use of the largest muscles in your body (hips, legs, buttocks). These exercises raise your heart rate, make your heart stronger and more efficient, and help keep your major

25

blood vessels supple throughout life. Endurance exercise is the single best way to burn calories and, for many, many Americans, walking is an effective and accessible choice. Surveys show that 60% of Americans who report undertaking regular physical activity identify walking as their first choice. Endurance exercise is more efficient and effective than strength training at helping to promote and preserve heart health. Conversely, it is less likely than strength training to preserve or build muscle strength and power.

- *Good nutrition* — As your mother used to say, "You are what you eat." You will also reap what you sow, and if you indulge in a diet high in saturated or trans fat, excess calories, poor quality carbohydrates, and insufficient fiber, you will certainly feel the effects in terms of increased risk of heart disease, stroke, cancer, and diabetes. We dismiss out-of-hand fad diets, diets that require you to join a program, eat special or proprietary foods that someone wants to sell you, and diets that rely upon supplements. As you will see in "Thou Shalt Eat From The Garden," God's creativity and abundance are on better display nowhere than in a garden; thus, we believe that, as in the Mediterranean diet, which has nearly five decades of research to support its value, a good diet starts with a cornucopia of fruits, vegetables, heart healthy fats, and whole grains. Because weight control contributes greatly to long-term health, we want to help move you away from the concept of dieting and on to the concept of eating better and being a better food shopper. Ours is a non-diet approach to healthy eating.

The Fitness Trinity is simple, memorable, and, we believe, quite biblical. Strength training finds its roots in, "Be strong in the Lord, and in the strength of his power" (Ephesians 6:10); endurance exercise is grounded in "Let us run with perseverance the race that is set before us" (Hebrews 12:1); and good nutrition is based on the words of God, "See, I have given you every plant yielding seed ... you shall have them for food" (Genesis 1:29).

26

Notice that God pushes us toward a diet rich in fruits and vegetables. He never says, "See, I have given you a hamburger!"

Know The Importance Of Keeping Body And Spirit Together

We have chosen to provide you with Ten Commandments of Faith and Fitness for more than the biblical reasons. Ten Commandments is also a widely recognized and memorable way of organizing ideas and concepts. At Amazon.com, you can find books titled the *Ten Commandments of Dating ... Financial Planning ... Parenting ...* and *Working in a Hostile Environment*. There is also *The Zen Commandments* and *The Ten Commandments of Golf*. The list is endless.

Ten is a manageable number of related ideas to learn and put into practice. As Moses did not quibble with God's prescription of Ten Commandments for living our lives, we will not alter the formula for our exploration of faith and fitness. We believe that our ten commandments are especially important because they ask you to honor God's first and greatest gift to you ... the gift of your mind, body, and spirit. This is a gift that should never be split into pieces, but always seen as a unified whole.

Unfortunately, Christians through much of the last 2,000 years have tried to drive a wedge between the spirit and the body. Neither Jesus nor the Jews wanted this split to exist, but a group of Greek thinkers in the early church introduced a dualistic philosophy that had a negative view of the body and a positive view of the spirit. Later theologians developed this theme: Saint Augustine believed that the soul makes war with the body, and the Protestant reformer John Calvin saw earthly human existence as "a rottenness and a worm." But recently, theologians and religious scholars have rediscovered the value of the flesh. No less an authority than Pope John Paul II gave a series of strikingly positive talks on the theology of the body.

There's ample precedent for this. Jesus, like his Jewish colleagues, saw the flesh as a good gift of God, and he rejoiced in the pleasures of touch and taste and other bodily sensations. "From the beginning Christianity has been an incarnational faith — 'the Word became flesh,' " says Father Bill Parent, a priest at Saint Peter's

27

Church in Waldorf, Maryland, "which means that there is something fundamentally good about our human flesh."

Today, people are more and more eager to make a connection between body and spirit, and many are pursuing this goal through diet and exercise. Marathon training has become a running meditation for many — it is a form of exercise that cuts through the clutter of life and offers the gift of simplicity, if only for a few hours a week. There are no phones to answer, no bills to pay, no reports to write — only the path that lies ahead. Many have come to love the freedom that running provides to think and dream and problem-solve. Marathoners find themselves becoming tense and irritable when the opportunity to exercise is taken away from them.

One of the mistakes we've made in religious circles is to define "salvation" entirely in terms of life after death when, in fact, the word can describe health and wholeness in this life as well. A Maryland-based ministry called Body & Soul has a holistic mission of promoting physical discipline, spiritual growth, and evangelism through exercise. It conducts classes in aerobics and strength training set to Christian music and advertises itself as the place "where faith and fitness meet." Created by aerobics instructor, Jeannie Blocher, in 1981, Body & Soul has grown to include classes in more than 30 states and 15 foreign countries.

The reunion of spirit and body carries with it the possibility of integrity — that is, the bringing together of different parts into a unified whole. As human beings, we long to be complete and undivided, enjoying integrity as physical, emotional, intellectual, sexual, and spiritual creatures. But there is much in life, in us and around us, that creates division and shatters this unity. One reason Dan Brown's book, *The Da Vinci Code*, has become such a hit is because it tells a story — fictional though it may be — of a spiritual movement that portrays the body and sexuality in a very positive light.

It would be wrong, however, to ignore the dangers that can arise from an excessive focus on the flesh. Integrity of body and spirit is healthy, but idolatry of the body is not. Gene McAfee, a United Church of Christ pastor in Ohio, observes that "body consciousness is very much media-driven, for males as well as for females." He had a conversation with a young evangelical friend who talked about the shopping trip he'd made to restock his bathroom with all sorts of hair and body gels, rubs, lotions, facials, toners, and the like.

This raises the question of what really motivates participation in diet and exercise programs. Is it a desire to honor God or a hunger to look hot? Even the most honorable religious movements can become corrupted by the narcissism prevalent in our culture. "Diet and exercise should glorify God through good stewardship of the physical gifts he has given us," says Bill Parent. "The danger is that they can become self-centered, self-serving ways of glorifying ourselves." There is always a risk, in church exercise programs, that the focus will shift from worship of God to worship of the "perfect bodies" presented by the entertainment, dieting, and advertising industries.

Moreover, as Gene McAfee points out with concern, it's chiefly only one level of our society — the relatively affluent and well-educated part — that is focused on diet and exercise (not to mention cosmetic surgery and gastric stapling), while the poor and less-educated part is sliding deeper into physical neglect. Bad food choices, tobacco, alcohol, drugs, disease, and violence are taking a serious toll on lower-class white, black, Asian, and Hispanic bodies. Fortunately, there is a movement underway to incorporate health ministries into many African-American churches. John K. Jenkins Sr., pastor of First Baptist Church of Glenarden in Landover, Maryland, reports that his church's "Health and Wellness" group is promoting health fairs, monthly blood-pressure screenings, eye tests, nutrition classes, sickle-cell screening, and exercise classes.

On balance, we believe that the incorporation of the body into spirituality is a positive development, and we hope that it continues to spread throughout our communities of faith. The body is simply too important to ignore as we try to figure out what it means to live with integrity. We offer you this book on faith and fitness with the hope that you will come to see that both worship on Sunday morning and exercise throughout the week are important to spiritual growth and a life of true integrity. When you are a whole and sound person, it is easier for you to reach out and extend your hand — indeed, God's hand — to someone in need.

29

Know What This Book Can Do For You

We begin this journey with a single concept that we want readers to grasp and hold throughout: that strength is a virtue, regardless of whether it is cast in spiritual or physical terms, and that, in fact, the two are deeply interrelated. Strength is not merely the absence of weakness. Rather, it is a proactive approach to daily life that aims to cultivate wholeness and integrate mind, body, and spirit in ways that maximize our opportunities to do God's good work. *God wants you to be strong*, and so do we.

Contemporary culture, with its secular, market-driven emphasis on fads and headlines, tends to disregard the valuable and time-tested principles that form the basis of both Christian life and physical well-being. In this book we propose that, rather than being at odds with one another, being physically fit and a follower of Jesus are two sides of the same coin. In fact, the two precepts support each other, and that diligence and achievement in one sphere facilitates success in the other, thus enhancing overall well-being in a personal sense, and empowering each person to then make a more powerful contribution to personal, family, and community life.

Spiritual and physical fitness are achievable goals, but only for those who are willing to put aside the cultural temptations to rely upon shortcuts, quick fixes, or denial as strategic options. While the paths to these two elements of fitness are likely clear, they are by no means easy to traverse. Traveling them successfully requires hard work, continual — indeed, sometimes painful — introspection, and a willingness to learn, sacrifice, and change. If you embark upon the journey that we outline here, you will participate in a real-life game of "truth or consequences." We will ask you to accept certain immutable truths about both faith and fitness and to understand that your choices have consequences, many times serious ones. For example, just as Christ's life provides a powerful example of how to live with faith and love, so, too, does exercise science tell us that our bodies will fall into disrepair if we do not care for them properly.

Each of us is part of God's creation. As such, perhaps the most fundamental element of Christian stewardship of God's creation is to begin by managing our own lives in a manner that respects and reveres the divine gift of life. Through conscious decision-making, each of us has the opportunity to take our imperfect physical beings and make them as strong and as fit as we possibly can, not necessarily for the purposes of vanity or competitive athletics, but because not doing so is, by itself, an act of disrespect and irreverence.

On the pages that follow, we provide a roadmap that we believe Christians can use to improve their physical and spiritual health, thus improving the quality of their lives. In doing so, we believe that Christians should regard neither faith nor fitness as endpoints. Rather, they are both ongoing, lifelong processes. A day in church or a moment in prayer are, by themselves, insufficient to constitute a Christian life. That comes from repeatedly exercising the principles of compassion, honesty, wisdom, kindness, and fidelity in our daily lives by making the Christian choice even when it is difficult to do so. Living a Christian life comes from taming anger, resisting temptation, and acting with compassion — not just once, but all the time — recognizing that God's imperative, as articulated by Jesus in the gospels, is not to pick and choose what feels right or easy, but to fully engage in God's challenge to every one of us that we can do better. And, in doing better for ourselves morally and spiritually, we elevate all those around us and become living, breathing, strong, working beacons of God's love.

Similarly, we hope to convince readers that fitness comes from repeatedly making good choices. One nutritious meal and one long walk are inadequate to meet the needs of a healthy life. A healthy life is one that derives from making consistent, rational, wise long-term choices in diet and exercise. It means, in large measure, being able to resist the temptations of a marketplace that wants to feed our most base desires and not our long-term needs. This is true not just in concrete terms (for example, an endless stream of "new and improved" snack products, or the absurdity of soda with vitamins), but also in conceptual terms (so-called "expert" companies and individuals shilling "magic" diet and exercise solutions that lack any scientific substantiation or usefulness for most people).

Over the last 30 years, there has been an explosion of research in exercise science and human nutrition. The studies from major universities, government agencies, and private research organizations, such as the Cooper Institute in Dallas, Texas, provide an abundance of rich and detailed evidence about what a regular person — not a world-class athlete — needs to do on a day-to-day basis to maximize his or her chances for a healthy life. Unfortunately, much of this information is quite unsexy and mundane; consequently, it does not grab the attention of the conventional media that flits from one "new" finding to another without providing appropriate context and guidance on how people can fit together what often seem to be disparate pieces of a complicated puzzle. We hope to clarify the muddle and give you useful starting points upon which you can build as new evidence emerges from studies yet to come.

We recognize that some Christians may view our approach with skepticism. Dispensationalists may contend that with the second coming of Jesus, it is pointless to engage in a rigorous pursuit of physical health, because in the long run, it will not matter. We disagree strongly. The divine gift of life carries with it a *current* obligation to live fully and well, so as to not waste life's most precious resource ... time. None of us can retrieve wasted time, and, we believe, God will judge each of us, in part, on whether we have used the life given to us wisely and in a way that allowed us to carry out the Lord's work every day. In addition, it is both arrogance and folly to believe that any one of us knows when Jesus will return. It may be tomorrow or perhaps not in the lifetime of anyone alive today; as it is not knowable by any one of us, we can only maximize the opportunities we have to manage our lives wisely. Seeking to live a Christian life, which includes alleviating suffering, uplifting the needy, and correcting the wrongs that arise from sin, in a world that abounds with it, takes energy, perseverance, and diligence. The stronger you are, the more you can do, and the more you can do, the closer you come to fulfilling Christ's charge to live a life grounded in faith and love.

Whether you are healthy but inactive, or are plagued by a chronic disease, such as diabetes, obesity, or high blood pressure, we believe that you will find both inspiration and practical guidance on these pages. As you begin this journey, we ask that you undertake it with patience, an open mind, and faith in both divine guidance and sound, scientific exploration. There is no more powerful combination for creating change in the world — or in ourselves as individuals — and we urge you to harness the energy of both for your benefit.

For many people, the fall into a state of physical disrepair, whether from poor eating habits, insufficient exercise, or both, has taken a lifetime. Likewise, it will take time to reverse the cycle of un-health and turn it into a cycle of health. Unlike many quick-fix books on diet and exercise, we hope to teach you not how to "lose 10 pounds in 10 weeks," but, instead, to live a healthier life in which your primary goals are not weight loss as an isolated goal, but both physical and spiritual vigor and vitality that can sustain your heart and soul for decades, not weeks. Making changes in small steps increases the likelihood that you will truly drop negative behaviors, start positive ones, and make your changes stick for the long term. After you have finished reading our *Ten Commandments of Faith and Fitness*, we hope that you have moved toward a healthier relationship with food and exercise, with yourself and those around you, and most importantly, with God. To that end, we hope that this book will play a powerful role in helping you to keep body and spirit together.

Your Action Steps From Commandment One

1. Make appointments with yourself for at least three periods of exercise per week (three if you are new to exercise, more if you are already active).

2. Commit the Fitness Trinity to memory.

3. List three activities that will help you to keep body and spirit together.

4. Identify your Covenant Partner, and make a covenant for the Ten Commandments of Faith and Fitness.

Sample Covenant
Between Your Covenant Partner And You

_____ (Covenant Partner)

makes a covenant with

_____ (Your Name)

to provide support in the pursuit of faith and fitness.

The Covenant Partner promises to communicate daily/weekly/ biweekly (circle one), to offer encouragement and help to measure progress.

The Covenant Partner will challenge, assist with learning and problem-solving, provide constructive criticism, and help instill a healthy sense of discipline and commitment.

Signed

_____ (Covenant Partner)

_____ (Your Name)

_____ (Date)

Commandment Two

Thou Shalt Be Self-Aware

Be Aware Of Good Information

No single factor is more important to making wise choices and succeeding in life than being aware of the best possible information. Regardless of whether your goals are material or spiritual, saving money for retirement or supporting a family in need in your community, you can enhance your confidence and maximize the chances of success when you do a bit of research beforehand. Ask good questions, and know how to differentiate between fact and fiction, and between hype and reality.

In exercise and nutrition, it is equally important for you to discern the differences between science and speculation. One of the most confusing aspects of trying to live a life of faith and fitness in our culture is that our information-drenched society is really a bundle of mixed, often confusing, messages. Government health agencies seem to change their opinions and their guidance at the drop of a hat, and the commercial marketplace is even worse. You can find a purveyor of almost every kind of exercise gadget or gizmo or nutritional theory or strategy ... but, you will rarely find gadgets, gizmos, potions, or plans that actually work and deliver the results that they promise.

For example, recent research shows that most commercial diet plans actually have very little credible, scientific evidence to support their claims.[6] How can this be so? These companies make tens of millions of dollars from American consumers, yet they apparently devote few funds to conducting honest, scientifically credible research that establishes the value of what they sell. When companies refuse to invest in critical and rigorous analysis of their behavior, products, or services, it is often because they do not want to see — or do not want others to see — the results of the analysis. A sales pitch is much easier to make when it is uncomplicated by valid and reliable data; conversely, if the products and services are truly useful and effective, their contribution to weight loss or weight management is measurable in a scientifically meaningful way, which would, of course, provide a powerful competitive advantage in the marketplace.

Other examples include the unceasing stream of exercise gadgets that enterprising entrepreneurs, whose enthusiasm perhaps overwhelms their actual knowledge of exercise, bring to market and sell as the next greatest solution to all your exercise ills. From continuous passive motion tables to abdominal exercisers and from electrical muscle stimulators to slow and static strength training, nearly all the latest and greatest gadgets and ideas share one important thing in common — none of them work, and, equally enterprising, scientists have actually conducted the tests to tell us so.[7][8][9]

Despite the marketplace confusion, we know what works to achieve fitness and faith ... making clear, rational choices every day of your life. In fitness, this means relying upon the best information that modern science can provide, and there is lots of it, some of which we will outline here. As you go forward in this program, you should endeavor to become a more skeptical information consumer, one who asks questions, understands the motivation behind sales pitches for different products and services, and most importantly, appreciates that developing a complete picture of faith and fitness is not unlike assembling a large, complex puzzle.

It is not always immediately apparent how a particular piece fits into the greater whole (for example, why you should lift weights at least twice weekly or ensure that you eat enough of the right kinds of carbohydrates). However, as you accumulate more knowledge, you will see more clearly how all the disparate pieces fit together and become more aware of how these components fit into your personal health situation. Science, like our understanding of God and the way he works, often proceeds incrementally and cumulatively, with a series of small insights that build upon one another. Because our approach to fitness is grounded in science and fact — after all, God endowed each of us with reason, skill, and memory, and it is our obligation to use these tools wisely — we will ask you to have patience and recognize that today's science

36

may not be able to address all your questions. But, as you will see, there is more than ample scientific information to support an approach to life that gives physical activity and good nutrition a prominent place in your day-to-day existence.

Be Aware Of The Value Of Exercise

Have you ever tried to change a tire on your car without the benefit of a jack? Can you imagine building a house without a hammer and nails, or planting a tree without a shovel to dig the hole? How about taking a photograph without a camera? Of course not. In these examples, and many others that you encounter every day, having access to the right tools and sufficient knowledge to use them wisely and safely will determine whether or not you can do the job. Without the tools that you need, your objectives — no matter how laudatory and regardless of whether they relate to work, church, community, or recreation — will remain out of reach. However, when the proper and necessary tools are at hand and you use them thoughtfully and carefully, your work goes smoothly, efficiently, and is ultimately much more likely to deliver the rewards that you seek.

We believe that you should think about exercise and its place in your life in this way — as a tool that you can shape to your specific needs, with the potential to improve many aspects of your being, from physical health to emotional outlook. It is, however, a unique tool in that it requires repetitive, consistent use in order to deliver effective and meaningful results. Just as faith is a process that requires daily repetition, so, too, is exercise a process and not only an endpoint.

When you give it the opportunity to do so, we are confident that you will find regular exercise to be a highly useful tool that enlivens, empowers, and energizes. The ultimate power of exercise is like the power of faith. As Saint Peter Julian Eymard said, "Faith is to believe what you do not see; the reward of this faith is to see what you believe." We are asking you to believe in the power of healthy, sensible, physical exercise as an ennobling process that will let you reach for greater things in your life, just as your faith in Christ brings with it the powerful belief that salvation is accessible to any of us and that our reward is everlasting life. Indeed, physical activity, whether it is formal exercise or an afternoon of lawn mowing and gardening is more than just useful; it is actually protective.

Physical inactivity is a quiet, corrosive killer — much like immoral behavior — and long-term epidemiologic analysis show that physically active people dramatically reduce their risk of death from a wide variety of causes by about 30% to 40%.[10] The greatest impact comes from reducing the risk of death from cardiovascular disease. No matter what your starting point, exercise has the power to deliver results and take you farther than you believed possible. Indeed, it is often the least fit people who benefit the most from making exercise a part of their daily devotion.[11] [12]

To be sure, exercise's full range of health-related rewards will not appear overnight. It will take time and toil for you to achieve your goals, and during this period, you will likely doubt yourself, your activities, and their power to transform you in the manner you desire. At one time or another, we, too, shared your skepticism and concern. Doubt is a natural part of the fitness process, just as it is part of faith. But, we believe that diligence, perseverance, and learned application of sound, scientifically grounded exercise principles form the most reliable and predictable path to long-term better health. God may not have provided an exercise plan in the gospels, but he surely provided each of us with the intelligence to learn, adapt, change, and choose, and we urge you to put these skills to use for both your own and God's greater interests.

Exercise is not an abstraction. It is a very real mechanism that has the potential to deliver you powerful, concrete, life-changing results. When you consider what you want from an exercise program, you should envision the real, discrete endpoints (often called outcomes by health professionals) that you would like to achieve. The endpoints that people desire from exercise vary as much as the individuals themselves. You might desire some of the things that we list below:

- a healthier body weight
- lower risk for major chronic ailments, such as high blood pressure, heart disease, diabetes, and some cancers

- reduced reliance on prescription medications, fewer visits to the doctor, and decreased risk of hospitalization
- more self-confidence and self-respect
- greater ability to live independently as you age, and reduced risk of things such as falls — a leading cause of death and disability in older adults
- less risk of depression, anxiety, and isolation from others
- increased ability to reach out to others through your church, including participating in the missions and ministries, both here and abroad, that matter most to you
- enhanced muscular strength, power, and endurance, which make it easier for you to participate in other recreational activities and enjoy them more
- setting and achieving specific fitness goals, such as running a mile in 10 minutes or less, or bench pressing more than your body weight
- more productivity at work and less likelihood of on-the-job injury if you work in a physically demanding field
- better sleep
- better sex life

Use our list or create your own. Sit down with your spouse, close friend, or Covenant Partner and ask them to help you develop a list of both short- and long-term goals for your fitness program. Start small, take modest incremental steps, and strategically build up to more complex goals as you progress. Studies show beyond any reasonable debate that exercise can help you along the path to achieving these outcomes. How much you ultimately achieve will depend on a number of factors, some of which you cannot control and exercise cannot affect. These include your genetic makeup (short, small-framed people are unlikely to ever bench press 400 pounds, nor is that necessary for good health); and, the severity of any illness that you already have (exercise is not magic and it may not be able to reverse or stem the progression of some problems, such as severe heart disease, cancer, or disabling joint problems).

Exercise may, however, make it easier for you to live with your diagnosis, allow you to reduce or eliminate use of some medications, and enhance your self-confidence and mood. Exercise offers benefits and hope for those who suffer from cancer, heart disease, arthritis, depression, diabetes, overweight, and obesity.[13] [14] [15] [16] [17] So, if you suffer from one of these or from another chronic condition, take heart. Even if your ability to exercise hard or for long periods is limited by your illness or treatment side effects, you may well find that small amounts of regular physical activity will be both suitable and beneficial. As always, check with your physician before starting an exercise program. Both healthy adults and those with chronic ailments need to engage in a thorough exercise planning process, which includes medical clearance. The planning process will challenge you to hone your ability to identify and set reasonable goals, and then design and implement a process for reaching them.

Bear in mind that your long-term success at using physical activity and diet to improve your health will be determined by the complex interplay of your current health and level of fitness, disease risk factors, physical capacity (determined largely by heredity), the equipment and facilities that you have access to, the validity of your plan, and your ability to stick to it. One thing that we believe you should work at diligently, no matter what your current state of fitness, is to try to limit weight gain as you get older. As we all know, people tend to gain weight as they age; taking the weight off is enormously difficult. You have a greater likelihood of lifelong health if you can develop and persist in a physical activity and diet strategy that helps to *limit* the amount of weight you gain rather than hoping to take it off after you accrue it. In most cases, this will mean committing yourself to gradually becoming more active as you get older, thus resisting the natural tendency to slow down and be less active. The latter is a formula for enslavement by the creeping onslaught of chronic disease. Of course, to maximize your health opportunities, you must endeavor to stop smoking.

Before we go any further, we should emphasize here what exercise is not and should not be. It is not about developing physical strength to diminish, demean, or humiliate others. It is not about developing an unhealthy narcissism or self-absorption about your physical appearance. Most certainly, it is not about using steroids, human growth hormone, erythropoietin (EPO), or any other performance-enhancing drug or supplement. As you will learn later in this book, we are completely confident that you can achieve an admirable and sustainable state of physical strength and endurance by relying on nothing more than the fresh foods available in your local grocery store and a store-brand daily multivitamin as a little bit of insurance.

Perhaps the hardest challenge you will face on this path is resisting the temptation of false idols, such as products and services that claim to have all the answers, the magic bullet, or the secret weapon. This is especially important for people who need to lose weight, which includes nearly two-thirds of American adults. When a person or company tells you that they have all the answers, you should ask for the *evidence* to support their claims. In contemporary science, the highest standard of evidence is a well-designed study that is reviewed by qualified professionals and scientists other than the author (a process called peer-review) and then published in a respected professional journal.

Very few products and services in the marketplace can meet this rigorous standard. Our approach to writing this book has been to rely on the peer-reviewed, published, exercise science and nutrition literature because it is the highest and most credible standard available. Thus, our recommendations are neither infallible nor necessarily comprehensive, but rather, accurately reflective of today's science on key fitness and nutrition issues as we understand it. Most importantly, we are not merely dispensing our potentially uninformed opinions, but relaying the research, findings, recommendations, and consensus opinions of thought leaders in these critically important fields. Bear in mind that many fitness and diet books published in the marketplace do not rely upon the peer-reviewed scientific literature, but just reflect the author's belief that he or she has an idea to sell that the public may buy. It is a remarkably low standard and one that we have worked hard to avoid.

We urge you to be a polite, persistent skeptic about claims that offer an easy way out. Before using any supplement or nutritional product, make sure that you speak with a physician or pharmacist to ensure that it will not adversely affect any illness you have or interact with any medication that you are using. Be aware, also, of the limitations of the people you speak with.

Physicians get little training in nutrition or exercise science; while many medical schools offer some formal instruction in nutrition, only a very small minority require it. Worse still, medical students appear to gradually lose interest in nutrition and nutrition education over the course of their training. First year medical students think highly of nutrition education for their patients, but their interest in it declines over the course of their training, and they especially lose interest if they plan to enter a subspecialty. Only 19% of medical students believe that they get sufficient training in nutrition counseling and by their fourth year only 17% are actually providing their patients with nutrition guidance. So, while two-thirds of Americans are overweight, less than a fifth of doctors-to-be believe that they are getting the nutrition training they need or actually imparting nutrition knowledge to their patients.[18] To the best of our knowledge, no medical school requires instruction in exercise physiology or exercise science. Detailed exercise planning advice is best secured from an American College of Sports Medicine certified Exercise Specialist or Clinical Exercise Physiologist. This is particularly true if you have, or are at-risk for, any chronic illness.

Be Aware Of Return On Investment

While exercise is not the only tool that can help you reach the quality-of-life endpoints that you value, it will play a critical, irreplaceable role in the process. This is primarily because exercise is one of those things in life that delivers a very high return on investment, a lot of bang for the buck, so to speak. No other activity offers the prospects of improving so many different parts of your life as does regular, moderate-to-vigorous exercise. Exercise is irreplaceable in this role because it is the only thing you can do daily, for yourself, that stimulates all the physiological systems in your body that are crucial to good health:

- **Cardiovascular system:** Exercise strengthens and improves the efficiency of your heart and lungs and can help maintain or improve the elasticity of your blood vessels.
- **Musculoskeletal system:** Strength training is the cardinal means to build and maintain healthy muscles, as well as strengthen bones and connective tissue, such as tendons (attach muscles to bones) and ligaments (connect bones to one another).
- **Neurological system:** Endurance exercise, in particular, can improve mood; while many endurance athletes describe feelings of joy and euphoria, often called runner's high, which occurs when your brain purportedly releases hormones called endorphins during prolonged activity, no one has actually proved the existence of this phenomena. Rather, it could simply be the case that people who enjoy endurance exercise are just really happy when they do it. Further, people who exercise regularly generally report feeling better about themselves, and have less anxiety and depression. In addition, preliminary research indicates that people who exercise regularly are at reduced risk for Alzheimer's disease, the incidence of which appears to be increasing at the same time that many of us are becoming less active as we age.
- **Immune system:** Moderate exercise stimulates your immune system, which includes white blood cells, antibodies, and other cells that kill or defend against invading bacteria and viruses, and potentially prevent the spread of cancerous cells. Be careful, however, because hard exercise can have the opposite effect of suppressing immune function, actually making your more susceptible to certain illnesses.

Thought of in these compelling terms, nothing else, not even prayer or the power of positive thinking (potent tools in themselves), can displace exercise as the key component of a healthy lifestyle. Human beings — created in God's image — thrive on movement, activity, and work; when denied these core needs, they slowly degenerate from disuse and complacency. This disuse — the lack of sufficient activity in the daily lives of American adults of all ages and even our children — is what lies at the root of the epidemics in our culture of heart disease, diabetes, overweight, obesity, and depression. This is a costly and deadly situation that robs people of their vitality and, often, the best years of their lives. Why is this so?

We believe that it is largely an educational failure. Our schools generally cut physical education to the bare minimum when budget priorities conflict, thus saving money in the short term and risking our children's health — and increasing medical care spending — in the long term. Further, young people right up through college age are strikingly ignorant about how their bodies work, because coursework in human anatomy and physiology or exercise science is not required. We are hard pressed to understand why learning how your body works and how best to care for it is anything less than essential. Culturally, we place an inordinate emphasis on competitive athletics, leaving out of the exercise discussion an entire cadre of children for whom competing is neither feasible nor desired. You do not need to be an athlete to be fit.

The fundamental requirement for fitness is a self-awareness of its necessity and a commitment to investing time, energy, sweat, and possibly some money, to get results. We believe, however, that like a life of faith, the return on investment for a lifetime of devotion to health-giving physical activity will ultimately yield a return that could far exceed even your own expectations and goals.

Exercise is as close as we can get to a magic elixir for a long and healthy life. Regular, moderate-to-vigorous exercise is essential for health and vitality, and there is no other intervention — no pill, powder, or potion — that can do more to improve your physical, emotional, and psychological well-being. If you plan exercise carefully, do it wisely, and progress in small increments as your body increases in strength and tolerance; you can do all this with a minimum of side effects and adverse consequences. Unlike many of the things that people use to improve their health, such as questionable nutritional supplements, unproven weight loss programs (that is, nearly every one for which you see ads), and even some dubious medical services, exercise's value as a tool to prevent disability or illness, improve quality of life, and help with recovery from sickness is scientific fact, not idle speculation or a baseless marketing claim.

The scientific support for exercise as an essential tool for modern life continues to grow daily. As the studies accumulate, we understand more about how exercise can help prevent or ameliorate disease. We believe that as you embark on the exercise program that appears later in this book, you should do so with a firm grasp of the scientific evidence about the value of exercise. You should, however, exercise some caution in your approach to exercise because, like all physical activities, it is not without its risks and adversities.

Strength Training

We gave you some brief exposure to strength training as one part of the Fitness Trinity in the First Commandment. Let's expand on it here. Strength training is a broad concept that comes down to this: working your muscles against resistance for the purpose of building muscular strength, power, or endurance, making your bones more resistant to fracture (critically important for aging adults), and getting some modest cardiovascular benefit.

Strength training is doable in a number of ways: weight-lifting machines, such as those you commonly find in gyms; free weights, such as dumbbells and barbells; elastic tubes and bands that vary in the amount of resistance they provide; and, finally, using your own body weight, in exercises such as push-ups, pull-ups, and similar movements. Strength training is something that children can learn (with proper adult supervision)[19] and that can dramatically improve the quality of life for seniors because it helps build healthy muscle that empowers older people to live with greater independence and require less help from others.

Strength training is also a primary means of keeping bones strong throughout life, helping protect against potentially debilitating and deadly hip and lower back fractures in later years.[20] Absent any serious medical disorder, such as severe high blood pressure, joint pain, or current injury, all healthy sedentary persons should learn this important lifetime fitness skill and continue it for as long as they live.[21] Even for people with many chronic illnesses, regular exercise, including strength training, is a good way to alleviate symptoms, build confidence and independence, and improve quality of life.[22]

Endurance Exercise

What strength training is to your muscles, endurance exercise is to your heart, lungs, and blood vessels. It is the essential tool for keeping your cardiovascular system young, flexible, and fit.[23] In turn, you can reduce your risk of heart disease, high blood pressure, stroke, diabetes, depression, and control your weight better than someone who does not do endurance exercise.[24] [25] [26]

What do we mean by endurance exercise? It is any exercise that puts you into motion and requires you to use the biggest muscles in your body (legs, hips, and buttocks) repeatedly for an extended period. Ideally, endurance exercise should last at least 30 minutes, but for people who need to lose weight, 60 minutes is a more appropriate target. However, research also shows that as you age, you might need to move your endurance exercise target higher as you get older to ensure that you do not gain fat around your waist, where it is especially deadly.[27] [28]

Endurance exercise burns calories more efficiently than does strength training, which makes it an essential weight loss tool. For example, a 150-pound man who lifts weights at a moderate intensity for 30 minutes burns about 100 to 125 calories; this same man who walks 2.5 miles in 30 minutes (a pretty brisk pace of 5 mph) burns 260 calories. This is because walking is continuous exercise, while most strength training workouts have periods of both work and rest; walking uses large muscles while some strength workouts might be restricted to smaller muscle groups, such as your arms.

As you consider your exercise strategy, it is important for you to remember that strength training and endurance exercise are not interchangeable. While you can get a modest cardiovascular benefit with circuit strength training (a series of strength exercises done in sequence with little rest between them), it is not nearly as great a training effect as doing a vigorous walk, jog, or bike ride for its own sake. Likewise, endurance exercise will do little to build muscle

46

strength and power. You must do both, because they are equally important, but also quite different.

This is known in exercise science as training specificity. That is, particular activities engage your body systems in specific ways and the net results of your efforts are very specialized attributes that reflect the kind of exercise you did. The concept of specificity is why it is important for you to have a well-rounded program of physical activity, so that you leave neither your muscles nor your heart by the wayside. You will also need to identify exercises that specifically support your other interests, such as golf, tennis, walking, or swimming.

Finally, everyone responds to physical activity differently. The elements that will determine how you respond are your age, gender, current level of fitness and training program (the less fit you are now, the more room you have for improvement), and your genetic makeup (some people do better with endurance activities, such as running or cycling, while others are genetically predisposed to do better at strength training). A tendency to do better at one thing (for example, running) does not mean, however, that you can neglect other important elements, such as strength training. While physical capacity gradually declines starting in the fourth decade of life, it is absolutely true that, at any stage in life, your muscles and cardiovascular system are trainable and you can improve your level of fitness or performance no matter what it is now.

Good Nutrition

Nothing appears to confuse Americans more than how to eat wisely. We are going to boil it down (no pun intended) to a simple concept that should resonate strongly with Christians — the Mediterranean diet, which comes from the region of the world that includes the Holy Land itself. The Mediterranean diet has over 50 years of research to support its value as a way of eating that, in conjunction with regular exercise and not smoking, helps people manage their weight, as well as reduce the risk of cardiovascular disease and, possibly, some cancers. Before we go too much further, however, we want to remind you that all the commercially successful diets of the past several years have virtually no *scientific evidence* to underpin them. And, the high-fat/low-carb craze was particularly fraudulent in scientific terms because it seduced people into thinking that somehow a calorie was no longer a calorie and that you could gorge on fat and make yourself healthy. Nothing could be further from the truth.

We want you to remember this critical nutritional concept — count calories because calories count. No dietary fad has changed the laws of thermodynamics, and there is in nutrition science, just as there is in faith, an immutable law: If you eat more calories than you need, you will get fat. If you eat fewer calories than you need, you will eventually lose weight. The question, then, is how do you eat well and still enjoy all the pleasures that good food provides? This is where we believe the Mediterranean diet is a particularly strong tool. The fundamentals of the Mediterranean diet are abundant fruits and vegetables, heart-healthy fats, such as olive oil, whole grains, and lean protein, such as fish and chicken breast.[29] We will explore the Mediterranean diet in greater detail in the Fifth Commandment, "Thou Shalt Eat From The Garden." Suffice it to say that for our purposes at this stage, we urge you to absorb these critical dietary truths.

- It is necessary to understand both how much you eat and what you eat. As Americans, we eat too much, and the consequence is widespread overweight, obesity, and all the diseases that they help bring about. Further, we eat too many of the wrong foods, indulging processed carbohydrates (white flour and sugar) and saturated fats, while underconsuming fruits, vegetables, and whole grains, which are all loaded with valuable nutrients, such as fiber, vitamins, and minerals.
- There are both good fats and bad fats, and knowing the difference will affect your health. Broadly speaking, you do not need the saturated fats found most commonly in meats, whole-milk dairy foods, and fried products. You need, and benefit from, the unsaturated fats commonly found in certain cooking oils such as canola and olive oil, some nuts

48

and seeds (such as flax seed), many kinds of fish, and avocados. It is important to identify and modify fat intake, replacing saturated and trans fats with either unsaturated ones or with proteins and whole grains.

- Taking supplements is not an answer to anything. There is very little credible, scientific evidence that taking supplements — beyond a basic multivitamin bearing the letters USP on the label — will do you any good at all.[30][31] As you will read later on, we believe that eating from God's garden will supply you with very nearly everything you need for good health, and the multivitamin is an inexpensive and easy health insurance against potential deficiencies, if you are eating a calorie-restricted diet, as many people are.

"About 40% of you need to lose weight," a Baptist pastor named Steve Reynolds recently told his congregation in Annandale, Virginia, during a worship service. "When you love potluck more than God, it's serious."[32] These are challenging words for Christians who want to make good choices about the nourishment of body and spirit.

Be Aware Of The Value Of Walking

We want you to get active ... NOW. Just as Jesus did not advocate a "go slow" approach to spreading God's word and doing God's work, we do not believe that complacency is a substitute for activity. Thus, we want you to start moving today, and if you are already exercising, then use this opportunity to step it up a notch.

We want beginners to go to their calendars and make a minimum of three exercise appointments with yourself for this week. In each appointment space, we want you to write the word "WALK" in bold letters, because that is your exercise goal this week: at least 30 minutes of walking on each of those three days, spread across many small walks, if need be.

Some people will undoubtedly find this approach of scheduled walks intimidating. But, we have chosen walking as the foundational activity for a reason. It does not require you to join a gym, takes little money, and provides an understandable, highly accessible point of departure for building a long-term, more sophisticated, and multifaceted exercise program. For the vast majority of Americans who are insufficiently active, this is the best place to start ... nothing more or less complicated than walking. We all know how to do it, it does not require any elaborate or expensive equipment, and you can do it indoors or outdoors.

If you are not walking already, we want you to commit yourself to completing walks that add up to 30 minutes during at least three of the next seven days. You should walk at a pace that allows you to just barely hold a conversation with another person or, if you are alone, you should be able to just barely recite a brief poem, scriptural passage, or other saying of about 20 words length. (To learn more about this Talk Test of exercise intensity, read Commandment Three: "Thou Shalt Endure.") If it is very easy for you to talk, then you are walking too slowly; if it is very difficult for you to speak, then you are working too hard, so slow down a little.

The only equipment you need is a pair of comfortable and supportive athletic or walking shoes and clothing that is appropriate to the weather in your locale. Many shopping malls open their doors early to allow people to walk laps in the mall's interior, so make use of this resource if you prefer to walk indoors rather than outside. Drink about a cup of water about 20 to 30 minutes before starting. You may wish to carry some water with you during the walk and sip a bit more after finishing.

Marketing claims notwithstanding, most people do not need to consume sports drinks before or during activity that lasts less than an hour. Water will do just fine. While commonly available, sports drinks typically have about half the calories per serving of soda (an advantage for the sports drinks), but for someone trying to lose weight these are still unnecessary calories. As your fitness improves and the duration of your endurance activity increases, you may wish to revisit the use of sports drinks, because scientific data shows that they can help prolong endurance exercise and allow you to work more intensely. The drinks are especially important when walks, runs, or bike rides last longer than an hour or if the weather is hot. In general, you should not be thirsty when you start your activity, and you should drink more water after it ends. Not only can water help you stay adequately hydrated, so can fruits and vegetables, because most of them have high water contents. Hence, if you consume sufficient amounts of fruits and vegetables daily, you can "eat" your water, as well as drink it on the side.

Walking is an ideal exercise for many people because you can modulate the intensity of a walk by moving faster or slower, and it is remarkably effective at doing several important things: raising your heart rate, thus making your cardiovascular system stronger and more efficient; burning calories, which will help you lose weight or control it better; and, providing activity with a relatively high level of comfort because walking places little stress on your body, given that it lacks the impact that comes with running.

Walking's chief disadvantage, ironically, actually stems from one of its main benefits — the fact that it does not involve the kind of ground impact that you get with running. The consequence of this is that walking is not as effective at keeping your bones strong as running or rigorous strength training; it will, however, help improve both muscle and bone health in a very unfit person. Generally speaking, walking requires supplementation with strength train ing, because we know from studies that weight lifting for your legs and lower back will help preserve the strength of those bones and prevent fractures in future years.

Despite this relatively modest drawback, we are confident in recommending that you should make walking your baseline activity. Once you master walking at different paces, over varying terrain, and build fitness, you can grow into any additional endurance activities that you wish, including adding some jogging to your routine to bolster bone health. If you are overweight or obese, you may find that swimming or cycling will suit you better, especially as you start your program. This is because the water or bike will support your body weight, making it easier for you to do the activity. As you lose weight, you can add walking to your mix of pursuits. An overweight or obese person will likely tire more quickly on a walk than will a lighter person. When this happens, do not despair. Sit down to rest your legs, feet, and ankles, but keep your arms moving. Then, after you recover a bit, resume your walk. As fitness improves, you will need fewer and fewer of these periods of active rest.

Walking's fluid, comfortable movement is something that many people can happily do day after day, and this concept is critical because over the course of this book we will repeatedly emphasize your need to make good exercise and dietary choices over and over again. So, it is essential for you to find an activity that you like enough to be able to do nearly every day.

If you already exercise regularly — by walking, running, cycling, or other activities — we want you to use the designated exercise appointments this week to break out of your routine and increase your exercise effort. There are three ways to increase your exercise effort: increase duration (how much time you spend doing it), frequency (how often you work out), or intensity (work harder during a given exercise session).

If you have days on your schedule when you are currently inactive, add an exercise appointment to at least one of them to increase the frequency of your weekly workouts. You can increase the intensity of each exercise session. For walking (or most other endurance exercises, such as cycling and running), you can increase intensity by varying one of these elements: moving more quickly, taking longer strides, or varying the terrain that you cover. As there is no such thing as a truly flat road, most of us live in locales that have hills, which are God's way of giving us a means to work harder without having to go very far to do it. Walking hills is a great way to raise your heart rate, build healthy muscle in your hips and legs, and the hard work actually will burn calories more quickly. Stairs also work very well to increase the intensity of a walking workout but they are difficult for people who have weak muscles and difficulty maintaining their balance — use stairs with great caution.

Be Aware That Jesus Was A Walker

One other elementary thing about walking that we, as Christians, can readily relate to is that Jesus was a walking man. Throughout the gospels, we read of Jesus traveling by foot from town to town — preaching, teaching, healing, and inviting people to follow him. Walking is not only an effective method of transportation, it is also an excellent opportunity to socialize, talk, think, and pray. It creates an opportunity for us to exercise not only our bodies, but our spirits. From the time of Jesus until today, walking has been an activity that clears the mind and expands the soul.

Over the course of these ten commandments, walking will be the core activity around which everything else is arrayed, including strength training, diet, and possibly even fast walking, running, and cycling. Use your walking time to meditate on how regular disciplines — such as 30- to 60-minute walks — can move you closer to your elusive personal goals. As an example, we offer the story of Roger Bannister.

In the spring of 1954, British medical student, Roger Bannister, stepped onto a track in Oxford, England, and broke a world record by running a mile in less than four minutes — a race that became known as "The Miracle Mile." The four-minute mile had long been seen as a barrier that no human being would ever be able to break.

What is it, in your life, that stands before you as a four-minute mile? What personal goal seems to you to be attractive, alluring, exciting, and enticing ... but also elusive and maybe even inconceivable? Is it satisfaction in the workplace, professional fulfillment, or a set of friends you can trust? Is it a course of study that fits your own gifts and interests, or a community of Christians that will support you in your spiritual growth?

The apostle Paul had a particular four-minute mile in mind: The goal of knowing Christ and the power of his resurrection, and eventually attaining the resurrection from the dead (Philippians 3:10-11). He was so committed to attaining this goal that he threw himself completely into the race, and said, "Forgetting what lies behind and straining forward to what lies ahead, I press on toward the goal for the prize of the heavenly call of God in Christ Jesus" (vv. 13-14).

Did he achieve his goal? No doubt about it. So can we. The good news for us today is that we can run a miracle mile. Let's begin our training by gleaning some tips from Paul the apostle and Roger the runner, and then take their insights with us into our own personal races. If we begin to think like runners, we'll develop some daily disciplines that can help us to move ever closer to achieving our elusive personal goals.

The first tip is to let go of any attitudes that can distract us, dismay us, or destroy us as we run the race that lies before us. For Roger Bannister, this meant rejecting the idea that running a mile in less than four minutes was inconceivable. For the apostle Paul, this meant tossing out his old religious orientation, because he discovered that it was rubbish compared to "the surpassing value of knowing Christ Jesus" (v. 8). For us, destructive attitudes might include the fear that we cannot find a meaningful career, or develop healthy relationships, or build bonds in a small group at church. When we encounter these attitudes, we need to trash them. They are rubbish and can get in the way of our goal.

The second tip is to train over time and stick to a schedule. Roger Bannister didn't decide on the spur of the moment to set a world record, but he worked long and hard in a disciplined way to prepare himself for the miracle mile. He had been a competitive runner for years, and then, in the weeks prior to the record-setting race, his training intensity increased. Every day, for one-half hour, during his medical school lunch break, he ran 10 quarter-mile races at a pace of 59 seconds apiece. He took breaks of only 2 minutes between each race. He did not sit around and enjoy a lazy lunch hour.

This is the same kind of discipline that we are challenged to show as we pursue our professional, personal, and spiritual goals. By doing good things a little at a time, week in and week out, we reach the point where we can achieve some very significant objectives. This means being punctual at work, dependable in our friendships, committed to daily prayer time, and faithful to our exercise periods. The key is to be disciplined and to trust that ordinary good efforts have a tendency to add up and even multiply — resulting in extraordinary progress.

A third tip is this: Expect bad days. Every runner knows that some training runs feel awful, and as an athlete you have to try to put them behind you. Will we face injuries? No doubt. Twisted ankles can be agonizing on the walking path, while gossip and unfair criticism can cause terrible pain at work, in social circles, and in the Christian community. Will we have setbacks? Certainly. It would be wonderful if our bodies looked better after a week of exercise, if promotions always came on schedule, and if relationships were marked by nothing but peace and joy and harmony. But we know that disappointment, pain, and conflict are part of the daily race we face. Fortunately, God always gives us what we need, and he will not let us be tested beyond our strength (1 Corinthians 10:13).

The key to success is to remember that daily disciplines can move us ever closer to our elusive personal goals. This is true in 30-minute walks, and it is true in the most important race we'll ever run — the one that ends in resurrection life. Straining forward to what lies ahead, we are challenged to keep our eyes on Christ and trust him to show us the way to go. He'll be with us as we move forward one day at a time, let go of destructive attitudes, train over time, and endure bad days. In the end, he'll run right along with us as we cross the finish line into resurrection life.

Be Aware Of The Need To Keep Records

Just as we wrote this book to transmit important ideas, facts, questions, and issues, we want you to become avid exercise and nutrition writers. Studies show that people who are persistently successful at diet and exercise write things down.[33] Get yourself the tools you need to write things down, whether that is a computer word processing or spreadsheet program or just a spiral-bound notebook and a pen. We suggest an excellent software for this purpose from Crosstrainer (www.crosstrainer.com). Today, we want you to start a diet diary, so that you, too, can have the eye-opening experience of seeing exactly what you eat every day.

Starting today, we want you to write down everything you eat for the next seven days and possibly beyond ... and we mean everything, approximating the quantities and calories as well as you can. This is easy to do with prepackaged foods, because they contain quantity and calorie information right on the label. This is also increasingly true with food served in fast-food restaurants. You can look up other foods on the internet (a very useful website is one run by the US Department of Agriculture at www.nal.usda.gov/fnic/foodcomp/search/, where you can look up virtually any food imaginable) or buy calorie guides in food and bookstores. In addition, food manufacturers and restaurant companies post nutrition facts about their products on their websites.

If you eat half an apple and 2 chocolate kisses for a snack, write "1/2 apple — 50 calories, 2 chocolate kisses — 60 calories," and so on for every single thing you eat. This will likely have two important effects. First, it will not surprise us at all if you spontaneously start to eat less because the act of writing it down makes you immediately self-aware of the fact that maybe, just maybe, you actually eat a lot more than you need. Second, every week you should review the diary, and we want you to use a red pen to circle all the items you ate that you did not need. Finally, when you make your food entries, we also urge you to note whether your eating was in response to some other stimulus. There is an important reason for understanding this issue.

Food is an important part of our lives and our culture. We use it to celebrate, grieve, and manage stress, not just to nourish ourselves. We want you to look at what you ate and how much you ate, and make some connections with other events in your life. Perhaps the half-pint of ice cream came right after your child came home with a bad (or good) report card; maybe the third beer of the evening came when you wanted to hang out in the bar instead of going home and settling a disagreement with your spouse. We suspect that you will find that you, as we ourselves do, use food as more than sustenance, but often allow it to fulfill some other need. These other needs are called "triggers," and we hope to help you find other ways to deal with your food triggers. Food is necessary for life, but it need not be the only tool that you use to mitigate your emotional responses to various stressful situations. We hope that, over time, you will increasingly come to rely on prayer and exercise as your primary stress management tools, setting aside more time and energy to pray, walk, run, or lift weights, and less time to lift up spoons and forks.

You may eventually become so adept at keeping track of your calorie intake that you can do it in your head. But, for most people, keeping a daily record, even on a humble index card that you throw into a recycling bin at day's end, will prove a powerful and visible form of personal accountability. Successful weight loss and maintenance mean knowing what you ate and making adjustments along the way, as well as catching and compensating for slip-ups. When you track intake and know that you have exceeded your daily caloric goal by 250 calories, you will also realize that one of your challenges for the next day is to try to recoup that amount either through better food choices or a bit more physical activity. Writing things down will also help you eliminate guessing about your calorie intake, because that is a notoriously inaccurate and error-prone process. Don't take the chance of underestimating your daily calorie intake — sometimes by as much as 30% to 50% according to some studies — write things down.

Be Aware Of The Need For Medical Clearance And A Personal Health Inventory

Before you embark on *any* exercise program, you should sit down with your physician and get medical clearance. This is vital if you are either sedentary (not active at all), returning to exercise after a period of inactivity, overweight or obese, or suffer from a chronic illness such as diabetes, heart disease, or depression. For our purposes, we believe that all adults and children should follow the guidelines of the American College of Sports Medicine and meet with your doctor, review your health history, as well as any prescription drugs that you are taking, and discuss other potential limitations, such as reduced range of motion in your joints.

This is a good point to take stock of your personal health history, not because we want to pass judgment on it, but because it serves a useful purpose for you to see it in writing. This will help enhance your understanding of your current health problems (or things for which you may have risk factors), and also help you envision how diligent devotion to exercise can help you change the current picture.

57

The PAR-Q

Before embarking on a more diverse and potentially more difficult exercise program, it is essential to understand your current state of health and your readiness for such demands. To that end, we want you to use The Physical Activity Readiness Questionnaire, also known as the PAR-Q. The PAR-Q is a tool that exercise specialists use to determine whether someone is ready for regular physical activity.

The PAR-Q is a valid and reliable tool for estimating whether someone is ready to start an exercise program or increase the intensity of their current workout routine. It asks questions that explore whether you have had signs or symptoms of problems with your cardiovascular, neurological, or musculoskeletal systems. If you ever decide to work with a personal trainer or other fitness consultant, do not work with anyone who does not, at a minimum, use the PAR-Q to screen you. A well-qualified fitness coach or exercise specialist will go beyond the PAR-Q and do a thorough health history. We want you to review and answer the questions in the PAR-Q, which, in turn, sets the stage for a more detailed health inventory. The more detailed health inventory may eventually lead you to see your doctor for additional follow-up.

The essence of the PAR-Q is seven straightforward questions, and here they are:

1. Has your doctor ever said that you have a heart condition and that you should only do physical activity recommended by a doctor?
2. Do you feel pain in your chest when you do physical activity?
3. In the past month, have you had chest pain when you were not doing physical activity?
4. Do you lose your balance because of dizziness or do you ever lose consciousness?
5. Do you have a bone or joint problem that could be made worse by a change in your physical activity?
6. Is your doctor currently prescribing drugs (for example, water pills) for your blood pressure or heart condition?

7. Do you know of *any other reason* why you should not do physical activity?[34]

If you answered YES to any question, you should see your doctor before you have any kind of fitness testing or appraisal or before you become much more physically active. In either case, you should follow your doctor's advice about pursuing an exercise program; in particular, you need to understand your medical limitations. A yes answer to one or more questions is not, however, the end of your exercise career; over the long term, you likely will increase your exercise capacity, but you will have to do so more gradually than someone who answered no to all the questions. Alternatively, you may need to restrict yourself only to activities that are medically safe, depending on the severity of your problems and the medications that you use.

If you answered NO to *all* the questions, you are probably ready for physical activity, and you should be able to increase the frequency, intensity, and duration of your activities gradually. You are also probably ready for a full-fledged fitness test, which is potentially a very rigorous process. If you decide to have a fitness appraisal, you should locate a fitness instructor who has at least a bachelor's degree in physical education, exercise science, or a related field, and is also at least a Health Fitness Instructor, certified by the American College of Sports Medicine.

Avoid becoming more active if:

1. You have a temporary acute illness, such as the flu or a severe head cold. Resume your program after your health improves.
2. You either are, or may become, pregnant. Discuss exercise during pregnancy with your ob-gyn physician.
3. Your health changes, and your answer to any question above shifts from no to yes. In this case, notify your fitness advisor and then see your doctor.

If you do not have a regular physician, now is the time to find one, get a thorough physical, and get immediate treatment for any problems that your doctor diagnoses. Diabetes, high blood pressure, elevated cholesterol, and even heart disease can grow quietly and insidiously and require medical expertise to diagnose and treat. These are not trivial matters for you to deal with before you embark on an exercise program, which we hope will ultimately make your life longer and better. If you already have a regular physician, you will want to share with him or her information below.

Be Aware Of "Risk Stratification"
For Exercise Testing And Planning
Many people who either have, or are at-risk for, chronic diseases need medical clearance before exercise testing or participation. The consequence of these ailments is that exercise testing and exercise participation carry some risks. The American College of Sports Medicine produces guidelines that outline the circumstances under which someone should get clearance from a physician before exercise testing or participation. The guidelines, which we reproduce in brief on page 61, categorize people as low risk, moderate risk, or high risk. Medical clearance is especially useful if you are either sedentary (not active at all), returning to exercise after a period of inactivity, overweight or obese, or suffer from a chronic illness.

Risk Stratification For Fitness Testing And Exercise Planning	
Low risk	• Men under age 45, OR Women under age 55, who have no symptoms and no more than one of the following risk factors: Family history of heart disease[35] High blood pressure Elevated cholesterol Smoking Impaired glucose metabolism Obesity (body mass index > 30) Sedentary lifestyle, or A good cholesterol (HDL) level of less than 40 mg/dL.
Moderate risk	• Men over age 45, OR Women over age 55, OR anyone who has two or more of the above risk factors.
High risk	• Any person with known heart, lung, or metabolic disease (such as diabetes), or who has one or more of the following signs or symptoms of disease: chest pain or discomfort, shortness of breath at rest, with mild exertion, or when lying down, dizziness, ankle swelling, rapid heartbeat, calf cramping during walking or other mild activity, heart murmur, unexpected fatigue or shortness of breath with typical daily activities.

Source: Adapted from *ACSM's Guidelines for Exercise Testing and Prescription*, Seventh Edition. American College of Sports Medicine. Lippincott Williams & Wilkins. Baltimore, Maryland, 2006.

In some cases, a physician should attend the fitness test to guard against medical complications. Below is the ACSM's guideline on if you should have a medical exam before you have a fitness test or start to exercise, or whether a physician should attend your fitness test.

ACSM Recommendations
On Having A Physician Exam Before Starting Exercise
Or Having Physician Attend Fitness Testing

Physician Exam Before Starting Exercise

	Low risk person	*Moderate risk person*	*High risk person*
Moderate exercise	Not necessary	Not necessary	*Recommended*
Vigorous exercise	Not necessary	*Recommended*	*Recommended*

Physician Attendance At Fitness Testing

Submaximal fitness test	Not necessary	Not necessary	*Recommended*
Maximal fitness test[36]	Not necessary	*Recommended*	*Recommended*

Source: Adapted from *ACSM's Guidelines for Exercise Testing and Prescription*, Seventh Edition. American College of Sports Medicine. Lippincott Williams & Wilkins. Baltimore, Maryland, 2006.

While the above table says that a physician visit is not necessary for low and some moderate risk persons, it is never a bad idea to get physician clearance for exercise. Take the time to be cautious and have your doctor sign off on your exercise plan. Ask your physician to advise you about whether, based on your medical and family histories, you should undergo an assessment by a cardiologist or exercise physiologist, potentially including cardiac stress testing or other cardiac screening, before fitness testing or starting an exercise program.

In addition to speaking with your doctor, you should also touch base with the pharmacist who dispenses your medications. A wide variety of prescription and over-the-counter drugs can have an impact on your ability to engage in an exercise program, and you should understand their effects, particularly on your heart rate, blood pressure, and breathing. For example, if you take a beta blocker, such as Coreg®, your heart rate both at rest and during exercise will be lower than expected. The drug will also lower your blood pressure during exercise and at rest. Likewise, calcium channel blockers, such as Norvasc®, may raise your resting and exercise heart rates. For asthmatics, a bronchodilator likely will not affect your heart rate, but it will open up your breathing passageways and improve your exercise capacity. In particular, ask the pharmacist or doctor about how to use the medication before, during, and after exercise.[37]

As you can see, it is essential that you understand these potential impacts, and that you also discuss your medication history with your exercise professional. If he or she looks quizzically at you when you do so, find another exercise professional to advise you. According to a recent story in the *Wall Street Journal*, most personal trainers have little more than a high school diploma and a few hours of instruction, so, in fact, you may do more to educate a personal trainer working with you about your medical issues than he or she will do for you.[38]

There are some important indications as to when you should stop any physical activity, particularly if you have a medical condition. If you have chest pain or tightness, shortness of breath or wheezing, dizziness, nausea or vomiting, leg cramps or other severe muscular discomfort, or break into a cold, clammy sweat, STOP exercising immediately and get medical help.

The final issue that we wish to address in this section on cautionary notes is the issue of sudden death during exercise. This subject is a persistent fixation with people who fear that exercise exposes them to an undue risk of dying. Many people remember Jim Fixx, who popularized running for an entire generation, yet died during a run at age 52. More recently, former NFL linebacker, David Little, apparently robust and healthy, died while lifting weights at home. There is a risk of sudden death during exercise. However, the risk is estimated to be about 1 death for every 15 million episodes of exercise.[39] Further, studies indicate that while there is a risk of sudden death during exercise, the more consistently you exercise, the less likely you are to die during vigorous activity. In other words, the risk of sudden death during exercise may be greatest for those who do not exercise regularly or those who have other risk factors or untreated underlying disease, then engage in strenuous activity for which they are not prepared. It is lower for people who exercise regularly and challenge themselves with vigorous activity.

Your underlying health status will also affect your risk of sudden death during exercise. Indeed, within days of the death of former NFL linebacker, David Little, at age 46, an autopsy showed that he had an undiagnosed cardiac condition that predisposed him to sudden death. In the case of Jim Fixx, he also had underlying heart disease, likely the result of strong family history of it, high cholesterol, and smoking earlier in his life. Thus, the lesson is not that he died while running, but that running probably extended his life for years, gave him a higher quality of life than he would have had without it, and provided the opportunity for him to spread his message about the joy of running to millions of people. Think of how many countless lives Jim Fixx's advocacy for running *has saved*, not that he died while doing it. We do not know what Jim Fixx's religious beliefs were, but perhaps God's mission for him was to spread his gospel about running, which opened the eyes of an entire generation.

We believe that the small risk of sudden death during exercise is far and away less worrisome than the risk of dying from any one of a number of ailments that exercise can help prevent or manage, including heart disease, high blood pressure, overweight/obesity, and diabetes. Remember that heart disease is the number one cause of premature death and disability in our culture, and it is so because we exercise too little, not because we die from exercising too much or too hard.

Be Aware That Jesus Has Power To Change And Heal Us

Jesus shows real transformative power — the power to change people — when he surprises the Pharisees with a call for mercy,

64

not sacrifice (Matthew 9:13). Jesus knew that it was a religious violation to break bread with tax collectors and social outcasts and misfits, not to mention to be in close contact with a diseased woman, but he did both. He did these things because he believed that showing mercy is *never* against the law of God.

We see this today in the work of organizations dedicated to helping children in South Africa survive the HIV/AIDS epidemic. A good number of these children have lost one or both parents to AIDS, and many are HIV-positive themselves. As easy as it would be to judge the South African adults who now suffer from HIV/AIDS, we're challenged to take another approach, and reach out with *chesed*, or covenant faithfulness. It is our covenant obligation to address the needs of the more than one million children who have been orphaned by AIDS in South Africa, and we can show them the love of Christ by supporting organizations devoted to the creation of orphanages, health clinics, day care centers, and other institutions that have a positive impact on children affected by AIDS. Jesus can change us, by making us more compassionate, generous, and merciful, and we, in turn, change the world around us.

Jesus can also heal us, as he exercises his illness-conquering and death-defeating power. Jesus was passionately committed to overcoming sickness and death throughout his earthly ministry, and his healing work continues today as we lift our needs to him in prayer.

All across the country now, churches are offering services for wholeness, and people are testifying to the power of prayer in the healing process. Researchers are assembling data on prayer and illness, and some doctors are even getting into the habit of praying for their patients.

Prayers are being offered for whatever is broken in people's lives, not just for physical illness. Craig Barnes, a Presbyterian pastor who has participated in many healing services, reports that prayers are being lifted up for healing of broken hearts, lost relationships, broken marriages, childhood abuse, and lost jobs. He believes that God may answer these prayers in different ways, even using the brokenness of the body to heal our spirits. "The promise is that God will give us himself, and that is what is needed," he concludes. "The spirit is healed, no matter what happens to the body."

In times of personal brokenness, God gives us the gift of himself — a gift that is seen most clearly in the life and ministry of Jesus Christ. We are never completely powerless in the face of illness or loss, because we can always tap into the power of Jesus — a power that can change us, renew us, and give us healing and hope. God wants our bodies to be as strong and healthy as possible, because God desires to use our bodies to advance his ministry and mission in the world. "Your body is a temple of the Holy Spirit within you," says Paul to the Christians in Corinth (1 Corinthians 8:19) — because of this, God has an interest in maintaining our spiritual and physical fitness.

The good news being revealed by recent research is that religious activity is good for our bodies as well as our souls. Decades of studies on the link between faith and health are leading researchers to conclude that:

- people who regularly attend religious services have lower rates of illness and death than do infrequent attenders or nonattenders.
- people who report a religious affiliation have lower rates of heart disease, cancer, and high blood pressure.
- older adults who participate in private and congregational religious activities have fewer symptoms, less disability, and lower rates of depression, anxiety, and dementia.
- religious participation is the strongest determinant of psychological well-being in African Americans.
- actively religious people live longer, on average, than the nonreligious.[40]

Clearly, we should not leave religious activity out of our weekly routines. God wants to change us in body, mind, and spirit, so that we will be his strong and healthy servants in the world.

Be Aware That You Can Feel Badly While Living Well

To some, faith and fitness might seem to be a luxury, available only to those with enough leisure time to join Bible study groups and exercise three times a week. The fact of the matter is that people can have lots of free time and money ... and still feel rotten.

Cash cannot create contentment, and possessions don't always provide us with a sense of peace. Sure, we may watch "The Fabulous Life of Celebrity Super Spenders" on VH1, and gawk at the extravagant shopping sprees of Hollywood's best-paid superstars, but we know that most celebrities are just a few steps away from having a meltdown and ending up in rehab. What Grandma always said is true: Money can't buy happiness.

Still, most of us expect that improvements in quality of life are going to make us feel better. But they don't — at least not by themselves. In his book *The Progress Paradox*, Gregg Easterbrook makes the point that life is getting better all the time: Our houses are bigger than ever, our incomes are growing, our health is improving, and the environment is becoming cleaner.

So why isn't all this good news making us jump for joy? Easterbrook has some intriguing ideas about why we feel rotten in the middle of our nation's great riches, and how we can be simultaneously healthy and unhappy. He makes the case that:

Bad news sells. It's always a disaster of some kind that draws us to television news reports, and bad news is what keeps us glued to the tube through many commercial breaks. During a snowstorm in Washington DC, in the early 1990s, the local NBC affiliate changed the name of the weather segment from WeatherCenter to StormCenter. Well, guess what? They never changed it back, not even for sunny days. Bad news sells. Indeed, one of the best things that you can do to lower your stress level is to turn off and tune out the seemingly endless 24-hour news cycle that saturates our lives. We don't want you to ignore the broader world, just place the news in its proper perspective.

We don't sleep enough. Americans sleep an hour less every night than they did a generation ago. If that's not bad enough, we sleep about two or three hours less per night than people did a century ago. With such sleep deprivation, no wonder we feel cranky!

We are full of envy. Award shows, feature films, celebrity internet sites, *People* magazine, and programs such as "The Fabulous Life of Cameron Diaz" are constantly bombarding us with information about how the more "fortunate" members of our society live, and this is bound to make us feel envy — even if our lifestyle is really quite comfortable.

The solution to one problem creates another. Easterbrook describes this phenomenon as "the unsettled character of progress," and his insight makes sense, when you think about it. We invent an anthrax vaccine, and then we fear that it has terrible side effects. We create a nationwide network of cell phones, and then we live in terror that some distracted driver is going to run us down in his SUV. We develop miraculous cures for diseases, and then we worry that we will not be able to afford them. The unsettled character of progress often leaves us feeling very anxious about the future.[41]

For these reasons, and others, we are experiencing a progress paradox — we are feeling bad while living well. But there is also a spiritual component to this problem, one that is addressed quite clearly by Paul in his second letter to the Corinthians. Writing to a group of Christians in the wealthy Greek city of Corinth, Paul reminds them that they have promised to give him a "bountiful gift" for the poor Christians in Jerusalem (2 Corinthians 9:5). Although he describes this as a completely voluntary gift, it is clear that he expects the Corinthians to be generous in their support, and he promises many rewards for their giving.

For Paul, you see, true happiness is found in what you give ... not in what you receive. "God loves a cheerful giver," he tells them, ramping up the very first Christian stewardship campaign (v. 7). Do you want to be enriched in every way? Then let's see some "great generosity" (v. 11). Are you interested in glorifying God? Then show your brothers and sisters "the generosity of your sharing" (v. 13). Are you looking for God to provide you "with every blessing in abundance"? Then don't hold tight to a miserly attitude — instead, "share abundantly in every good work" (v. 8).

The apostle is laying out for us another paradox — what we might call "The Stewardship Paradox." In any true paradox, you are faced with a statement that seems to be contradictory, but turns out

68

to be true. In Paul's words to the Corinthians, he is saying that personal enrichment comes from great generosity, and that blessings in abundance come from sharing abundantly with others. His point is that we are to be good managers — good "stewards" — of the things that God has given us, and that we actually receive the most when we give the most. It's a paradox — The Stewardship Paradox.

How can such a contradiction be true? "The point is this," says Paul, using an agricultural image, "The one who sows sparingly will also reap sparingly, and the one who sows bountifully will also reap bountifully" (v. 6). Whether you are growing melons or trying to improve your physical fitness, Paul is absolutely right — you cannot expect significant results without making a significant investment. There will be no great harvest of melons in the fields, or increases in personal strength and endurance, or improvements in the health and safety of our communities, unless forward-thinking men and women are willing to sow bountifully by making significant investments of time and talent and treasure in the areas that matter to them ... and to God.

The key to personal happiness is to make a commitment to sowing bountifully, as individuals and as members of the community. In the economy of God, we find that we receive the most by giving the most, and as we give, we discover that God is truly able to provide us with every blessing in abundance (v. 8). As we put time and money into physical fitness, we find that we feel happier and healthier, and we do not have to invest so much money in medical care. As we develop our physical strength and endurance, we find that we are better able to serve our neighbors by pushing wheelchairs into church, swinging hammers in mission projects, and carrying canned goods to the community food pantry. As we share our resources with people in need, we find that we are enriched in every way for our great generosity, and we find ourselves filled with the "surpassing grace of God" (vv. 11-14). As we make sacrifices for others, we come to see that money cannot buy happiness, but generosity certainly can.

Cash cannot create contentment, and possessions cannot give us a sense of peace. But happiness can be ours if we are good stewards of the bodies that God has given us, and if we look for opportunities to share with people in need, out of the great abundance that our Lord has given us.

Your Action Steps From Commandment Two

1. Take your personal medical inventory, and get your physician's clearance to begin an exercise program.

2. Follow Jesus in being a walker.

3. Establish your exercise and diet diary.

4. Volunteer for a community project in which you can be a good steward of the body God has given you.

Commandment Three

Thou Shalt Endure

What Is Endurance Exercise?

In spiritual terms, endurance exercise is something that, quite literally, can save and prolong your life. It is essential to the prevention or management of heart disease, diabetes, high blood pressure, elevated blood lipids, depression, and some cancers. No activity will offer you as great a return on your time and effort invested as endurance exercise.

For our purpose, endurance exercise is an activity that you can do continuously for at least 30 minutes and (eventually) up to 60 minutes for many people. It should be sufficiently hard work that it causes you to breathe somewhat hard and break into a light sweat and, occasionally, it should be very vigorous. Shortly, we will explore some options for achieving this level of work. But first, let's look at what science tells us about the benefits of endurance exercise and what it can do for you.

The Benefits Of Endurance Exercise

The most direct and meaningful benefit of endurance exercise is its impact on your cardio-respiratory system, which includes your heart, lungs, and blood vessels. Endurance exercise also requires, and contributes to, healthy bones and fit muscles. Endurance exercise is essential to keeping this crucial infrastructure healthy and strong well into later life. Here are some of the things that endurance exercise will do for you:

Reduces Your Risk Of Dying From Heart Disease

Cardiovascular disease (CVD) is the number one cause of premature death and disability in our society. It affects huge numbers of people, making its clinical and financial impact far reaching. Consider these statistics from the American Heart Association's 2005 Heart Disease and Stroke Statistics — 2005 Update:[42]

71

- 13 million Americans live with coronary artery disease. Of these, over half (7.1 million) had a heart attack; the others have chest pain during exertion, called angina.
- 65 million Americans have high blood pressure, which increases their risk for heart attack, stroke, and kidney failure.
- About 5 million Americans live with the effects of stroke each year, and nearly 5 million suffer from congestive heart failure.
- Of the 70 million Americans who live with some form of cardiovascular disease, over 60% of them are younger than age 65, which means that the issue here is not simply chronology, but choices. According to the AHA, nearly 40% of Americans are physically inactive, which is a key part of the CVD-related data that we point out above. Some other estimates say that up to 70% of Americans are sedentary, which makes the picture all the more problematic.

Regular physical activity is essential to reducing your risk of CVD, and if you already have it, to helping preserve or improve your quality of life. The effect of endurance activity on the risk of dying from CVD is compelling. For example, in its recent position statement on the cardiovascular health of women athletes, the International Olympic Committee's group on Women and Sport confirmed that women who engage in endurance exercise reduce their risk of dying from heart disease by nearly 40% ... that is, they cut their risk nearly in half.[43] This point was reinforced in a recent analysis, which showed that even modest daily physical activity can help women cut their heart disease risk by 38%.[44] The data is equally compelling for men. In fact, a great deal of benefit for both men and women comes with a relatively modest increase in endurance activity, such as walking. In a recent review of the literature, Slentz and colleagues point out that people who are sedentary (and, thus, poorly fit) and start to walk regularly actually get a very substantial reduction in their risk of chronic diseases such as diabetes.[45] This is especially important because diabetes greatly increases the risk of developing heart disease. Exercise can help with the prevention or management of heart disease in several important ways:

- **Helps improve your cholesterol profile, especially by raising your HDL (good) cholesterol and changing key characteristics of your LDL (bad) cholesterol, which, in turn, lowers your risk of coronary artery disease and a heart attack.**[46] [47] Managing your cholesterol — whether it is presently elevated or not — is complex. Let's take this in stages. First, we cannot emphasize enough the importance of raising the HDL cholesterol. According to the American College of Sports Medicine and the American Heart Association, raising HDL, which endurance exercise can help you do, is essential to helping reduce your risk of heart disease. In fact, every point your HDL goes up, your risk of heart disease could go down as much as 2% (men) or 3% (women). Thus, a man who increases his HDL from 50 to 60 could theoretically reduce his risk of heart disease by 20%. An HDL level of 60 or more is actually cardioprotective, meaning that it reduces your risk of heart disease. Further, there is a relationship between HDL and LDL. If you have a high HDL and high LDL you may be better off than someone who has a low LDL, but also a low HDL.[48]

  Second, exercise has an important additional impact on your LDL cholesterol. Exercise can help lower your LDL cholesterol, provided that it is of sufficient duration. In addition to lowering LDL cholesterol, exercise exerts a dramatic effect on some of the characteristics of your LDL. One of the characteristics of LDL cholesterol that concerns heart specialists is the size of the particles. The smaller the particles, the higher your risk of developing heart disease. Exercise not only helps reduce LDL overall, it increases the size of LDL particles. A pioneering study at Duke University showed that exercise — especially up to 3 to 4 hours per week at a moderate to high work intensity — reduces LDL and makes a significant difference in the size of the LDL particles in your blood, making

73

them markedly bigger.[49] The bigger the LDL particles, the better it is for you.

And, of course, as we have said before, exercise is critical to losing weight, which also helps you manage your cholesterol.[50] Keeping your cholesterol in a healthy range matters: a person with a total cholesterol over 300 has a five times greater risk of developing heart disease as someone with a total cholesterol of less than 200.[51]

- *Keeps your blood vessels supple and flexible as you age.* This can help reduce your risk of high blood pressure, stroke, and aneurysms, which are the abnormal ballooning of arterial walls. If we stay sedentary as we age, our blood vessels pay the price; arteries gradually lose their flexibility as a normal part of aging, but inactivity hastens and worsens the process. Between ages 25 and 75, arterial wall stiffness can increase by up to 50%. The most effective way to nip this process in the bud is to do regular — and vigorous — endurance exercise. Studies show that middle-aged and older adults with a history of endurance exercise have arterial walls that are nearly as flexible and healthy as people much younger. Endurance exercise helps increase the amount of elastin in the blood vessel walls and may help reduce the amount of calcium deposited there, which can contribute to stiffness. The data is not so clear whether strength training has the same effect.[52] Further, Japanese researchers have reported that in animal research, endurance exercise actually appears to turn some genes on or off; these genetic changes may help maintain the supple youthfulness of key blood vessels, such as the aorta, which is the major artery that carries blood from your heart to the rest of your body.[53]

- *Helps preserve critical heart function as you age, ensuring that your heart beat remains regular and strong.* As we get older, there is a phenomenon know as heart rate variability (HRV), which reflects how many heart rhythm disturbances you have. As HRV gets worse, meaning that there are more irregular beats, your risk of a heart attack goes up. A substantial body of research shows that moderately and vigorously active adults have less HRV and, consequently, a substantially

74

lower risk of death from heart rhythm disturbances than do less active or inactive adults.[54] [55] [56] The reason is that they did more moderate to vigorous exercise, which helps maintain vagal tone, the critical connection between the heart and central nervous system. You do not need to be an Olympian to achieve this highly desirable level of heart health. You can reach it through activities such cycling at 8 to 10 mph, or walking at 4 mph. These activities, incidentally, will also go a long way toward helping you manage your weight, and, thus, reduce the risk of being overweight, obesity, and diabetes. And, importantly, even people who already have heart disease get a boost here. They benefit from being as active as possible, within medically safe parameters, because activity helps them also reduce the number of aberrant beats that they suffer.[57]

- *Makes your heart bigger and stronger, allowing it to pump more blood with each beat and beat fewer times per minute.* Health professionals call this improved left ventricular function. The left ventricle is the heart's main pumping chamber. We know that athletes have bigger, stronger hearts than sedentary people, which allows them to pump more blood with every beat. Thus, their hearts beat fewer times per minute. As people age, the amount of blood they pump with every beat, called stroke volume, gradually drops because the heart muscle gets stiffer and less compliant. Regular endurance exercise is essential to keeping your all-important left ventricle healthy and hard working. Studies show that master athletes (technically defined as athletes older than age 35, but most often the terms applies to athletes in their forties and beyond), have left ventricles that are as strong and as efficient as people much younger than they are.[58] Reducing your resting heart rate may pay long-term benefits even if you are a senior citizen. A recent review of studies of left ventricle function in older people found that regular endurance exercise (4 times weekly for up to 40 minutes) can lower resting heart rate by about 8% or 6 beats per minute. Doesn't sound like much, does it? It adds up to over 8,600 fewer heart beats daily, which means that both stroke volume has gone up (that is, your heart is stronger, more flexible and able to eject more blood with each beat) and your heart requires less oxygen at rest because it now has to work less.[59]

- *Helps you lower or control your weight, and, especially, limit the build-up of fat around your waist.* When your waist circumference increases, your risk of heart disease goes up. In a very interesting survey of experienced runners, scientists from the Universities of California (Berkeley) and South Carolina, found, not surprisingly, that the men who ran the most had the smallest accumulation of fat around their waists. More importantly, they concluded that in order to limit fat build-up, it is important to gradually increase the amount of exercise you do every year.[60] By consciously adding activity in your later years, you help compensate for the fact that most people gradually tend to be less active as they get older.[61] Thus, when you add activity, you help maintain an energy balance and reduce the risk of weight gain. The activity helps you control adiposity, which is how exercise scientists refer to the amount of body fat you have — a serious risk factor for heart disease and dying young.[62][63][64] Remember, however, that activity alone cannot prevent weight gain; you must also eat wisely, a topic that we will cover in another section.

- *Reduces your risk of sudden death from a heart attack.* As we noted early on, many people worry that by exercising they risk sudden cardiac death, which distorts the fact that exercise actually protects against sudden cardiac death. More to the point, however, French researchers recently reported that how a person's heart responds to exercise (in the form of an exercise stress test) provides very important clues as to their risk of sudden cardiac death during exercise or at rest. People with low resting heart rates and those whose heart rates go up sufficiently during exercise and come down quickly afterward have a significantly lower risk of sudden death than those without these characteristics.[65] All three of these measures of heart health — low resting heart rate (less than 75 beats per minute), appropriate increase in heart rate during exercise (an increase of at least 89 beats per minute higher than resting heart rate),

76

and rapid reduction in heart rate afterward (more than 25 beats per minute) — get better with regular exercise.

* *Lowers your risk of developing metabolic syndrome.* Metabolic syndrome is a dangerous collection of signs and symptoms that, collectively, indicate someone is at a much higher risk for diabetes and heart disease. The indicators are a low HDL (good) cholesterol (<40), increased waist circumference (>40 inches for men, >35 inches for women), high fasting blood sugar (>110), elevated blood triglycerides (>150), and high blood pressure (>130/85). According to the National Cholesterol Education Program (NCEP), if you have at least three of these elements, you have metabolic syndrome. While there is some academic debate about the meaning of this diagnosis, it provides a readily understandable reference point for understanding your own personal risk factors.[66][67] Of these risk factors for metabolic syndrome, endurance exercise can have a direct impact on all of them. If you are at-risk for metabolic syndrome, even if your numbers in these characteristics are only borderline (ask your doctor to be sure), you should set about developing an endurance exercise strategy. It is highly likely that doing so will help you improve your odds of NOT developing this serious and dangerous disorder. Endurance exercise works and matters when it comes to metabolic syndrome.[68]

Lest you think that exercise neglects the rest of your body, have no fear. Endurance exercise is what we call an equal opportunity benefactor. It bestows benefits and opportunities for growth on everyone who is willing to take the risk of sticking with it ... not unlike a life of faith, when you come to think of it. Let's take a quick look at the benefits of exercise on other major body systems.

Keeps All Your Important Parts Healthy And Strong
Exercise is the only thing we know of — outside of specific prescription drugs — that can do so much for so many important body systems. The consequence of this broad reach is that endurance exercise is a powerful quality-of-life enhancer.

- *Lowers your risk of some kinds of cancer, particularly colorectal cancer.* In a major review of the state of the science, the American College of Sports Medicine's flagship journal, *Medicine & Science in Sports & Exercise* reported in November 2003 that exercise plays an important role in cancer.[69] For example, exercise may reduce the risk of colon cancer by up to 30% to 40%. In addition, women who are physically active may have a 20% to 30% lower risk of breast cancer than sedentary women. Finally, people with cancer who exercise have notably better quality of life than those who do not exercise.[70]

- *Assists with glucose metabolism.* The most common disorder of glucose metabolism in our society is diabetes. Type 2 diabetes, which typically happens to people over age thirty, is strongly linked to being overweight or obese. In turn, being diabetic greatly increases your risk of heart disease and kidney failure. The key characteristic of Type 2 diabetes is insulin resistance, which happens when your body either produces insufficient insulin or your body does not use the insulin properly to store excess glucose. Exercise is an important and well-accepted tool in helping to manage Type 2 diabetes. Large, long-term epidemiologic studies, which examine the presence of disease in big populations, document persuasively that regular endurance exercise helps reduce the occurrence of diabetes Type 2.[71] (In fact, not only is endurance exercise useful for this, but so is strength training.)[72] [73] [74]

- *Manages your stress level.* Most of us know intuitively that exercise is a good stress manager. But, more recently, scientific studies have started to put some data together with this widely accepted notion. People who exercise regularly — even those who have already had a heart attack — tend to report a stronger sense of well-being and confidence.[75] In addition, over time, people who exercise regularly may be at lower risk of depression than those who do not.[76] And, new research offers hope that regular exercise can help with the treatment of depression.[77]

- *Helps build healthy strong bones (in younger people) and slows the rate of bone loss in older people.* Exercise is critical

78

to bone health. For endurance exercise, this is a bit complicated, however. That's because the endurance exercise most often touted by government agencies and health groups is walking. The bone-health benefits of walking are modest, at best. Certainly, walking is better than doing nothing at all. Swimming is also problematic for bone health; it could actually increase bone loss because of your buoyancy in the water. For endurance exercise to contribute to bone health, it must involve striking the ground with a force greater than your body weight (this is called ground reaction force). So, walking will not do much for your bones, but jogging, running, jumping, and sports that involve sprinting (such as soccer, basketball, lacrosse) will.[78] Strength training also helps support bone health, and we will cover that in the next chapter. Even if you do not want to run, you can gain some benefit for your bones by jogging from time to time on your walks. The extra impact with the ground will help stimulate your bones and slow the rate of loss, which reduces your risk of fracture, disability, and early death.

- *Keeps your mind sharp.* People who exercise regularly have a lower risk of Alzheimer's than do those who do not exercise.[79] [80] [81]

This is a pretty good list of the benefits of endurance exercise. We are confident that, as the research evolves, scientists will find more and expand on the things that we already know. Now that you know *why* you should do endurance exercise, we want you to understand what to expect when you start.

What To Expect When Starting Endurance Exercise
The first and most important thing to anticipate is that your introduction to endurance exercise will be imperfect and, at times, frustrating. You will progress in small increments, not great leaps and bounds; you will often find the process challenging and physically and emotionally uncomfortable, and that is a good thing. Overcoming discomfort and challenges is critical to success in any life venture, whether it is following a difficult hiking trail or

following Jesus. The key to sustaining your progress will be understanding and overcoming your weaknesses, building on your strengths, and making wise choices from the options before you. Thus, the process of making endurance exercise a part of life will, like you and us, be imperfect ... but ultimately worthwhile.

As in faith, persistence has its rewards. As you overcome the initial fits and starts of doing endurance exercise on a regular basis, you will feel and see noticeable results. First and foremost, what once seemed difficult — your first walk around a lake at a moderate pace, for example — will gradually feel easier and easier as your heart, lungs, and muscles get stronger and fitter. Next, you will probably also start to notice that some of your clothes fit more loosely (especially after you start to follow our nutrition guidelines), which means that you are losing weight. We also expect — consistent with the research findings that we outlined above — that you will start to feel stronger and more confident. Exercise is a momentum play: the more you do, the better you get at it, and the more confident you feel about increasing your efforts.

You should expect that at times you will feel aches and pains that frequently accompany physical activity. In most cases, these will turn out to be minor disturbances that resolve with rest. If, however, you have an injury that results in redness, swelling, joint immobility, pain to the touch, or any other severe symptoms, seek medical care at once. Likewise, if you have shortness of breath, cramping pain in your calf muscles, chest pain of any kind, dizziness, nausea, or vomiting, STOP exercising and get medical help immediately. Never exercise if you have a fever, diarrhea, vomiting, or any other serious systemic symptom or illness. If you are ever uncertain about whether exercise is safe when you do not feel well, ask your health care provider.

Options For Endurance Exercise

Your options for endurance exercise are very diverse: walking, running, jogging, swimming, cycling, rowing, stair stepping, jumping rope, dancing, aerobics, and jazzercise are all feasible and suitable. Really, however, only two things matter. First, you must choose an activity (or two) that you enjoy doing. The reason for this is very straightforward: the more you like the activity, the more likely you are to stick with it. Second, you must be active long enough and work at it hard enough for the activity to make a difference for you. This is a particularly crucial point for people who are novices; casual exercise at a low-intensity work effort is highly unlikely to burn enough calories to allow you to lower or manage your weight and reduce your health risks. The same is true for more fit people who want to enhance their endurance. There is a relationship between exercise intensity and results.

When you consider your options for endurance exercise, remember also the importance of bone health. As we noted above, if you swim or walk, you will not exert sufficient force on the long bones of your legs (your thigh bones or femurs), or on your hips and spinal vertebrae to help protect against fracture later in life. If you walk or swim, it is critically important that you learn how to lift weights — and do it like you mean it — in order to stimulate your bones to stay strong as you get older.

We also want to put to rest here the myth that running is bad for your knees. It is a just plain factually wrong statement. Except for intense, competitive running, or running that involves twisting, torsion, and impact, such as you get in football and basketball, there is *no evidence* that low to moderate intensity jogging or running will do anything to harm your knees. So, if you enjoy jogging or running, have no pre-existing injury or structural problems with your knees, ankles, or hips, by all means get out there and, as the commercials say, "just do it." In fact, the stress of moderate intensity running is not only good for your bones, but it also benefits your joints, causing the cartilage that lines the ends of your bones to rebuild itself in response.[82] This is known as remodeling and is a normal, healthy, and beneficial response to running. If you are presently a walker, or new to exercise, the best way to introduce yourself to jogging is to start jogging for brief periods during your walks, gradually building up the distance that you jog or run, compared to walking.

Since Henry turned forty back in the year 2000, he has been doing a lot of running. He had never been a runner back in high

81

school, and he avoided it pretty successfully during his young adult years. Then his friend, Bill Parent, challenged him, on his fortieth birthday, to join him in running the Marine Corps Marathon. Henry thought Bill was crazy.

The marathon was still six months away, however, and Bill convinced Henry that he could train for it in that amount of time. Henry started out slowly, *very* slowly — he would go out and exercise for an hour at a time, running for 3 minutes, walking for 7, running for 3 minutes, walking for 7. Three minutes of running at a time was about all he could endure. But the next week, he ran for 4 minutes and walked for 6, ran for 4 minutes and walked for 6. After seven weeks of training in this way, Henry made it to the point where he could run for a full hour.

That was the key to his ability to complete a marathon: starting slowly, and building up his running time ... 1 hour, 2 hours, 3 hours, 4 hours ... and finally completing the Marine Corps Marathon in 4 hours, 12 minutes. He would sometimes let the words from the letter to the Hebrews cycle through his mind, "Let us run with perseverance the race that is set before us, looking to Jesus the pioneer and perfecter of our faith" (Hebrews 12:1-2). Over the years, his marathon training has become a running meditation for him, and he has been amazed by the clarity of thought — along with the occasional agony of the body — that he experiences during his workouts. Long runs with church members have led to some heart-to-heart conversations that might not have occurred at any other time, and Henry has found himself growing closer to these men and women through the pursuit of shared physical activity goals. Mike Watson is a member of Fairfax Presbyterian who once led Henry up a mountain in a grueling training run. Mike says that he appreciates the chance that running gives him to "be thankful for the nature God gave us and the ability we have to get out and move about."

Endurance exercise can be enormously satisfying, spiritually and physically, but no matter how well you plan and choose, you will inevitably encounter some roadblocks to get around. These include time (the biggest and most important potential roadblock), the weather, injuries, and illness.

- Make time your friend, not an enemy. To those of you who believe that you do not have time to exercise, we propose that reality is quite the opposite: you don't have time *not* to exercise. To help manage your exercise time, we suggest that you schedule it for yourself each day, just as you would an important meeting, family event, or church service. When you see your exercise appointment in black and white, it is a visual reminder for you to take time for yourself. You are less likely to forget to exercise or to put it off; and, if you need to reorganize your day, your exercise time will be right there along with the rest of your obligations awaiting your attention. Further, being fit makes time, it doesn't diminish it, simply because fit people move more efficiently, think more clearly, are sick less, and are generally more optimistic in their outlook. And remember, too, that short workouts are as good for health as longer ones. Don't despair if, on a busy day (and they may all be busy), you need to do 2 or 3 or more short workouts (10 to 20 minutes each), instead of one longer one. You will still get the health benefits you need and want.[83]

- It is a question of whether, not weather. No matter where you live, weather complicates exercise opportunities. To be flexible and still stay fit, we encourage you to have options for yourself. Whether you exercise on a bad weather day is really a function of your own creativity. If you walk, for example, see if you can pick out a nearby mall as an alternate spot to exercise on very hot or cold days. Cyclists should consider buying an indoor trainer on which they can mount their bicycle for quick, intense indoor spins. If you cannot get to the pool or hiking trails for your daily jaunt, then consider spending that inclement weather day in the gym lifting weights. Remember that it is NEVER safe to be outdoors during a thunderstorm, extreme cold or heat, or in icy conditions. Pay attention to weather warnings about wind chill and heat indexes. Opting for a rest day is a far better choice than risking serious injury.

- Fatigue and injuries mean rest, not risk-taking. If you are sick or hurt, it is time to take a break. Build rest days into your exercise schedule. If you have one or two rest days per week, that should be more than sufficient; and, the rest days will help you break your exercise routine into manageable blocks and let you fit in all your other life activities. Any injury that causes swelling, bleeding, redness, inflammation, or appears infected, requires medical attention. Also, as we have noted previously, do not exercise with a fever, nausea, abdominal or chest pain, difficulty breathing, or any other potentially serious condition. In these cases, get immediate medical care, and resume your exercise routine only after you get medical clearance to do so.

Understanding Your Heart Rate During Endurance Exercise

As you already know, the primary purpose of endurance exercise is to give your heart, lungs, and blood vessels a good dose of physical activity. The question arises, then, of how to keep track of how your heart is doing during your workout. The main reason to know this is so you can determine how hard you are working. As we have already noted, working hard enough — not too hard or too easy — is your long-term target. Work insufficiently hard and you may not get the results that you want. Work too hard and you run the risk of burning out or hurting yourself.

Your heart rate during endurance exercise is the most easily understandable and accessible tool you have. There are two ways to monitor your heart rate during a workout. One is to buy a heart-rate monitor and learn how to use it. Most often, this includes a wristwatch and a chest strap. The chest strap has a sensor for detecting your heartbeat and transmits that information to the wristwatch, allowing you to look at the watch at any time during your workout to know how hard you are working. Many of these devices are programmable and have alarms to let you know when you are working above or below a target threshold. Recently, Reebok came out with a heart-rate monitor that does not have the chest strap. It is a wristwatch with two touch points surrounding the watch face. Place two fingers on the touch points and the watch takes your pulse. Obviously, this watch will work well for runners and walkers, but not cyclists! We believe that a heart-rate monitor is a sound investment that will help you build a good feedback loop, providing useful data on how hard you are working during your aerobic activity. Prices range from about $70 to several hundred dollars depending on the complexity and sophistication of the devices and whether the one you are considering connects to your computer. For most people, we believe that a simple one, such as the heart-rate-sensing wristwatch from Reebok, will more than suffice.

An alternative to using a heart-rate monitor is to use the Talk Test. This requires no equipment other than your own voice. To use the Talk Test, first identify a poem, song lyric, or scriptural passage of about 25 to 30 words that you can easily memorize — the verse from Hebrews that Henry uses is close to the perfect length: "Let us run with perseverance the race that is set before us, looking to Jesus the pioneer and perfecter of our faith" (Hebrews 12:1-2). Then, during exercise, say it to yourself, speaking the words out loud, not under your breath. How easily you can say them is the measure of how hard you are working, which is why you must try to say them at your normal volume, and whispering does not count. If you can speak comfortably, as in a casual conversation, you are working at a very low intensity, which is typical of warm-up or cool-down. When speech is somewhat difficult — you have to catch your breath to continue — you are probably in your workout range. Most of your endurance exercise, no matter what it is, should happen in this range. If you cannot speak at all, you may be working too hard. If you have a workout partner, the Talk Test is easy to use because you have someone with whom you can converse. When you are exercising by yourself and use the Talk Test, those around you may look at you a little funny, but rest assured this is a scientifically valid tool that will serve you well over the long term.[84]

Calculating Your Heart Rate For Endurance Exercise

You can use a relatively straightforward formula for calculating a rough estimate of what your heart rate should be during endurance exercise:

220 minus your age = your estimated (theoretical) maximum heart rate (MHR)

For a fifty-year-old man or woman: 220-50=170

Most healthy people should plan to do endurance exercise at about 70% of their estimated MHR. Thus, this fifty-year-old person should generally exercise at an intensity that produces a heart rate of about 120 beats per minute. If you are using the Talk Test to gauge exercise intensity, this should allow you to speak with difficulty and require that you occasionally catch your breath. The formula that we used above is not perfect, and your actual MHR may vary by as much as plus or minus 10 to 12 beats per minute. Regardless, this is a good place to start. As you build fitness, you can work harder during some workouts and strive to get your heart rate up to 80% to 85% of your estimated MHR. If you ever have an exercise stress test in a heart specialist's office, he or she may be able to tell with great precision your actual MHR.

More recently, exercise scientists from Oakland University (Rochester, Minnesota) published a proposed new formula for calculating an estimated MHR. Importantly, their work intimates that the relationship between MHR and age may not be as uniform as we once believed (i.e., as you get older, your MHR declines in an orderly, or linear, fashion). Based on their research, they propose another formula that might more accurately estimate a person's MHR. That formula is: MHR = 207 - (0.7 x age). Thus, in our example of a fifty-year-old person, this formula would yield an estimated MHR of 172 (172 = 207 - 0.7 x 50). Notice that this is only slightly different from the estimate of 170 derived by the other formula. You can use both formulas and take an average, if you wish. If you would like to read more about this issue, we suggest that you read the work of Ronald Gellish and colleagues in the May 2007 issue of *Medicine & Science in Sports & Exercise* (volume 39; number 5).

Tips For Safe And Effective Endurance Exercise

When you start your endurance exercise program, you will need to consider three essential questions about your workouts:

1. How frequently should you exercise?
2. How long should you exercise?
3. How should you measure the intensity of your workouts?

How Frequently Should You Exercise?

In general, you should plan to do at least three or four sessions of endurance exercise weekly. This is consistent with the government's widely touted recommendation for basic physical activity. It is, however, insufficient for many people. This is because 30 minutes of endurance exercise three times a week may not be enough to help you change your body composition or manage it successfully for the long term. For that laudable and healthy goal, you should plan on four or five times per week — at a moderate intensity level for about 60 minutes. You can build gradually and aim for endurance exercise of three or more hours per week, which is what's necessary to elevate your HDL (good cholesterol), and protect you against heart disease.

A plausible way of building your fitness and tolerance for endurance activity is to add 10% to your activity each week. So, in week 1, your 30 minutes of physical activity per day is your baseline. In week 2, assuming no injuries or other problems, aim for 33 minutes per day ... a 10% increase over week 1. (And, yes, you can still do several short workouts per day.) In six weeks or so, you likely will reach the desirable daily target of 60 minutes of physical activity. You can add time more slowly if you need to. This is not unlike Henry's strategy to teach himself to run ... add a manageable amount of time over a period of weeks or months, and you will soon reach your targets.

If you do endurance exercise three to five times weekly, bear in mind that you should reserve some time and energy for strength training, which we will discuss in the next chapter. When necessary, you can double up, that is, lift weights and do endurance exercise on the same day. If you do this, you may wish to take care of your strength training first, as a vigorous strength workout is probably less likely to interfere with your endurance exercise than vice versa.[85]

There is no compelling evidence that exercising at a particular time of day matters. What counts is that you exercise at a time that is convenient and sustainable for you, given all the other things you must attend to in your life. For many people, morning workouts are best because that allows them to get their exercise done reliably and then move on to other commitments. Deferring workouts until later in the day, unless you are very disciplined and organized, runs the risk of letting other demands impinge upon your exercise time. You may also be more tired at day's end. You could alleviate some of your late-day fatigue by drinking a cup of coffee or tea before activity, as caffeine is a useful workout booster. But do this only if you tolerate caffeinated drinks well and know your limits. Alternatively, when you are tired, you should reduce the intensity and/or duration of your activity.

If you are good at juggling things when demands change, then having a relatively stable and predictable exercise time may not matter. For most people, however, we recommend the following procedure. Every Sunday, after church, sit down with your calendar for the coming week, whether you keep it on paper or on your computer. You may also wish to have the weekly weather forecast at your fingertips. Then, considering both the weather and your other meetings, make all your exercise appointments with yourself for the coming week. Once everything is on paper, it becomes a more tangible commitment, and, symbolically at least, it becomes equally important as all your other tasks and commitments.

How Long Should You Exercise?

In general, for healthy adults who need to lose weight or want to manage it successfully for the long term, we support about 60 minutes of endurance exercise most days of the week.[86] As noted above, this duration is more consistent with the 2002 recommendation of the Institute of Medicine (IOM).[87] This recommendation is not overbearing, lofty, or unachievable. Rather, it is aggressive, challenging, and life-saving even though it demands considerable dedication and commitment. In our culture, however, which is increasingly inactive, overweight, overstressed, and depressed, we think that the recommendation makes sense on a number of levels.

First and foremost, it really is a call to reorder priorities. In the large scheme of what's important in life, we think people should have enough self-respect for themselves to devote an average of one hour daily to the betterment of their own health. This may require limiting some other commitments, but, in the long run, that may turn out to be healthy and useful as well.

There is another reason that we support the IOM recommendation, and it is a spiritual one. Living a Christian life requires reaching for the highest possible ideals of compassion, honesty, integrity, commitment to others, and obedience to God. It is not a life for the timid of heart. Why should striving for health be any different? We believe that giving people an easy way out encourages them to do just that ... take the easy way out. If you tell people to walk — just walk — three or four times weekly, without guidance about intensity of effort, or outlining the benefits of longer and more vigorous exercise, you will encourage a population that is willing to do just enough and not all that it can. In our view, our culture suffers enough from the "let's just-get-by syndrome," and we have stopped striving for excellence in our personal, work, spiritual, and physical lives.

The consequences of this cultural attitude are people who have, among other things, "spare tires" around their waists, but insufficient spare time, because they are too tired, or running off to the doctor for problems often remediable through diet and exercise; children who know how to guide gun-wielding thugs through their video games but who cannot guide a mountain bike over a leaf-covered trail; high rates of divorce and domestic violence; and, according to a recent report from the Pew Charitable Trusts, college graduates who can neither read a credit card statement nor balance a checkbook.[88] Maybe challenging the notions of what constitutes a *good* — not just an acceptable — exercise and nutrition program is the best place to start changing a slavish cultural devotion to complacency and mediocrity.

If your body weight is normal and you wish to keep it there, you may be able to do so by staying in the range of a regular routine of 30 to 45 minutes of endurance activity. As we have noted, however, you must be watchful of weight gain as you get older and the way to limit it may be to either add time to your exercise sessions or gradually make them harder.

How Should You Measure The Intensity Of Your Workouts?

One of the most important means of judging how hard you are working is to assign each workout a numerical rating. Studies have repeatedly shown that this system, called the Rating of Perceived Exertion or RPE, is a valid tool in helping people who exercise estimate how hard they worked on any given day. Knowing this can help you plan for future exercise, and, thus, help you avoid burnout or prevent injury because you can thoughtfully integrate low, moderate, or high intensity exercise into your program.

It is neither helpful nor necessary to work at the same (high) intensity every time you exercise. Rather, variety is useful, and workouts typically differ along one of two parameters: duration (how long you exercised) and intensity (how hard you worked).

The RPE scale that is easiest for most people to remember and work with is a 0 to 11 scale. Each of the numbers on the scale means something:[89]

0	No intensity at all, such as sitting at rest
1	Very weak effort, a barely noticeable amount of work
2	Weak effort that is slightly noticeable
3	Moderate effort
4	
5	Strong effort
6	
7	Very strong effort
8	
9	
10	Extremely strong effort, requiring a high level of intensity of work
11	
>11	Absolute maximum, highest possible effort

About 5 to 10 minutes after every workout, rate it using the 0 to 11 RPE scale. Doing the rating a few minutes after finishing helps prevent a biased assessment based on your effort during the last few minutes of activity. If you finished your walk or run on an easy stretch, you would tend to assign the workout a lower rating, even though you may have worked quite hard at several points. Conversely, if you finish a 45-minute walk with a hard, fast sprint, you will tend to assign it a higher rating than it might deserve.

In most cases, we want you to stay in the 3 to 7 range of effort; if you are a bit tired, back off and do a workout that is closer to a 3. Feel strong today? Push yourself and see if you can do a workout that is a 7 or 8. The RPE should reflect your overall perception of how hard the exercise was, accounting for physical and psychological perception. For example, say you have a consistent loop that you like to run, which has two substantial hills. You will find that some days you will traverse this route and rate your run a 4 or 5, while on other days, it may seem like it was a 7 or 8. When you estimate your RPE score, focus on your impression of the overall difficulty or ease of the workout, not just isolated components. You should take into account the psychological as well as physical stress of the workout.

Many things can affect your RPE, including fatigue, state of mind, physical effort expended, whether you ate and drank appropriately before and during your workout, and even weather. The most important way for you to use the RPE is to space your harder workouts. If you have had two or three workouts in a row that you rated at 6, 7, or 8, it is time to do a less intense workout that you will end up rating a 3, 4, or 5. Once you get comfortable with this scale, you will find that it is a very useful tool for learning how hard you can push yourself and what your limits are. Studies show that RPE accurately reflects the physiologic demands that physical activity places on your body. It closely tracks your heart rate (that is, exercising at a higher heart rate, say 80% of your maximum, feels harder than working at a lower heart rate). As such, it is a reasonable substitute for a heart-rate monitor for many people, especially when coupled with the Talk Test.

After you get in the habit of assigning an RPE to each workout, you can add a level of sophistication by using the Foster Index to rate and plan your endurance exercise. This is easy to do; all you do is multiply your RPE times the number of minutes spent exercising. So, for a moderately intense walk with an RPE of 5 that took 40 minutes, your Foster Index is 200 (5 x 40). The Foster Index is a handy tool because it allows you to see, in one number, the relative intensity of a workout and the time expended. We strongly recommend that you start using the RPE to rate your endurance workouts, because we will ask you to use it as well when you start strength training, which we discuss in the next chapter.

Testing Your Current Fitness Level

Before you start on any exercise program, you should understand how fit you are now. There are two ways to do this. If you belong to a gym, you can ask the staff there about exercise testing. If you do not belong to a gym, you can test yourself. Because this commandment is about endurance exercise, we will cover only endurance testing here. We will discuss strength testing in the next chapter. In the paragraphs below, we outline things you should know before getting an exercise test done at your gym, as well as how to do it yourself.

Exercise Testing At Your Gym

Following the American College of Sports Medicine guidelines, we recommend that everyone have baseline fitness testing done before beginning an exercise program. This will help you fully understand your overall fitness level, as well the potential impact on your exercise program of any underlying disease or health risk factors, such as smoking or a strong family history of heart disease. Fitness testing can be done by a qualified exercise professional, such as an ACSM-certified Health Fitness Instructor or Exercise Specialist.[90] Your exercise professional should take a thorough health history and, at the very least, complete a Physical Activity Readiness Questionnaire (also called the PAR-Q) with you. At the end of the health history and PAR-Q process, the exercise professional should do a risk stratification, which will tell you what risk category you fall into both for fitness testing and an exercise program.

Many commercial gyms offer what they call fitness or exercise testing. You should ensure that the gym follows ACSM protocols. Ask them to show you the source material for the exercise testing that they do. The ACSM protocols for exercise testing are thorough, scientifically sound, and evaluated regularly for updates and improvements. If done according to ACSM protocols, your exercise testing process should take about 60 to 90 minutes, going from body composition (body fat assessment) to endurance testing (using either a treadmill, exercise bike, rowing machine, or step bench), and testing for both muscular strength and endurance.

Many people cannot afford the expense of formal exercise testing. Fortunately, there is good data that supports doing simple self-tests that require very little, if any, fancy equipment. About the only thing that we cannot teach you to do for yourself is take body fat measurements using calipers. However, there is a reasonable proxy for determining your body composition.

Let's start this process by getting baseline data on your body composition. We will assume for our purposes that you do not have access to body-fat testing with calipers, which, in the hands of a qualified professional, would tell you what percentage of your physical being today is fat. In general, for adult men, a number in the 8% to 17% range is considered healthy, while for women, the healthy range is 12% to 20%. You can be too thin; men should not be below 5% body fat and women should not sink below 10% to 12%. Inadequate fat stores can interfere with a number of important body systems, including your nervous system, heart, hormones, and bones. The goal of an exercise and nutrition program is not to be as skinny as possible. It is to be fit, strong, and physically and emotionally healthy — that is unfortunately not the case for many people with eating disorders who seek excessive thinness.

The best and easiest way for you to estimate whether you need to lose weight is to understand your body-mass index or BMI. Simply, this is the ratio of your height to your weight. The formula for BMI is:

Your weight (in kilograms [kg]) ÷ Your height (in meters^2)

If you want to complete this formula manually, you will need to do a couple of conversions:

- To convert your weight in pounds to kg, divide the pounds by 2.2. So, if you weigh 170 pounds, divide this by 2.2 to get 77.3 kg.
- To convert your height into meters, multiply your height in inches times .0254. Thus, a 5'6" tall man is 66 inches tall, which equals 1.68 meters (66 x .0254). To square this number, multiply it by itself (1.68 x 1.68), which gives you 2.79.
- This person's BMI then is 77.3 ÷ 2.79, which equals 27.7, making him overweight.

BMI categories:
Less than 18.5 = too thin
18.6 to 24.9 = normal
25 to 29.9 = overweight
Greater than 30 = obese

If you do not want to compute your BMI manually, you can find a calculator on the internet at the website of the Centers for Disease Control and Prevention at www.cdc.gov/nccdphp/dnpa/bmi/calc-bmi.htm or the website of the National Heart Lung and Blood Institute at www.nhlbisupport.com/bmi/bmicalc.htm.

After you calculate your BMI, write it down on your calendar. Recalculate it periodically, perhaps once per month. You should also weigh yourself and measure your waist and hips. Men should have a waist less than 40 inches and a waist to hip ratio that is less than 1.0. Women should have a waistline less than 35 inches and a waist to hip ratio of less than 0.8. Write all these measurements in your exercise and diet diary and get in the habit of retaking the measurements regularly, a process known as self-monitoring. Good, steady self-monitoring helps greatly in the battle to lose weight and keep it off.[91] [92] You will know quite clearly if your weight-loss program is working by how your clothes fit. So, while weight loss may cause you to spend money on new clothes, we believe that will be a much happier expense for you to endure than continuing to spend money on medical care or prescription drugs.

Next, we want you to do one of two different tests of your cardiovascular fitness, called field tests because they are not done in a laboratory. All you need for either of these is a safe place to walk or run. In our experience, a high school or college running track is the best place because you know the distance (each lap is 1/4 mile or 440 yards/402.3 meters), it is flat, and tracks are readily accessible. You could also use a walking path, jogging trail, or other course, as long as it is relatively flat, you can determine distances, and you feel safe there. It is helpful to have a test partner who can time you, help take your pulse at the end of the test, and assist you in the event of an injury or other problem that arises during the test.

The 1-Mile Walk

This test is most suitable for people who are either new to exercise, or are returning to it after a prolonged absence. In either case, you should have medical clearance from your physician before doing the test. As the name implies, the test is very straightforward, requiring you to walk 1 mile as quickly as you can, following these steps:

- Warm-up for your 1-mile walk by walking first slowly and then at a moderate pace for about 10 minutes.
- Have your partner time your walk with a stopwatch; you should start your timed walk when he or she says, "Go."
- Get to a fast and steady speed and try to maintain it. Do not try to reserve some of your energy for a sprint to the finish.
- If you are walking on a track where you will pass your partner more than once, he or she can read out your intermediate times to you, or remind of which lap you are on and how many remain.
- When you come to the finish, your partner should stop timing you, read out your time to the nearest second, and write it down.

- Immediately upon stopping, take your pulse for 10 seconds and multiply that number by 6. The product of those two numbers (your end-of-walk heart rate x 6) is your maximum heart rate for the walk.

Make a note of how fast you walked the mile and what your heart rate was immediately upon ending the walk. By dividing this number by your estimated MHR, you can estimate how hard your heart worked ... the greater the percentage of MHR, the more fit you are.[93] Keep this information in your exercise and diet diary because we will ask you to re-test yourself annually and see whether your are improving by doing the walk in less time and reaching higher percentages of your estimated MHR. Generally speaking, a person who walks the mile in 25 minutes (2.4 mph) has a relatively low level of fitness, while someone who walks it in 12 minutes (5 mph) has a good fitness level. Where are you in this range?

The 12-Minute Or 1.5-Mile Run

This is another popular and easily administered test, in which you can opt to run for 12 minutes or 1.5 miles. This test is more suitable for people who exercise regularly, are familiar with the mechanics of running, and have a greater level of fitness. As with the 1-mile walk, we recommend using a track or other relatively flat terrain, where you know the distance that you will cover.

The test itself is fundamentally the same as those outlined above for the 1-mile walk, except that you will run for either 12 minutes and measure the distance you covered, ideally to the nearest 1/10 of a mile *or* you will run 1.5 miles as fast as you can. In either case, we recommend working with a partner who will time you, call out your intermediate times or distance, and help you take your pulse immediately upon stopping. Note down your time or distance and your heart rate. You can also look at the tables on page 97 to see how your distance walked translates into an estimate of your fitness level.

96

12-Minute Aerobic Test
Number of miles traversed, by age group

Men

Age:	20-29	30-39	40-49	50-59	60+
Superior	1.81	1.77	1.71	1.62	1.57
Excellent	1.65	1.61	1.54	1.45	1.37
Good	1.54	1.49	1.42	1.33	1.24
Fair	1.45	1.39	1.33	1.25	1.15
Poor	1.34	1.29	1.23	1.15	1.05
Very Poor	1.06	1.13	.98	.92	.82

Women

Age:	20-29	30-39	40-49	50-59	60+
Superior	1.61	1.53	1.45	1.33	1.35
Excellent	1.45	1.38	1.32	1.21	1.18
Good	1.33	1.27	1.21	1.13	1.07
Fair	1.25	1.21	1.13	1.06	.99
Poor	1.16	1.11	1.05	.98	.94
Very Poor	.94	.93	.89	83	.81

Source: WashingtonPost.com; downloaded 1/27/06; originally published January 26, 1999.

A qualified and knowledgeable exercise professional can help you calculate your estimated cardiovascular capacity based on the results of your walk or run. Using credible, scientifically valid formulas, you can get a good picture of your estimated VO_2max, which is a measure of how fit you are. Your VO_2max tells how efficiently your body uses oxygen during physical activity. The more fit you are, the more oxygen you are able to use. You can also use an online resource to determine your fitness level. The website ExRx (www.exrx.net) is very useful and is run by exercise professionals. Click on the Fitness Testing link on the left to go to the section that has different calculators. You can enter your walk or run data into the appropriate calculator and get an assessment of your performance and fitness level. The site also provides guidance on activity programs.

Your self-testing of aerobic capacity will teach you a great deal about yourself, particularly if you are able to identify where you are on the tables above. Ideally, we want everyone to have an aerobic fitness level that is "good" or better. When you achieve that plateau, you are making a meaningful reduction in your health risks, most pointedly reducing your risk of cardiovascular disease.

Learning about yourself is a large part of the process of faith and fitness. Just as we want to help you understand your physical self and how to improve it through endurance exercise, we also want you to assess your spiritual self and understand where you are headed for the long term.

Living A Christian Life For The Long Term

The book of Genesis tells us about a man named Methuselah who lived a record-breaking 969 years. He had what's called "the marathon mentality," which is the wisdom you gain as you grow older, wisdom that takes the long view and sees the big picture. We can learn from this biblical character, because faithful Christian living is not a sprint — it is a marathon!

But guess what? The man named Methuselah was a mere *baby* compared to the "Methuselah Tree," a bristlecone pine tree that is now more than 46 centuries old. Yes, this tree, which is part of Inyo National Forest in California, was a seedling way back before the Egyptian pyramids went up — and it's still alive today. Talk about endurance!

What's its secret?

You're going to be surprised by the conditions under which the Methuselah Tree has accomplished this extraordinary feat. You might think that the environment would have to be extremely friendly to support a tree for 4,600 years — but you'd be wrong. Conditions are actually horribly harsh at the 10,000-foot elevation where Methuselah and other ancient bristlecones grow. These trees face cold temperatures, strong winds, minimal water, and almost no nutrients.

98

So, what's Methuselah's secret? How can it survive, much less thrive, in a place that would strike fear into the trunks of virtually any other trees?

It turns out that the bristlecone pine has evolved survival strategies that help it to cope with one of the most austere and unfriendly environments on the planet. Methuselah's adaptations include extensive roots, disease resistance, and small size.[94]

These strategies are the basis of the tree's marathon mentality — and maybe Methuselah has something to teach us today.

The prophet Isaiah certainly wasn't afraid to look to *trees* for inspiration. In Isaiah 55:10-13, he speaks of God's word as a force that comes down from heaven like the rain and the snow, bringing refreshment and growth and nourishment to the earth. God's word always accomplishes its goal, inspiring us to go out in joy and be led back in peace, and joining our jubilation are mountains and hills that "burst into song," and trees of the field that "clap their hands" (Isaiah 55:12).

Yes, the trees of the field actually "clap their hands." Don't ask how — just use your imagination.

The cypress tree and the myrtle shrub shall grow up, says the prophet, and they "shall be to the Lord for a memorial, for an everlasting sign that shall not be cut off" (v. 13). These plants are a sign of the wonderful new things that God is doing in human life — the days of judgment are over, says Isaiah, and new life is now available to all who repent.

It's probably no accident that the tree growing up in this biblical passage is a cypress. These particular trees were used extensively for shipbuilding in the ancient Middle East and grew abundantly in the area. Many believe that Noah used cypress wood for the ark — a vessel that carried faithful people and God's creatures safely through a time of judgment and delivered them to a place of new life.

So what are the trees saying to us today? What is the lesson of the cypress and the bristlecone pine, trees that want to teach us how to be safe in a stormy sea? In short, these trees encourage us to adopt "the marathon mentality."

This means no quick fixes — no trendy twists — no gaudy gimmicks — just a focus on extensive roots, disease resistance, and small size.

Extensive Roots

Bristlecone pines know that if they live in challenging environments, then they must put down extensive roots to maximize the intake of scant resources. For us, this means putting down roots into holy scripture, so that we can take full advantage of the guidance of the Bible and embrace God's promise that his word will not return to him empty. This word shall accomplish that which God intends, promises Isaiah, like the rain and the snow which come down from heaven, and do not return there until they have watered the earth (vv. 10-11).

Read the New Testament and you discover that Jesus comes on the scene as a man of action: curing the sick, casting out demons, cleansing a leper, and healing a paralytic — clearly, he cares deeply about the health of human bodies (Mark 2:13-19). Jesus goes around saving people from illness, destruction, and death, and then at the very end of his ministry he gives us the gift of his very own body, saying, "Take, eat; this is my body" (Matthew 26:26). He doesn't say this is my *mind*, or this is my *spirit* — he says, this is my *body*. When we put our roots into holy scripture, we discover that God came to earth in a human body — "the Word became flesh and lived among us," says the gospel of John (1:14). There is something good and important about our human flesh, according to scripture, so we should take proper care of it. Our worship on Sunday morning *and* our workouts throughout the week are critical elements in a life of health and spiritual growth.

Disease Resistance

A true marathon mentality, for trees and for people of faith, must also include a strategy for resisting disease. The Methuselah Tree has a dense, highly resinous wood that is an effective barrier to invasion by insects and bacteria — and in similar manner we are challenged to create barriers to crippling invaders. These can be as simple as setting limits on alcohol and junk food consumption, adding internet filters to our computers to screen out pornography, and taking the time to get to know the friends of our children and others in their social group. Insects are no problem for us, but physical inactivity, alcohol abuse, pornography addiction, and dangerous social circles can quickly cripple even the healthiest of individuals and families.

Exercise has a role to play in sin resistance as well. Many people have found that the best way for them to control sexual temptation is to put on their exercise clothes, lace up their running shoes, and hit the road. It always gets the blood flowing to the proper muscles and gets the head in the place it needs to be. In addition, working on physical fitness can have a very positive effect on sexual relations between husbands and wives. If both are working out on a regular basis, the result is a great deal more enjoyment in each other. The apostle Paul does a nice job of pulling this all together when he writes to the Ephesians, "husbands should love their wives as they do their own bodies. He who loves his wife loves himself. For no one ever hates his own body, but he nourishes and tenderly cares for it, just as Christ does for the church, because we are members of his body" (Ephesians 5:28-29). That's a remarkable summary, isn't it? It captures the kind of health and wholeness that we are all hoping to obtain. Paul pulls together the relational, the physical, and the spiritual in his talk of husbands, wives, bodies, Jesus Christ, and the church.

Small Size

Finally, bristlecone pines teach us that small size is one of the greatest of survival strategies. In fact, it is an approach that has allowed certain individual trees to live longer than entire civilizations. When the green part of a tree dies from a lightning strike, for instance, the tree copes by letting an equally significant part of its tissue and bark die as well. This way, the remaining greenery has a smaller total organism to support. Some particularly ancient bristlecones have only a thin strip of living bark left, which sustains a single living branch bearing but a few living twigs and needles.

101

In a sense, these ancients have gone back to being seedlings. The bristlecone allows most of itself to die, so that a small part of it can live.

What's the lesson for us? First, to allow old and unhealthy practices and patterns to die, so that new and healthier patterns can emerge. As Christians, we are in a constant process of confessing our failings and receiving forgiveness, dying to sin and being raised to new life. Next, we are challenged to assemble a small group for support and accountability, whether we are trying to complete a marathon or study the entire Bible. Christianity is a team sport, one that requires good coaching and camaraderie — from Covenant Partners and others — in an intimate community of faith where we are known and supported and challenged. Finally, we are invited to see our success as being measured over the course of years, not over hours or days or months. Our Lord is looking for us to be faithful and productive disciples over the course of a long and fruitful life, so that when our time on earth is over we will hear our Master say, "Well done, good and faithful servant" (Matthew 25:21).

If we take these tips from the trees, we'll be able to live a Christian life for the long term. With such a marathon mentality, we'll be able to draw deeply on the gifts of God, and join the world of nature in clapping and growing and giving glory to our Creator. With the same kind of endurance and strength as the bristlecone pine, we'll be able to go out in joy and be led back in peace.

Old Methuselah would be amazed at the changes you can make in your own life, to help you both endure and thrive in the years to come.

Your Action Steps From Commandment Three

1. Do a walk or run test to establish your fitness level.

2. Calculate your body mass index and measure your waist.

3. Reflect on "the marathon mentality," and list the ways that you can develop extensive roots, disease resistance, and small size.

4. Contact your Covenant Partner, and discuss your progress on Commandments One through Three.

Commandment Four

Thou Shalt Be Strong

The Simple Goodness Of Strength

We begin this chapter with a simple and direct message: Strength is a virtue. Indeed, it is even more than that. Strength, whether it is physical, intellectual, emotional, or spiritual, is an intrinsic good. It requires no other justification than itself.

Think about it ... intellectually strong people are less likely to be swayed by fads and trends. Instead, they ask tough questions to deepen their understanding about issues and they take a well-crafted, disciplined approach to learning. Emotionally strong people endure both hardships and joys with grace and dignity, never letting themselves get too high or too low. They are slow to anger and they don't bury themselves in bitterness and recrimination.

None of us would ever question the fact that Jesus was a man of strength. From resisting the temptations of Satan to standing up to the criticisms of religious and political leaders, Jesus showed incredible personal strength. His strength came from his sense of mission and purpose, his relationship with his disciples, and most of all from God himself. Jesus tapped into the very same divine power that is available to us — the power that Paul speaks of when he says, "I can do all things through him who strengthens me" (Philippians 4:13).

Spiritually strong people seek out a stronger relationship with God, look for ways to do God's work in their community and the world, treasure the gifts in their lives, and understand that life's trials are also opportunities for growth. And, last but not least, physically strong people live fuller lives, are better able to enjoy recreation and sports, live independently (especially important in the case of older adults), and dramatically reduce their risk of many illnesses, from osteoporosis to metabolic syndrome. If nothing else, people who are physically strong are better able to complete what clinicians call activities of daily living (ADL), which can be as simple as shoveling snow from a driveway to moving a piece of furniture.

So, rather than ask, "Why should I bother developing strength?" we think that the much more important question is, "Why would you not want to be as strong as you possibly can?" We think that you can and should be an intellectually, emotionally, spiritually, and *physically* strong person. One important tool for achieving physical (and possibly emotional strength) is to become a devotee of strength training. Indeed, building physical strength through a conscientious strength-training program may also help you uncover intellectual, emotional, and spiritual reservoirs of resilience and tenacity that you never knew you had.

What Is Strength Training?

Strength training, also called resistance exercise or resistance training, is defined as follows by the American College of Sports Medicine: "Training the muscles of the body to increase strength, power, or muscular endurance through moving a load or weight; the most common form is weight training."[95]

The load that the definition refers to can come from your own body mass (as in a push-up), a weight (such as a dumbbell or weight machine), or from resistance bands or tubes made of highly elastic rubber. One afternoon, Henry went to visit an elderly member of his church who was living in a retirement facility. When Henry walked in the door, the man immediately showed him the elastic bands he was using for strength training. He was proud of his work-outs and wanted Henry to see how he stretched the bands in his exercise class. So, you see, it can be done by *anyone*, at *any age*.

Strength is the ability of a muscle to contract with force. Power is that same muscle's ability to contract forcefully and quickly — that is, power really has two qualities, both strength and velocity. You will learn later, in this chapter, and in chapter 7 (Thou Shalt Periodize), that using a strength-training program to develop strength and power is potentially very useful because those characteristics immediately contribute to quality of life. For example, think about how you must move when attempting to cross a busy street just as the light is about to change. Need to move quickly or slowly? You are walking down a set of stairs, start to lose your balance, and instinctively reach for the banister. Need to move quickly or slowly? Very few activities of daily living (ADL) and sports require slow movement. Thus, using examples such as these, we will help you understand why so many commercially popular strength-training methods are both scientifically implausible and, often, just plain wrong. We hope to teach you to train your muscles for strength, endurance, and power.

How Strength Training Can Help You

Many years ago, when Vik was an undergraduate student at SUNY Cortland in upstate New York, one of his exercise science professors disparaged his interest in strength training. He told Vik that weight-lifting would never prove to have substantial benefits for either athletes or the general public; that it would always be a second cousin to running, cycling, and other aerobic activities, which happened to be the professor's main interests. Something intuitive told Vik that the professor was wrong, even though, at the time, no one's prediction could have possibly been more incorrect. The professor was categorically wrong, and over the last three decades, exercise science researchers have quantified Vik's intuition that strength training is indeed critical to both athletic performance and long-term physical health and well-being.

Over those three decades, there has been a virtual explosion of scientific information about the benefits of strength training. It is now part of training regimens for virtually all athletes, from weekend warriors to elite competitors, both in sports where its contribution is obvious (think football), and those where the contribution is more subtle (for example, endurance athletes such as runners, rowers, cyclists, and cross-country skiers).

Strength training's benefits are numerous and important.

- *It makes your muscles more efficient.* Surprising to many people is the fact that the immediate increase in strength they experience after starting to strength train comes not from having bigger muscles, but more efficient ones. New-comers to strength training increase their muscular strength

107

by about 30% simply because the complex connection between their muscles and nervous system starts to work better. In exercise science terms, this is known as improving muscular economy, meaning that you move more efficiently. Only after you accomplish this initial bump up in strength does your body shift to the next step.

- *It makes your muscles bigger.* The next way that your muscles respond to strength training is that they get bigger. Most of the increase in size comes from a boost in the cross-section of individual muscle cells. However, there are some scientific hints that, in some people, there is actually growth of new muscle cells as well, which contributes marginally to an increase in muscle size.

- *It supports more forceful muscle contractions.* Strength training builds your muscles' tolerance for exercise and one of the ways they adapt is to contract more forcefully. You can also use strength training to build endurance in specific muscles. So, for example, if you paint houses for a living, you might benefit from a regimen of shoulder and arm work aimed at making those muscles not only stronger, but also giving them greater endurance, which would probably make your job easier and more efficient. Likewise, a runner, walker, or cyclist might want to engage in some strength training that builds the power or endurance of his thigh muscles, thus making the running, walking, or bike riding more efficient.

- *It can help with the prevention or management of serious diseases.* Done properly, strength training is a vigorous form of exercise that can help you manage your risk of cardiovascular disease, diabetes, arthritis, depression, and other ailments. It can help people with cardiac disease,[96] diabetes,[97] high blood pressure,[98] and metabolic syndrome (a potentially deadly precursor of heart disease and diabetes).[99] [100] It is even useful as a part of an exercise regimen to help cancer patients recover from both their disease and their often debilitating treatment regimens.[101] However, in the case of cancer, it appears from the literature that the

108

doctors who devised the studies of exercise in cancer were largely ignorant about appropriate strength-training guidelines and essentially made up their strength-training programs instead of relying upon the exercise science literature.[102] Indeed, there is a lot that we still do not know about the importance of muscular health, but it is suffice to say that there is substantial evidence that maintaining as high a level of muscular strength as you can, particularly throughout middle and later life, will ultimately prove critical to your long-term health and quality of life.[103] [104] [105]

What To Expect When You Start

One of the great rewards of being a strength-training beginner is that you will see results very quickly. Novices who lift properly, consistently, and with determination and planning can dramatically increase their strength in a year. After that, the gains come more slowly. Very experienced strength trainers rarely see substantial gains in strength. For them, maintaining muscle strength, power, and endurance earned is the primary goal.

People who are untrained (weight-lifting novices) gain strength very quickly after initiating their program. In fact, many increase their strength by 60% to 70% within the first year of effort. Think about that ... if you bench press 100 pounds on the day that you start your weight-lifting program, bench pressing 160 by the end of your first year of work is within reach. How many other things that you do have that kind of return on investment? The challenge for people who start a weight-lifting program is to stick with it for the long term, because as time passes, your gains will come in smaller increments and your strategic focus will eventually shift from gaining strength to maintaining the muscle mass and strength that you built.

The goal of a lifelong weight-lifting program is to maintain the strength and muscle mass that you build during the initial phases of work. Studies of master athletes show that men who lift weight persistently over a long period are able to maintain considerable physical strength even well into their sixth and seventh decade of life.[106] Overall, everyone loses strength and power with age, but people who strength train regularly will retain a higher absolute level of strength. This is in marked contrast to men and women who do not lift weights regularly; they progressively lose both strength and muscle mass (and with it bone strength), which as we have discussed, is a recipe for deconditioning, disability, and dependence on others, instead of vitality and independence.

We also want you to lift weights because you can continually increase the load — in small increments — as you get stronger, and there is an almost endless variety of weight-lifting exercises, which will not only allow you to work all the major muscle groups in your body, but also let you isolate specific muscles when you need to concentrate on them. As such, strength training is an infinitely adaptable training tool that you can tailor to meet particular needs and goals. While many of the detailed adaptations are beyond the scope of this book, you should know that you can use strength training — with knowledgeable guidance from an experienced exercise specialist or health fitness instructor — to do things as diverse as rehabilitating an injured joint, improving your golf game, and making your walking or running more efficient.

For the purposes of this book, we will presume that everyone participating in the "Ten Commandments of Faith and Fitness" is new to strength training. Thus, you will need to start slowly, and perfect your techniques. Good technique is critical to avoiding injury and maximizing both results and enjoyment from the exercises. Gyms across the country are filled with people who lift with terrible technique — throwing weights instead of lifting them, and contorting their bodies to raise weights that are much too heavy for them to lift properly. These approaches are all about ego and not exercise.

In faith and fitness, we believe it is imperative to set ego aside and strive for excellence and purity of effort. What matters — especially now — is not how much you lift in any particular exercise, but whether you learn to do movements properly, learn how they feel when done correctly (and incorrectly), and that you add weight in manageable but challenging increments.

110

Strength Training Myths And Misconceptions

Few topics in exercise are as misunderstood or dominated by myths and misconceptions as strength training. There are two reasons for this. First, as we have already noted, exercise scientists were relatively slow to appreciate the conditioning and general health benefits of strength work and, consequently, slow to validate them in well designed and published studies. Second, strength training is a big target for all the quick-fixers in our culture, each of whom believes that he or she has discovered the "new, best" way to strength train ... or at least wants you to buy their product to find out. Because so few people understand strength training — or even how their musculoskeletal system works — this is an area ripe for everything from the dubious to the outright fraudulent. Here is the reality ... strength training done properly is hard, demanding, and incredibly productive. Here are some myths and misconceptions that we want you to remove from your thinking right now.

- *I don't need to lift weights.* Yes, in fact, you do. Starting in our fourth decade of life (the thirties), we all slowly start to lose bone and muscle mass. Along with the muscle mass goes strength, about 5% per decade of life. In particular, you lose the kind of muscle fibers most responsible for strength (called type IIx); you generally hang on to the ones that help you walk, cycle, or run (type I), until much later in life, when they, too, will break down if you do not work to keep them healthy and vibrant. The only way to stem this tide is to engage in some form of strength training. It will help keep your bones strong, your muscles powerful, and give you a regular, healthy health-producing exercise that you can do for as long as you live, thus helping forestall unhealthy weight gain and disability.[107]
- *My aging mom/dad should not lift weights.* Yes, they should. As long as there is no medical impediment to their doing so — such as a cardiovascular, neurological, or orthopedic problem. Older people are among the groups that benefit the most from building strong, healthy muscles. The pioneering scientific work in this field goes back many years

111

and is ongoing today.[108] In addition, new research shows that older adults can lift — and benefit from — heavier weights.[109] [110]

- *My children should not lift weights.* At the risk of being repetitive, yes, they should. Both the American College of Sports Medicine and the American Academy of Pediatrics support strength training for children as young as age ten. The caveat is that they need a responsible and well-informed teacher, and that the goals of children's participation until puberty is to learn proper form and build a healthy, lifelong fitness habit — not to develop super-sized muscles.[111] [112] Children younger than age fourteen should not do more than 1 or 2 sets of work per muscle group, with a concentration on moving smoothly and evenly throughout each activity's range of motion (2 seconds to lift and about 3 to 4 seconds to lower a weight). Strength training as a competitive activity is inappropriate in children of this age, and the impetus for training should be to successfully teach a healthy skill — one that can also support future success in sports — but not to encourage children to try maximal lifts or try to maximize muscle size.

- *I don't want big muscles.* When people start to strength train, they quickly start to notice a marked change in the muscles that they have worked — the muscles are bigger and more firm ... that is, they have greater tone, even when relaxed. You will not, however, suddenly explode into a world-class bodybuilder. First, whether you gain weight or not will be determined largely by two things: your genetic makeup and how you eat during your strength-training program. The overwhelming majority of us lack the genetic makeup to become world-class athletes, regardless of whether or not we strength train. We can, however, improve our strength and vitality a great deal within the God-given genetic framework that we all live with. So, relax, you will not develop Arnold Schwarzenegger-type muscles from the strength program outlined here.

112

The other wild card in strength training's impact on you is diet. If you eat a few more calories each day than you need to keep your body weight stable — and if those calories are predominantly high-quality protein — then you will gain muscle mass. Believe it or not, despite the persistent media drumbeat about obesity, there are some people in our culture who actually need to gain weight, especially muscle mass. Alternatively, if you keep your calorie intake at or below your daily requirements, you will gradually lose weight and simultaneously find that your muscles have greater tone, strength, and endurance. Rigorous strength training may lead you to lose somewhat less weight than you initially thought you needed to. Fear not. Muscle mass is good for you, even if it means that you do not reach your absolute weight-loss threshold. Someone new to strength work, who does it in conjunction with walking, may lose a lot of body fat and add some muscle. The magnitude of the changes will vary from person to person. Incidentally, if you stop strength training, muscles do not turn to fat. Rather, because they are mostly water and protein, your body simply metabolizes them and what you have worked so hard to build just disappears.

The biggest place you will notice a change after beginning to work out with weights is your clothing. Even as you get stronger, you will likely find clothing fitting more loosely, particularly if weight loss was a goal and you are managing your intake. This is because muscle is more dense than fat and takes up considerably less space. Thus, as you build healthy muscle and lose body fat, you may find that clothing fits more loosely at your waist, but is more snug in your arms and shoulders; you are losing body fat, which most of us deposit in the waist and hip region, and your previously understimulated arm, chest, and shoulder muscles are growing and getting stronger. Do not let this potential circumstance scare you away from lifting, because we think it is a good problem for you to have. There is, in our minds, no question about the trade-off: having a smaller, trimmer waist in exchange for stronger, bigger torso muscles is a good thing, even if it means buying a few new shirts and pants!

- *I don't have time to strength train.* Nothing could be more wrong. The two parts to our answer are: 1) you don't have time not to, because every day that you defer strength training is another day of opportunity missed as the natural aging process gradually robs your muscles of both strength and mass; and 2) few workouts are as time efficient as strength work. After some practice, you should be able to complete a solid, vigorous whole body strength workout in 30 minutes.

- *I can get just as much benefit from yoga, Pilates, and other activities.* Yoga, Pilates, and other calisthenics-type activities are generally light to moderate in nature (although more advanced varieties are very strenuous) and certainly can have their place in a well-rounded physical activity program. Yoga can provide substantial benefits for flexibility, stress management, posture, balance, and joint stability, particularly in older adults or those who are new to regular physical activity. Based on current research, however, it is doubtful that the most popular forms of yoga (such as Hatha yoga) are actually *exercise*.[113] Likewise, the evidence about the benefits of Pilates is scant and almost completely anecdotal.[114] That is, it may not be an activity that raises your heart rate, energy consumption, and neuromuscular activity in ways that will prompt the important — and absolutely necessary — muscular changes that we outline here. It is up to advocates for Pilates, yoga, and other activities — which have their rightful place in an active life — to demonstrate the value of their pursuits in good, controlled studies and get them published in good, quality exercise science journals. Until then, we believe that they are best regarded as things that are nice to do, if time, energy, and financial resources allow, but they are certainly not the physical activities that are essential — and proven — steps to reducing your health risks and improving your quality of life. No one suffers premature death and disability because they have tight hamstrings ... people suffer premature death

114

and disability because they have clogged arteries, weakened muscles, and bones that break. If you correct the latter, you will have plenty of time to work on the former.

- *Building big muscles will help me burn calories at rest.* This is not so much a myth, as it is a misunderstanding. Adding muscle will allow you to modestly increase your resting metabolism (the rate at which you burn calories). This is simply because muscle is more metabolically active than fat. However, unless you add very substantial amounts of muscle mass (possible for some people, but not everyone), your resting metabolism will pick up only modestly after you start a regular, rigorous strength-training program. It is true, however, that if you keep your diet under control, the modest increase in resting metabolism will add up over the course of a year and contribute to your weight-loss or weight-management efforts. What changes very dramatically, because of your stronger and bigger muscles, is your ability to burn greater numbers of calories when you are active. A strong, fit person — male or female — can engage in more and higher intensity physical activity than a weaker, less fit person. Thus, strong muscles most emphatically increase energy expenditure during physical activity. Their contribution to energy expenditure at rest is small because, well, they are resting.

- *Strength training will work for me no matter how I move or the level of resistance I use.* The popular media abounds with notions and ideas about strength training, few of which are grounded in science, but more often based on hype, saleable ideas, or fashionable trends. The level of resistance that you use in strength training matters profoundly because strength is both a function of, and measured by, the load lifted. (In exercise science terms, load = intensity.) Beginners will, logically, lift relatively light weights (less intense workouts) compared to more experienced strength trainers, the better to perfect technique and prevent injuries. However, once you achieve a baseline of fitness and are able to lift a particular weight successfully and safely 8 to 12 times,

115

you must add weight to keep improving. More to the point, at any stage in your strength-training experience, you should ensure that the weight that you use challenges you sufficiently; if your target is 10 repetitions, but you use a weight that you could actually lift many more times, then you are not using sufficient resistance to make your muscles adapt and get stronger. Likewise, pace of movement matters. A strength-training repetition should be done smoothly, crisply, and efficiently. No major exercise-science organization or body of scientific evidence endorses moving slowly during strength work (injury rehabilitation or special needs excepted).[115] [116]

Options For Doing Strength Training

You can strength train in a lot of different environments, which adds to its appeal. A commercial gym is certainly an option, but one that many people shy away from. If you have space at home, there are many kinds of home gyms that you can buy, some quite simple and straightforward and others very complex. Vik has maintained a home gym full of free weights and dumbbells for about 30 years and has not set foot in a commercial gym since he graduated from college. The weights never wear out or break, and he has all that he needs for a consistent and varied strength-training program.

The simplest option for strength training at home is a set of dumbbells and two exercise balls. We recommend dumbbells because they allow for a variety of movements, are easy for both men and women to use, allow you to increase weight in gradual increments, and, coupled with the exercise balls and some basic exercises, such as push-ups, will allow you to effectively exercise all your muscles.

We recommend the exercise balls because they are somewhat more versatile than a standard weight-lifting bench, and many come with illustrated guides that teach you how to exercise on them both with and without weights. You can get high-quality exercise balls from fitness stores and online from e-retailers such as www.performbetter.com. We suggest that you buy two, one that is specific to a person of your height and weight, and another larger

116

one that is expressly designed to support you during weight-lifting movements.

As for the dumbbells, you can find them at many sporting goods and fitness stores. We recommend that you buy fixed weight pairs (pairs of them from 5 pounds up to about 35 or 40 pounds to start with). By having multiple pairs, you will not have to spend time changing the weight on adjustable ones. This will let you set up more creative and challenging exercise routines because you will not have to stop to change weights, but can simply grab the next pair that you need. Initially, few people need pairs heavier than 35 or 40 pounds. When you get stronger, you can buy heavier ones or consider investing in a more elaborate home gym. The nice thing about fixed dumbbells is that there are no moving parts, they never wear out or break, and they take up very little space. When you buy the dumbbells, get yourself two pairs of Plate Mates, which are 1.25 pound magnets that you can attach to the sides of the dumbbells that you are using. Thus, you can move up in smaller increments than 5 pounds at a time.

Certainly, if you have the resources, you can buy a full-fledged home gym with barbell, bench, and other workout stations. Depending on options and configuration, you can spend from a few hundred to several thousand dollars on home gyms. Some of the more grand units are multistation machines that allow you to do a wide variety of exercises using a central weight stack. Shop carefully, make sure you ask about warranty and services (for elaborate home gyms, the manufacturer should provide at least one year of on-site service). You may also want to pay a little extra to have the store deliver and set up the gym. Some of them are quite complicated and come with a lot of weight, which can make the transportation and assembly process very difficult. You may find useful reviews of home gyms at resources such as Consumer Reports. You can also look into widely advertised products such as Bowflex, but be forewarned that they are expensive and, despite marketing claims, have no established benefit over traditional weights.

There are useful alternatives to dumbbells and other home gyms. Resistance tubes and bands are made from strong rubber materials and come in varying lengths and degrees of resistance. They take up virtually no space, rarely break or wear out, pack easily for travel, and typically come with illustrated guides to exercises that you can do with them. They are a good pairing with exercise balls. Remember, however, that resistance bands and tubes are, by nature, limited in scope, and you may rapidly outgrow them.

Many beginning strength trainers wonder whether they get greater benefit from working with free weights (such as dumbbells or barbells) or with machines (Cybex, Nautilus, and Life Fitness are three popular brands). This is really a "six-of-one" versus "half-dozen of the other" kind of argument. Both training options can work. Your diligence, devotion, and consistency ultimately matter more than the choice of equipment. You may get the most from your strength training by learning to use free weights and machines. However, keep these points in mind when you choose:

- Machines have a more fixed range of motion, but are safer because you cannot get trapped under a heavy weight. This is a critical point, because beginners need to learn, first and foremost, how to lift correctly. Strength always follows technique, and machines are a more controlled environment for good teaching of strength-training techniques.
- Using free weights will require you to use muscles in addition to the one that you are actually trying to work. This is because with free weights, you have no machine to provide support to you during the movement or to help you balance the weight as you lift it. You must work to keep the weight from moving side to side, forward, or backward, while you lift it up and down to complete the movement. For example, if you do a shoulder press with dumbbells while seated on a workout bench, your legs, hips, back and torso muscle will have to work to keep you stable and upright during the movement. Conversely, if you do a shoulder press on a machine designed specifically for it, you will put most of the onus on your shoulder and arm muscles that are actually lifting the weight. The stability that machines offer can be especially helpful for older people or those who are very frail.

118

- Free weights offer a bit more adaptability than do machines. Because the movement on a machine is fixed, you will have few options to modify an exercise to meet a specific need. For example, if you are rehabilitating an injured arm, you may find it more useful to work with dumbbells, because you can use different weights for each arm or use slightly different motions, allowing the weak one to work with a lower weight and eventually catch up to the stronger one. You may not have this flexibility with a machine that does not allow you to exercise each limb independently.

No matter whether you start small with dumbbells or exercise bands and balls, you are not sentenced to using these tools forever. As your fitness level improves and as you are better able to judge your finances, you will find an ever-expanding universe of exercise equipment and options at your disposal. What matters most is that by the time you reach the point when more complex (and expensive) equipment is the right choice for you, you will have already completed the most arduous part of this journey. You will have established a healthy, regular, and hopefully vigorous exercise routine, giving physical health and well-being a prominent place in your life. This means that, unlike many other people who buy expensive exercise gear that they never use or join gyms that they never visit, you will actually get a return on the investment that you make because you will grasp the fundamental importance of what you are doing. Like all successful investment processes, starting big is often not the key to success ... what drives success is starting small, sticking with your plan, building slowly, and challenging yourself to go to the next level when you are ready.

When you set strength-training goals, they should be achievable and build upon one another so that you can track your long-term progress. It is important to set aside ego and be realistic in your goal setting, remembering that the goal of our program is not performance, but fitness. Thus, it is less important to try to reach absolutes (for example, bench pressing 300 pounds, which is not something everyone can do) than it is to identify incremental goals that are more individualized and based on scientific data that lets us understand what fitness means in quantitative terms.

For example, if you are a forty-year-old who is new to exercise, instead of seeking to bench press 300 pounds, it is more important for you to first learn to lift weights safely and effectively, then bench press 100 pounds, and then seek to bench press your own body weight. We know from normative data that if a healthy forty-year-old man bench presses an amount equal to his body weight, he has upper body strength that exceeds that of 80% of his peers. If his bench press progresses to his body weight plus 10%, he is stronger than 90% of men his age. Conversely, if he bench presses half his body weight, he is weaker than nearly all other men his age.[117] The stronger you are, the more resistant you will be to disease and disability; the weaker you are, the more susceptible you will be.

If you start out this program considerably overweight, take heart. Because sound strength-training goals are relative to body weight, things actually get easier as you lose weight. For example, if you weigh 270 pounds now, with a high percentage of body fat, bench pressing your body weight (270) will seem daunting indeed; if you bench press 135 pounds (50% of your body weight), you may be disappointed with your performance. However, when your weight drops to 225, and your bench press rises just 40 pounds to 175 (as it likely will if you are new to strength training), you rapidly go from bench pressing 50% of your body weight to 78%. For long-term health, what matters is your relative performance over time, compared to population-wide data, not whether you bench press more than your neighbor.

To help you visualize and understand strength-training exercises, we strongly recommend that you purchase *Strength Training Anatomy*, Second Edition, by Frederic Delavier. This excellent, well-written, beautifully illustrated exercise guide is the only one you will need. The new edition even comes with special pages that discuss common strength-training injuries and how you can avoid them. Although most of the illustrations show men and women working out with machines or free weights, we think that you will

120

readily understand how to translate many of the exercises to whatever equipment you have available, such as dumbbells and resistance bands or tubes. Finally, if you exercise in a gym, be wary of people who want to teach you exotic, potentially dangerous strength-training movements that can place undue amounts of stress on sensitive joints such as your lower back or knees. Stick with the fundamental exercises in Delavier's book.

If you wish to learn more about strength training and especially delve into the science behind it, the book that we strongly recommend is *Optimizing Strength Training* by William J. Kraemer and Steve J. Fleck (Human Kinetics Press, 2007). This information-rich, science-based, highly readable text will give you the data that you need to take your strength-training efforts to their next stage of development, after you lay the foundation that we recommend here. It will help you grow beyond basic fitness into the realm of performance improvement, giving you the resources that you need to not only continue building strength, but to also cultivate power and muscle endurance, and use strength training to support other activities.

Workout Planning

Doing strength work properly means first understanding how strong you are now. Just as we asked you to do a self-test of your aerobic fitness, we encourage you to self-test your strength fitness as well. In general, the simplest, most direct measure of muscular fitness is to test upper body strength, using the bench press (a weight-lifting exercise) or push-ups, which measure chest muscle strength and endurance. You should not do any weight-lifting tests unless you have experience lifting weights and can complete the tests in a well-equipped gym where you can use either machines or free weights on benches and stands that have appropriate safety mechanisms built in. DO NOT complete the weight-lifting tests of strength at home by yourself, or at a gym, without the help of an experienced training partner.

The goal of the weight-lifting test is to learn your 1 rep maximum (1RM) in the bench press (or any other exercise). You should warm up thoroughly by lifting a light weight that you believe is about one-half the weight you will ultimately lift, about 8 to 10 times. Then, after a rest period of a minute or two, add sufficient weight so that the amount is now about 70% of what you think your maximum is. Lift this 3 to 5 times. Then, after another few minutes of rest, add weight in increments. Within 3 to 5 attempts of 1 repetition each, you should reach your 1RM. Rest about 4 to 5 minutes between attempts to give working muscles adequate time to prepare for the next attempt. The last weight that you can lift properly (without arching your back or using other moves to add leverage and lift the weight) is your 1RM. You can repeat this process with any strength exercise to determine what your 1RM is.

Another way to assess muscular fitness with weights is to complete a test of muscular endurance, which involves bench pressing a specific weight (80 pounds if you are man, 35 if you are a woman), until you cannot complete another repetition. The last one that you do correctly is your final number. Whether you do the 1RM or the endurance bench press, or both, make sure you write down these numbers, because we will revisit these tests.[118]

We anticipate that, for many people, it is simpler, safer, and more efficient to do basic strength testing at home, using push-ups. The push-up test involves doing a standard push-up, lowering your body with your back straight, until your chin touches the floor (or a book placed under your chest that is about 2.5 to 3 inches thick), and then pushing back up until your arms are straight. Some men and women need to do a modified version of the push-up, pivoting not on their toes, but rather on their knees. In either case, your stomach should never touch the floor, and you should breathe regularly, paying particular attention to exhaling as you push up from the floor. Your score in this test is the total number of push-ups that you can perform without stopping. As with the tests of cardiorespiratory endurance, your performance varies by age and gender. Thus, if you are a fifty-year-old man, and completed 25 push-ups, you have excellent upper body strength, while this would be only average for a 25-year-old man. As we noted previously, www.exrx.net is a good place to check your performance.

There is a very logical progression for safe and effective strength training, which we summarize in the charts on the following pages.

For maximum efficiency, you should keep your workouts short and simple. Use the chart below to find your experience level. Everything in your strength-training program, like the rest of this program, is an incremental progression. You must master safe weight lifting techniques before adding weight. And, you should add weight only in small, manageable increments that sufficiently challenge your muscles, but do not overwhelm them. (Important terms of reference — a repetition or rep is a single movement of any exercise; a set is a group of repetitions performed in succession.)

	Beginner (< 1 year experience)	Intermediate (1 to 2 years experience)	Advanced (> 2 years experience)
Number of workouts per week	2 or 3	2	2
Number of sets of work for each muscle group	1 or 2	2 to 4	5 to 8
% of your 1 Rep Maximum	60%	70%-80%	80% or greater
Target number of reps	8 to 12	6 to 10	3 to 5

Note that as you progress to greater strength and heavier weights, the number of repetitions that you do falls. After you complete your first 6 to 8 weeks of training — and have learned to lift safely — you also need to get in the habit of varying your workouts, a process called periodization, which we discuss in greater detail in Commandment Seven. Kraemer and Fleck's book offers an excellent discussion of how to periodize a strength-training program, and we highly recommend it for that reason. Even very advanced strength trainers should periodize their workouts and sessions in the gym should not all take place at the same intensity.

These are broad guidelines taken from the exercise science literature. They are important, however, because they are evidence-based indicators of what work intensity is most likely to elicit the greatest gains in strength.[119] Mastering strength training requires using lighter weights as a beginner to learn exercises properly, perfect your form, and develop some initial strength through the improvement in neuromuscular function. As an intermediate lifter, you need to add weight to get the full benefit of the activity. While continuing to lift a relatively modest weight, say 60% to 70% of your 1 repetition maximum will confer some health benefits, it will always limit your development and restrain you from maximizing your strength potential.

These are useful, functional evidence-based thresholds for strength work, and we believe that at a minimum, everyone (with at least intermediate level experience) should work every muscle group at least twice weekly, doing 2 to 4 sets of work, using about 70% to 80% of your 1 rep maximum for any given exercise. In most cases, this means you will do in the range of 6 to 10 repetitions, which is sufficient to actually build strength. In our view, the conventional advice to do about 12 reps of an exercise is nebulous ... it is too many reps to build strength and too few to build local muscle endurance. If you need to build endurance in a muscle group, you will need to use a relatively light weight, such as 30% of your 1 repetition maximum and endeavor to do many repetitions, shooting for 20 to 30 or more. Regardless of whether you seek muscular strength, endurance or both, you will need to stimulate your muscles enough to encourage them to adapt to the training load.

You can do either whole body workouts or divide your body into muscle groups and work two or three together at each session. Regardless, always start with the largest muscle group you plan to work and progress to the smaller ones. In a whole body workout, this means starting with your legs and hips (the largest muscles in your body), progressing in descending muscle size to your chest, back, shoulders, biceps, and triceps. Use Strength Training Anatomy to guide your exercise planning. A sample workout would look like this:

1. Leg press (thighs, hips, buttocks, some lower back)
2. Bench press (chest, shoulders, triceps)
3. Behind the neck pulldown (upper back, shoulders, biceps)
4. Lateral raise (shoulders, upper back)
5. Bicep curl (biceps, forearms)
6. Seated triceps extension (triceps, forearms)

Rest about two to three minutes between sets of work. In general, if you keep the weight constant from one set to the next, the less time your rest between sets, the fewer reps you will do in subsequent sets. If you rest more, say 3 to 4 minutes, you will be able to do more reps in subsequent sets or add weight to the remaining sets. If you rest a minute or less between sets, you will not be able to lift as much but will build some muscle and cardiovascular endurance especially if you are doing endurance lifting that requires many, many repetitions. For each set, you will need to use a trial and error process to determine what starting weight is right for you, especially if you have not done any maximum-strength testing. If you cannot complete 6 to 8 repetitions correctly and safely, then the weight is too heavy. If you can do more than 10 to 12, it is too light.

As you gain strength, you will eventually be able to do 12 or more repetitions with weights that previously felt challenging at 8, 9, or 10 reps. When this happens, you MUST add weight in order to keep making progress. You can do core exercises, such as abdominal crunches and low-back bridges between your strength-training sets. There is an excellent illustrate guide to core exercises at the website of the Mayo Clinic. You can find it at www.mayoclinic.com/health/core-exercises/SM00071. Make sure that you read the introduction page, and review the exercises done both with and without an exercise ball.

When you start lifting, you will get sore. If you are, do not be alarmed. The overwhelming majority of people are sore after their first one or two sessions of strength training. This is true even when novices lift relatively light weights, compared to people with more extensive exercise experience. It makes you appreciate how physically undemanding our daily lives have become that even a 20- to

30-minute novice strength-training workout can leave us feeling aches in muscles that we did not even know we had.

If you are still sore from a previous workout, you should use lighter weights than you typically would, and rest more between sets. It is also fine to skip a workout if you are sore. Missing an occasional workout to allow your body sufficient time, rest, and nutrition to rebuild from a prior exertion will not cost you anything. Indeed, the day off may do more to preserve the integrity of your long-term strategy than will doing a workout when you are uncomfortable, which may leave you frustrated, confused, or worse, injured. Get medical attention if the soreness persists for more than a day or two, becomes debilitating, or your urine turns dark.

Do not fear success or strength. It is a popular, but foolish and unsubstantiated, myth that you should persist in lifting relatively light weights. You should seek to be as physically strong as you can be, and you can achieve this goal only if you are willing to challenge both your mind and your body. If you lift the same weights over and over, you will eventually stop getting stronger long before you reach your genetic potential, simply because you will have ceased to challenge your muscles with progressively more difficult loads. Even older adults — people you might think must limit their work to very light weights — can get more from their strength training when they challenge themselves with moderate to heavy weights. Not only do they get markedly stronger, they also get much better at functional activities (activities of daily living), such as crossing a street or carrying groceries.[120] [121] [122] They also gain self-confidence and self-respect. Weakness and fear are not virtues — in particular, they are not Christian virtues. Strength and perseverance are. We want you to be strong and to persevere.

Keep in mind that your strength work and endurance go together, but they serve very different purposes. They work well together to build and maintain different body systems. Endurance exercise benefits primarily your cardiovascular system and type I muscle fibers; strength-training benefits primarily your bones and muscles, in particular type IIx muscle fibers. There is some overlap. You can build very strong and muscular legs and strong hip/leg bones with extensive endurance exercise, and, likewise, you can

126

build limited cardiovascular endurance using strength training.[123] You cannot, however, use endurance exercise to achieve the main goals of strength training (making your lower and upper body muscles and bones as *strong* as they can be). Nor can you use strength training to get the most out of your heart and lungs. Recall that this is called the specificity principle in exercise science. It means, simply, that particular exercises (or in this case, exercise routines) challenge different body systems in specific ways. Strength training and endurance exercise even use different kinds of muscle fibers and stimulate them in unique ways. So, realistically, you should not pick and choose between the two; you really do need to do both.

These two kinds of exercises are not only specific, but they are complimentary. You may recall an interesting and amusing set of television commercials a few years back featuring former pro football and major league baseball player, Bo Jackson. Bo was the first and most successful two-sport athlete in the modern era. The commercials played on his athletic virtuosity, with the theme "Bo Knows" showing him doing everything from playing other sports to working as a musician. What we all learned from Bo and the Bo Knows commercials was the concept of cross training — using different skills, muscles, and body systems to accomplish diverse goals in very distinct sports. We want you to keep this principle in mind as you go forward with faith and fitness. Not that you will become Bo Jackson, but that you, too, will rely on unique muscles, body systems, and skills to develop expertise in two fields of fitness: endurance exercise and strength training.

By cultivating experience in two endeavors, you are also actually building an exercise safety net for yourself. By knowing how to do two different kinds of fitness activities, you will always have the resources at hand to get some exercise done, even when other life events conspire against you. For example, suppose you sprain an ankle while working around the house. You probably can still do your upper body strength work while your ankle heals. If you have pulled a shoulder muscle, that should not stop you from walking, or possibly running. If you don't have time today for your 60 minute walk because of the last-minute meeting scheduled by your boss ... chances are, you can still squeeze in 20 minutes of lifting sometime during the day. You get the idea ... the more you know and know how to do, the more you can accomplish.

Below is a table that summarizes a set of useful tips that can help guide your strength work.

Range Of Motion
- Use as full a range of motion (ROM) as you can, but if you have a painful joint or muscle, limit the ROM only to what is pain-free.
- If you have joint pain of any kind, limit your range of motion only to what you can do pain-free.
- Do not stretch to warm up; gently stretch your muscles after your workout. Warm up by doing one or two sets of 12 to 15 reps of the exercise you would like to perform with a *very light* weight. Alternatively, spend 10 minutes on a treadmill or exercise bike to warm up before lifting. This will raise your body's core temperature and heart rate, boost circulation, and loosen up your muscles. Remember, stretching per se does not prevent injury and stretching a cold muscle is a terrible prelude to activity. Warm-up does prevent injury. A warm-up can include stretching, but it is better for stretching to happen after your activity when your muscles are warm and pliable.

Speed Of Movement
- Lift a weight in about a second, pause for just a moment, and take up to 2 seconds to lower the weight, but not more than 4 seconds; don't let gravity lower the weight. (In other words, don't drop it.)
- Moving more slowly than is noted above is inconsistent with the guidelines of the American College of Sports Medicine. People new to strength work can maximize their skills development by moving at this pace, which is slower than the pace used by many advanced-strength trainers. However, as you progress from a novice to an intermediate strength

128

trainer to an expert, you will find that you can benefit greatly from learning to move faster (but always under control), because this is the mechanism necessary to build power. Building power through more rapid movements in strength training is highly productive, but requires extensive instruction and practice to perfect. It is not appropriate for anyone who is a novice.

- Never throw a weight or cheat to lift it, and don't use momentum.

Breathing

- Never hold your breath.
- Breathe through a relaxed, open mouth.
- Do not clench your jaws.
- Exhale when lifting; otherwise breathe normally.

There is also a progression to follow in terms of exercise order. Follow this progression when you plan your workouts.

Large muscle groups (such as thighs, chest, back) ⟩

Smaller muscle groups (such as hamstrings, calves, arms) ⟩

OR, when you are already working a muscle group, go from ...

Compound joint exercises (two joints are moving as the bench press or leg press) ⟩

Single joint exercises (only one joint moves, such as a leg curl or a bicep curl) ⟩

Then, within each muscle group, always start with exercises that require movement at two joints before doing ones that move a single joint.

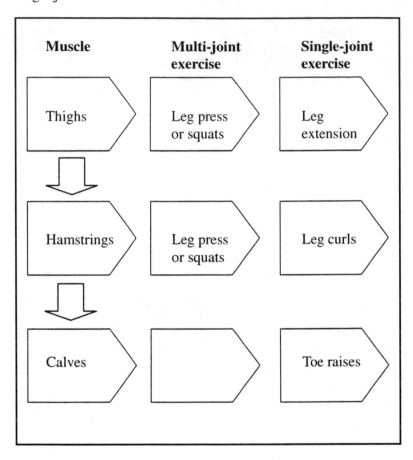

Here are the same kind of progressions, but this time for your upper body. Exercises for the biceps and triceps require movement only at the elbows (hence, single-joint exercises).

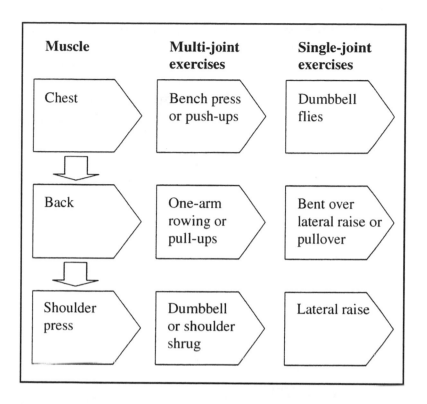

Muscle	Multi-joint exercises	Single-joint exercises
Chest	Bench press or push-ups	Dumbbell flies
Back	One-arm rowing or pull-ups	Bent over lateral raise or pullover
Shoulder press	Dumbbell or shoulder shrug	Lateral raise

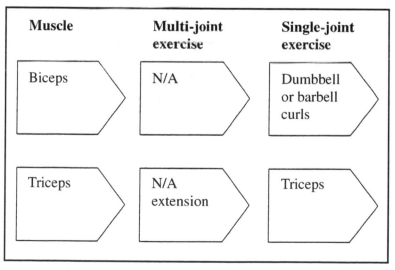

Muscle	Multi-joint exercise	Single-joint exercise
Biceps	N/A	Dumbbell or barbell curls
Triceps	N/A extension	Triceps

As we noted early in this text, we firmly believe that strength is a virtue. In both physical and spiritual terms, being strong is an empowering process that provides you with both the bodily and moral frameworks necessary to not only cope with difficulty and challenge, but to fully engage in life and enjoy it with far fewer limitations than those who choose not to build moral and physical muscles.

Jesus: The Source Of Our Spiritual Strength

Superman may have died back in 1992, in the pages of DC Comics, but now he's back, and he's stronger than ever. Turn on the radio, and you'll hear contemporary songs about Superman. Punch your TV remote, and you can see the popular series *Smallville*. Go to the theater or DVD store, and you can catch *Superman Returns*. Superman's shield was worn by the real stars of September 11 — firefighters and police officers — talk about your superheroes.

Of course, if you want to soar through the sky like a bird or a plane, you need to act like Clark Kent and put on a Superman suit. This is not just a comic book fantasy — scientists are actually hard at work on developing the necessary outfit. According to *Wired* magazine, a team at MIT has developed materials with properties closer to human muscles than anything yet seen. They believe that their innovative muscle material will be perfect for the anti-gravitational suits needed by fighter pilots, as well as for therapeutic and commercial devices.

The team has recently launched a company called Molecular Mechanisms to develop the technology. They expect to produce a variety of working prototypes that may even lay the foundation for a Superman suit for the armed forces. Such a suit — made of materials that are 100 times stronger than natural muscle — could enable soldiers to run, jump, and lift to a nearly superhuman degree.[124]

In fact, just about all of us would love to have this kind of strength. Not just physically ... but emotionally, morally, and spiritually. One of the most discouraging dimensions of day-to-day life is our ever-present human *weakness*. We collapse in exhaustion

132

before our everyday tasks are finished, we break down emotionally when confronted by severe stress, we give in to temptation instead of showing moral strength, and we take the path of least resistance instead of the demanding road of dedicated discipleship and leadership.

None of us is a Superman ... or a Superwoman. We're human. We wobble and wear out; we fall down and mess up.

Even the superheroes of the Bible have serious limits to their strength. In the third chapter of his letter to the Philippians, the apostle Paul looks back over his life and boasts, "If anyone has reason to be confident in the flesh, I have more: circumcised on the eighth day, a member of the people of Israel, of the tribe of Benjamin, a Hebrew born of Hebrews; as to the law, a Pharisee; as to zeal, a persecutor of the church; as to righteousness under the law, blameless" (Philippians 3:4b-6).

Circumcised, Israelite, Benjaminite, Hebrew, Pharisee, blameless — that's a powerful package. For a Jew of the first century, he was a regular Man of Steel.

But as a Christian, Paul admits that "whatever gains I had, these I have come to regard as loss because of Christ. More than that, I regard everything as loss because of the surpassing value of knowing Jesus Christ my Lord. For his sake I have suffered the loss of all things, and I regard them as rubbish, in order that I may gain Christ and be found in him" (Philippians 3:7-9).

Paul is ready to jettison all of his old sources of strength in order to gain the "surpassing value" of knowing Jesus Christ as Lord. Knowing Christ, trusting Christ, and having faith in Christ has become the most important dimension of his life. Paul is willing to deep-six his membership in the tribe of Benjamin, his status as a purebred Hebrew, his accomplishments as a law-abiding Pharisee, his spotless record as a passionate persecutor of the early church — trash them all in order to have a personal relationship with Jesus Christ. These qualities may have strengthened him in the past, he admits, but now he sees them as worthless, and he is ready to flush them all away. In place of these old characteristics, Paul craves a righteousness that comes through faith in Christ, the righteousness from God based on faith. He says, "I want to know Christ and the

133

power of his resurrection and the sharing of his sufferings by becoming like him in his death" (Philippians 3:10).

Suddenly, Paul sounds suspiciously like Clark Kent, doesn't he? He's an ordinary man who dreams of extraordinary things — the power of the resurrection and the sharing of his Lord's sufferings. Fortunately, for Paul and for us, this is no fantasy: We really *can* gain Christ and be found in him, we really can get wrapped up in our Savior through faith. For Paul, and for each one of us, Jesus can be a Superman suit.

When we clothe ourselves with Christ, we trust our Lord to give us a whole new set of powers. Not the ability to run, jump, and lift like a superhero, sailing over walls in a single bound, but instead the truly superhuman powers of compassion, kindness, humility, meekness, patience, forgiveness, love, peacefulness, and thankfulness (Colossians 3:12-15). When we clothe ourselves with our Savior's suit, we are protected not by synthetic muscles but by the whole armor of God: The belt of truth, the breastplate of righteousness, the shield of faith, the helmet of salvation, and the sword of the Spirit (Ephesians 6:13-17).

It's all about the outfit — the Superman suit that is given to all who have faith in Jesus Christ. When we put on Christ, we perform a critical act of spiritual strength training.

But clothing ourselves in this way does more than give us a personal benefit. As people who are empowered and protected by this extraordinary outfit, we have a mission to perform in this world. "I do not consider that I have made it my own," admits Paul to the Philippians, "but this one thing I do: forgetting what lies behind and straining forward to what lies ahead, I press on toward the goal for the prize of the heavenly call of God in Christ Jesus" (Philippians 3:13-14). Paul presses on, like a Man of Steel on a mission, determined to live out everything that Christ has called him to do: To spread the truth, to fight for justice, to liberate the oppressed, to share the gospel, and to anticipate — through it all — the heavenly prize that is waiting for him at the end of his earthly mission.

The same is true for us, ordinary men and women who have been given an extraordinary power. We feel it when we hear God's word, when we experience the Spirit's presence, and when we receive the body and blood of Jesus in holy communion. For those who believe in Jesus, this meal contains nothing less than the power and the presence of our risen Lord, a strength that helps us to leap any obstacle. As the apostle Paul discovered, "I can do all things through him who strengthens me" (Philippians 4:13).

I can do all things ... through him who strengthens me. That's super power. That's super strength. That's a priceless personal quality, available to all who have faith in Jesus Christ. We can be strong in the Lord, "and in the strength of his power" (Ephesians 6:10).

Your Action Steps From Commandment Four

1. Establish a strength-training program based on your current level of experience.

2. Develop your personal strategy for combining your strength training with your walking or other endurance exercise.

3. Set aside 15 minutes each day for prayer and reflection on scripture — a regular period of spiritual strength training.

4. Participate in an activity this week, in your church or community, that puts you in touch with the power and presence of God.

Thou Shalt Eat From The Garden ... (Of Eden, That Is)

Good Nutrition Supports A Good Life

Good nutrition comes from eating from the garden — a diet grounded in fruits, vegetables, whole grains, heart-healthy fats that are predominantly vegetable and seafood-based, and lean protein. This goes right back to the book of Genesis, in which God says, "See, I have given you every plant yielding seed that is upon the face of all the earth, and every tree with seed in its fruit; you shall have them for food" (Genesis 1:29). Although you might not have noticed it before, God recommends a vegetarian diet to Adam and Eve. Nowhere in the Garden of Eden does God say, "Adam, I am giving you a New York Strip Steak."

While there is no reason to avoid the modest consumption of animal protein, we are skeptical that Americans need to continue eating the amount of red meat (beef, pork, lamb) that we currently consume. The challenge is to eat abundantly from the garden — the Garden of Eden, that is — and to emphasize fruits, vegetables, whole grains, and heart-healthy fats, which, except for fish, come from plants (such as olive or canola oil).

To start the process of eating wisely, we want you to complete a very important homework assignment. When you next go to the grocery store, we want you to head first for the produce department, and slowly wander through each aisle, taking the time to look carefully at each fruit and vegetable display. Nowhere in our culture will you find better and more compelling evidence of the wonderful abundance and variety of foods produced in farm fields and orchards here and around the world. The sensory impact of this tour is striking ... there is a myriad of textures, flavors, colors, and tastes ... something for everyone. From the starchy, dense texture of bananas, plantains, and potatoes to the countless varieties of apples, oranges, berries, peppers, and salad greens, the produce section provides the most dramatic evidence conceivable of the cornucopia of nutrition and eating enjoyment that comes from the garden ... the Garden of Eden.

Next, we want you to go to the meat section and cruise the cases stocked with chicken, beef, pork, and the like. Not quite the same visual impact, is it? A rainbow of colors versus a few kinds of drab dead flesh ... we don't mean to be so blunt, but that is the reality of what you are looking at, and we want you to appreciate it as such. We do not say this as non-meat eaters. We both eat and like different kinds of meat (and fish). However, there is not the same variety of texture, color, flavor, and nutritional content in the meat case. In many ways, good nutrition comes from eating what *looks good*, in a colorful selection of foods.

As odd as that might sound, it actually fits with what a retired Navy cook once said to Henry. The man was a member of Calvary Presbyterian in Alexandria, Virginia, which Henry served before moving to Fairfax. He would always be working in the kitchen for church suppers, and Henry noticed that he would always garnish his plates with parsley or something else to add color. Henry was surprised to see a grizzled old Navy cook doing this, and so he asked him, "Kyle, why do you add color to the plate?" He said, "Henry, if it looks good, it will taste good." Something similar could be said for good nutrition: If it looks good, with a variety of shapes, textures, and colors, it will probably be good for you.

While the meat case certainly does provide an abundance of protein, as well as B vitamins and minerals, it is also where you will get a great deal of saturated fat and cholesterol, two of the great health-robbing substances in human diets. (Cholesterol, by the way, comes only from animal products ... red meats, fish, poultry, and dairy. There is not a single molecule of cholesterol in any vegetable, fruit, or grain. These foods are also naturally low in fat generally, and, specifically, low in saturated fat.) With the exception of avocados, fruits and vegetables are largely fat free, loaded with vitamins, minerals, fiber, and water, and have far fewer calories per ounce, which, as you will see, is a good thing for lifelong health.

When you think about how to eat, for both spiritual and physical health, we want you to really focus on the Garden of Eden. Eating a diet that has as its foundation abundant fruits, vegetables, and whole grains not only puts you closer to the way God intended us to eat, but it also happens to very nicely put you on the cutting edge of nutrition science. When you think about the dietary approach that we advocate, we want you to never lose sight of Genesis 1:29: "See," says God, "I have given you every plant yielding seed that is upon the face of all the earth, and every tree with seed in its fruit; you shall have them for food."

Before their fall from grace, Adam and Eve had pretty clear guidelines on how God expected them to eat, because the above passage sounds an awful lot to us like a diet rich in fruits, vegetables, and grains. Eating a healthy-fat, calorie-controlled diet built upon these nutritional components can help to dramatically reduce your risk of being overweight, which, in turn, lowers your risk of diabetes, heart disease, stroke, and some cancers. This is not without some work, however, as adhering to this approach requires diligence — not just for a day, but for a lifetime. You must be strong enough to resist the frequent clarion calls to rush headlong into yet another unsubstantiated, potentially foolish, and probably unproductive fad diet. You also need to resist the temptation of depending on processed foods. Commercial baked and fried goods, such as packaged cakes, pies, chips, and French fries may have started out in an orchard, field, or garden, but they are a very long way from it by the time they hit your plate and start clogging your arteries.

Get The Fad Out Of Your Diet

In our society, nothing appears to unite people of all stripes as much as the cross-cutting desire to somehow, someway, sometime lose weight. We are the heaviest culture in human history, and we pay the health consequences for our profligacy ... our arteries are clogged, our hearts strained, our joints ache, and we often suffer disabilities that rob us of both quantity and quality of life. While some ailments and diminished quality of life come naturally with aging, our poor diets amplify their impact and cause us to age more quickly than we otherwise would. Indeed, we may become the first of several American generations to come that will actually die younger than its predecessors. This is the wrong kind of progress.[125]

People who are vulnerable, anxious, and unhappy with themselves make great targets. While our free enterprise system gives us an abundance of useful ideas, products, and services, it also makes us ripe for the picking by contemporary charlatans selling quick fixes. From eating diets rich in fat, to eating diets with no fat, to using all manner of unproven and potentially dangerous nutritional supplements, Americans are good at nothing if not chasing the latest, greatest, and most likely useless quick dietary fix. To which we say simply ... STOP.

Get off the diet fad merry-go-round — now — today — and stay off it. In this chapter, we are going to teach you how to eat using what is commonly called the Mediterranean diet, which is built upon the nutritional elements that we outlined briefly above. In addition, there are over 50 years of nutrition science to support eating the Mediterranean diet; there is virtually no scientific evidence to support any other fad or commercial diet. What all these and many other commercially popular diets have in common is that they want to sell you something ... food, supplements, books, videos, or subscriptions. That should be the first red flag that arises in your mind when a coworker or neighbor exclaims the "awesome results" derived from the latest, greatest diet ... what does it cost and how much of it do I have to buy? If these diets are so great, why do you have to buy so much of their "stuff" for their diet to work, and why do their purveyors not fund good studies of them?

For all the tens of millions of dollars that these companies make, they fund little or no independent research of their products, services, or theories. And, we suspect we know why. As scholars from the University of Pennsylvania recently learned and wrote — they don't work.[126] If we were pitching and selling faulty notions and services, we would not want to measure their value or utility, either.

140

Even the marketplace has passed judgment on one of the most outlandish fads of recent years, the Atkins diet. The Atkins Company went bankrupt when people finally realized that: a) eating a diet loaded with protein and fat is unpleasant, boring, possibly dangerous to your liver and kidneys and nearly impossible to stick to, and b) beyond some dramatic short-term results, no one can really say that the Atkins diet works or even has a plausible scientific basis. If it did, the cardiology community would have heartily (no pun intended) endorsed it, but heart physicians did not.

The companies that trade in dietary fads want you to believe that eating well and healthily is so complicated that you cannot possibly do it without their help. This is incomprehensible marketing gibberish, an intentionally disingenuous sales pitch that is designed to get you to spend your hard-earned money, not empower you with information that can help you become a smarter, savvier, more independent consumer who can make good choices in any environment. Intellectual and emotional dependence on the false hope of "special" foods and diets is not a recipe for success.

Indeed, as we were writing this chapter, we wondered how much it really cost to eat using one of the commonly available commercial programs. Thanks to an analysis by *Forbes* magazine, we now have some insight on this question. In September 2006, MSNBC.com carried an analysis by *Forbes*, which compared the cost of eating using one of the popular — but largely unproven — diets, versus how much a typical American adult spends on groceries each week (about $54). On the next page is a table summarizing those results.

Diet Name	Cost of using it weekly (for a single person)	Costs how much more than a typical weekly grocery bill
Atkins	$100.52	85%
Jenny Craig	$137.65	152%
NutriSystem	$113.52	109%
Ornish	$78.74	45%
Slim Fast	$77.73	48%
South Beach	$77.61	44%
Subway	$68.60	26%
Sugar Busters	$69.62	28%
Weight Watchers	$96.64	78%
Zone	$92.84	71%

To further validate our point, we want you to carefully and diligently read, watch, or listen to ads for commercial diets, especially those that tout very substantial weight loss or rely upon the testimonials of celebrities. Typically in these ads, you will see, read, or hear the phrase, "Results not typical," which is a reference to the great success of the ad's subject. Well, if the results are not typical, why should you buy the product or service? Would you buy a pre-scription drug that claimed its ability to heal an infection or steady a heart rhythm was "not typical"? Would you buy a car if the manu-facturer claimed that the design of its safety systems meant that the airbag's ability to deploy at the right time to prevent death or in-jury was "not typical"? In other words, why should you use a prod-uct or service that has not established its effectiveness well enough to provide the intended benefit for the majority of people who want to use it? We think you should not use it at all, unless the manufac-turer can produce a good quality, randomized controlled study that is published in a respected journal. This is not a perfect or fool-proof standard of excellence, but it is better than no standard at all. Do not confuse celebrity with credibility; just because someone is famous does not mean that what they are pitching is not *fatuous*.

Another limitation of commercial diet programs is that they may ask you to buy their products, and then you fill gaps in the program by buying some of your own groceries. The fact that you now have to buy food from two sources means that you probably will need a celebrity's disposable income just to survive using this strategy. The reality of popular diet programs is that they all work and they all don't work. This is because, in the short term, many succeed at helping you manipulate your calorie intake so that you eat less and lose some weight. However, cultivating an addiction to a proprietary diet is not a recipe for lifetime good health, and, in many cases, unless you reorient your relationship with food, you will simply regain the lost weight over time. Great for the diet industry that gains a repeat customer, but bad for you and your wallet.

Our approach to dietary health is grounded in science, com-mon sense, and, importantly, reality. One reason that you may not see headlines about the Mediterranean diet is that it is not particu-larly sexy ... lots of fruits and vegetables, whole grains, seafood, nuts, and modest amounts of alcohol. More pointedly, it enables you to eat successfully and well with the food you can get from a good, well-stocked grocery store or farmer's market — not from a website, catalog, specialty retailer, or subscription service.

143

Buying "special foods" enriches the seller, but impoverishes you both financially and intellectually by encouraging dependence and discouraging a rational, thoughtful, industrious approach to diet and good health. We want you to be a strong person whose approach to diet is not to diet at all, but rather to change your thinking about food so that you eat well, eat for health, and enjoy doing it. You cannot do this when you are trapped on a dietary fad roller coaster lurching from one unsubstantiated claim to another. It is not where you buy, but how you make buying decisions; it is not just what you eat, but also how much you eat (yes, calories still matter). Most importantly, what counts is that you exert intellectual control over this process. Not only do calories still matter, but thinking about what you are doing matters, too.

What the diet companies don't want you to know is that while obesity and being overweight are incredibly complex — and often difficult — problems to solve, there are many important data points about what works.

- Watch your calorie intake. No commercial diet overturns the fundamental laws of thermodynamics ... a calorie is a calorie is a calorie.[127] If you eat more calories than you need, you will gain weight; eat fewer than you need, and you will gradually lose weight. Most diets are simply fancy and expensive ways of manipulating your calorie intake and food choices by convincing you that you simply cannot do the job yourself.
- Set modest, but specific, goals. A useful goal for any overweight or obese person is to lose 10% of your present weight and keep it off for a year.[128] While that may be your long-term goal, you should also have short-term goals that address both diet and exercise. For example, good short-term goals are to first start keeping a diet diary and to make three exercise appointments with yourself for the week. Resolve also to start every meal with a broth-based soup or serving of vegetables or fruit and not fried foods, breads, or cream-based soups. When you achieve one set of goals, then set

more, but remember to continue the behaviors that helped you achieve your initial targets.

- Have faith in what you can achieve and be diligent. Data from the National Weight Control Registry and other studies show that up to 20% of obese people can maintain their weight loss. Keep a diligent diet diary, weigh yourself regularly, and pay attention to how tightly or loosely your clothes fit. This is called self-monitoring and, as we already noted, is essential to long-term success.

We cannot overemphasize the importance of eating an abundance of fruits and vegetables. The story of Daniel from the Old Testament is instructive here. After Daniel and a number of other Israelite youths are taken as prisoners to Babylon, to be servants in the king's palace, they are given the opportunity to enjoy food and wine from the king's table. But Daniel resolves not to defile himself with the royal food and wine. He makes a request to their guard, "Please test your servants for ten days: Give us nothing but vegetables to eat and water to drink. Then compare our appearance with that of the young men who eat the royal food, and treat your servants in accordance with what you see." The guard agrees to this and tests them for ten days. At the end of the ten days, they look healthier and better nourished than any of the young men who eat the royal food. The guard then takes away their choice food and the wine they are to drink and gives them vegetables instead. Daniel and his colleagues eat from the garden and are much healthier as a result! (Daniel 1:1-16).

The Seven Keys To Successful, Lifelong Nutrition

Consistent with the biblical theme of this book, we want to make our nutrition discussion concise, pithy, and informative. Because Americans are bombarded nearly every day with sometimes confusing messages about diet, we want to boil our lessons down to a manageable number ... 7. If God could create the heavens and earth in 7 days, we are confident that you can remember — and, more importantly, implement — 7 keys to eating a healthy diet.

145

Step One: Keep moving.

Believe it or not, the first step in eating well is not about eating at all. The first and most vital element of a good diet is to stay physically active. No matter whether you walk, run, row, lift weights, ride a bike, ballroom dance, hike, or combine a number of activities, physical exertion — enough to breathe hard and work up a sweat at least several times a week — is the cornerstone of your healthy diet and trump card in your quest for long-term health. In large measure, this is because we want to teach you to eat a diet that supports your physical activity, thus helping you think differently about food and what it does for you. While food fills many interesting and welcome roles in human culture, it is first and foremost fuel, and we want you to think of it as fuel for activity. We use food to celebrate, mourn, bond, and sometimes just to make ourselves feel good (think of chocolate ice cream). In all cases, however, our bodies, which are first and foremost biological entities, use food as the source of nutrients that support a healthy life, fueling all of our physiologic operations from building healthy muscles and bone to ensuring that our nervous system works correctly and our heart beats regularly.

Step Two: Do the math.

Understand how many calories you need to maintain your present weight, which is really quite easy to estimate. Once you know this number you can calculate how much of a calorie deficit you need every day to lose weight, or, as is true for some people, put on a little bit of weight, in the form of healthy muscle, of course. To determine your estimated daily caloric requirements, follow these steps:

- Divide your weight (in pounds) by 2.2 to get your weight in kilograms (kg). A 150-pound man weighs 68.2 kg (150 ÷ 2.2). In general, people burn about 1 calorie per hour per kg of bodyweight when we are at rest.
- Multiply your weight in kg, 68.2 in our example, times 24 (the number of hours in a day). This equals 1,636 calories. For the purposes of our example then, a 150-pound man

who wants to maintain his current weight would eat this many calories per day, if he was at rest the entire time. Most of us, however, do not spend our day at rest. So, you need to modify this figure.[129]

- Add calories in 10% increments depending on how much physical activity you do daily.

    a. If you live a sedentary life and just go about your daily activities (that is, you do not exercise), you burn relatively few additional calories beyond what you require at rest, so add 5% to 10% (82 to 163 calories) to the total above, for a total daily caloric requirement of 1,717 to 1,800 calories.

    b. If you are moderately active, say you walk 3 miles daily at 15 minutes per mile in addition to daily activities, add 20%, because you are burning more calories. In our example, this means adding 327 calories for a total daily caloric requirement of 1,963.[130]

    c. If you are vigorously active — for example, you ride your bike for an hour daily at 12 mph, add 30%. In our example, this means adding about 480 calories for a total daily calorie intake of 2,126. You get the idea ... once you can estimate your baseline caloric needs, it is simple algebra to determine how much you need to eat (or not eat, as the case may be) to maintain, lose, or gain weight. A very useful website for these kinds of calculations is www.exrx.net, where you can estimate the number of calories you burn in a wide variety of activities, and estimate your resting metabolism.

    d. Now, write these numbers down in your diet diary, because they are your baseline data. If you want to lose weight, you need to create a daily calorie deficit. When you have a daily calorie deficit, you will have burned more calories in a 24-hour period than you ate ... this is how you lose weight. Let's stick with our hypothetical 150-pound man and say that he needs to lose 10 pounds. Losing 10 pounds of fat means burning 35,000

147

calories because a pound of fat has 3,500 calories in it. If our guy wants to lose a pound a week, he has to have a daily calorie deficit of -500 calories. You can achieve a calorie deficit by eating less, exercising, or doing both, which is the ideal route. Creating a daily deficit of 500 calories is actually quite easy ... it is giving up one 12-ounce can of soda and a small bag of chips (300 calories combined) and walking two miles in 25 minutes (200 calories). That's it. Now that you know how to do the math, this should not seem quite as daunting as everyone who wants to sell you a book, food, supplement, CD, DVD, program, service, or how-to guide would like you to believe. Below is a chart that summarizes the cumulative effects of a daily calorie deficit for someone who needs to lose weight.

If you reduce your daily calorie intake by this much	And burn this many calories by exercise	This will be your total daily calorie deficit	And you will burn this many calories per week	Which will lead you to lose this many pounds of fat (on average) ...			
				Every week	Every month	Every six months	In a year
100	100	200	1400	0.4	1.6	9.6	20.8
150	150	300	2100	0.6	2.4	14.4	31.2
200	200	400	2800	0.8	3.2	19.2	41.6
250	250	500	3500	1	4	24	52
250	300	550	3850	1.1	4.4	26.4	57.2
300	350	650	4550	1.3	5.2	31.2	67.6
350	350	700	4900	1.4	5.6	33.6	72.8
400	400	800	5600	1.6	6.4	38.4	83.2
450	450	900	6300	1.8	7.2	43.2	93.6
500	500	1000	7000	2	8	48	104

e. Some people actually need to gain weight, particularly lean muscle mass, because they are too thin for their own good. Adding muscle is not the same as losing fat. A pound of muscle has only about 600 calories worth of energy, because muscle is mostly water. Thus, to gain muscle mass, you must do two things ... strength train to stimulate the proper changes in your muscles, and eat a small amount of extra food each day, mostly in the form of a well-rounded, protein-rich snack (such as a turkey or tuna sandwich), within an hour of completing a strength workout. You can expect to add — at most — about a pound of muscle every couple of weeks. The extra calories you eat should come from a mix of foods that include carbohydrates, protein, and fat. For example, after strength training, a turkey breast or tuna sandwich on whole grain bread will meet your needs, as would a cup of low-fat cottage cheese with chopped fruit or vegetables.

A number of popular publications, and even some physicians, really misunderstand the influence on energy expenditure of adding lean healthy muscle.[131] They unfortunately believe that adding a few pounds of muscle — while very good for you — will cause you to somehow magically burn *many* more calories at rest than you would without the muscle mass. Having muscle is important for reasons that we have already discussed, but muscle tissue accounts for about 30% of your resting caloric expenditure. Your organs burn about 65% of your calories at rest, and fat, which is not as inert as you might think, burns the remaining 5%. When you exercise vigorously, this energy balance shifts, and your muscle accounts for 65% of your caloric expenditure. Experts estimate that the resting energy expenditure of 10 kg of muscle tissue (about 22 pounds) is 100 calories, or about 5 calories per pound per day.[132]

Hence, as we told you in "Thou Shalt Be Strong," the value of healthy, strong muscles is less what they do for you when you are sitting still (called resting energy expenditure by exercise scientists) than what do they do for you when you are moving (called physical activity energy expenditure). Strong, healthy muscles are the engine that allows you to be active, and being active is what really burns calories. So, yes, you should want to lose fat and build a few pounds of healthy muscle, which will burn some additional calories each day, but it will not make you a caloric furnace while you are sitting your desk.[133] Instead, it will help you become a strong, efficient calorie burning machine when you are physically active. The stronger you are, the more you can do; the more you can do, the greater the number of calories you can burn. The greater the number of calories you can burn, the more likely you are to maintain a healthy body weight and keep your heart and lungs fit.

Step Three: Eat it all ... well, almost all.

Here is some earth-shattering nutritional news ... carbohydrates and fats are good for you ... in the proper quantities and the right kinds. Your highest priority is to manage your calorie intake based on the calculations that we described previously. Within that context, the next priority is to eat a wide variety of foods conscientiously and in moderation. Gluttony was one of the Seven Deadly Sins articulated by Pope Gregory, and successful weight management does not include gluttony as one of its key components. A brownie, eaten by someone who understands how that affects his or her daily calorie intake, is not a bad thing. We are highly skeptical, however, about eating an entire plate of brownies.

In its revised guidelines for good nutrition in 2003, the US government recommends that most people get about 60% of their daily total calories from carbohydrates, about 15% from protein, and about 20% to 35% from fat. From these recommendations, the government outlined a new food pyramid, which you can find online at www.mypyramid.gov. Like most government products, the food pyramid is a compromise, and in some ways a concession to, food manufacturers and producers who played a role in its development, because so much food production is federally subsidized and regulated. In fact, we find it hard to give credence to any treatise on living a healthy life that does not even get around to discussing physical activity recommendations until page viii of the Executive Summary. Physical activity is the baseline and everything builds on that.

150

We believe that there are better, healthier alternatives to the government's recommendations, and we specifically embrace those expressed in the book *Eat, Drink, and Be Healthy* by Walter Willett, M.D., of Harvard's School of Public Health.[134] It is a gem of a book — science-based, but easy to understand — and filled with useful information from studies done around the globe on the actual choices people make that enhance health. We recommend that everyone get and read Dr. Willett's book; until you do that, however, here are our comments.

- Build your daily diet around fruits and vegetables and eat them in abundance. Fresh, frozen, or canned vegetables in virtually any form (except breaded, fried, or creamed) are a nutritional blessing and a goldmine of good things ... fiber, vitamins, minerals, phytochemicals, and even water.[135] A plate of vegetables, sautéed or lightly grilled in olive oil, is a terrific foundation for any meal. Eating veggies on the run is also easier to do these days, as grocery produce departments overflow with bags and containers of cut, washed, ready-to-eat fruits and vegetables.[136] Don't diminish the benefits of eating vegetables, however, by drenching them in fat-laden dressings. Low-fat dressings are better options, as are olive oil/canola oil, balsamic or red wine vinegar, or fresh lemon or lime juice.

  We also recommend that everyone use the face-of-a-clock imagery for meal planning. Imagine your plate as a clock. Fill it from 12:00 noon to 6:00 with vegetables, both raw (salad, for example) and cooked (lightly steamed, sautéed, grilled, broiled, or roasted). From 6:00 to 9:00, have your lean protein (discussed in greater detail later); and, finally from 9:00 to 12:00 a whole grain carbohydrate. If you combine this approach with using a slightly downsized dinner plate, you will start the process of changing both the quality and quantity of your daily consumption. A typical dinner plate is about 11 inches in diameter; try using an appetizer plate, about 9 inches in diameter

151

instead. Unless you are trying to win an engineering prize by seeing how high you can stack your food, you will put substantially less food on the smaller plate than the larger one. Further, if you try this approach and stick to it, you will likely find that you fill up more quickly because fruits and vegetables, with their high water and fiber content, fill you up, leaving less room for other things.[137]

If you start meals with vegetables (green salads, vegetable-based soups, or fruit salads), and snack on these things as well, you are much more likely to get a satisfying sensation of fullness when you eat. This is called "satiety" and is essential to long-term weight loss. If you never feel full, you are likely to continue consuming foods that you don't need, such as refined grains (see below). Fruits and vegetables, with their fiber and water content, help with satiety.

- Enjoy carbohydrates ... just eat the right ones. The notion that carbohydrates are uniformly bad for you is foolish and unsubstantiated. Carbohydrates are an essential source of fuel and important nutrients, especially fiber. Your body converts carbohydrates into fuel for living and moving more easily than it does fats or proteins. Nothing is a better fuel for exercise, by the way, than carbohydrates. Since our primary objective is healthy, vigorous physical activity, it is important to consider carbohydrate consumption in that context. About 50% to 60% of your total daily caloric intake should come from carbohydrates.

There are important differences between carbohydrates. We recommend that you keep to a minimum consumption of refined grains. Examples of refined grains include the vast majority of baked goods, such as cakes, pies, white breads, cookies, pastries, and the like. The better carbohydrate options are whole grains, which have not been stripped of their vitamin, mineral, and fiber content. It is important for you to shoot for a daily fiber intake of 25 to 30 grams. Food labels all identify the fiber content. The more you can do to get refined grains — and conventional

152

white potatoes — out of your diet, the better. You will be much better off with an emphasis on whole grains, sweet, and gold-flesh potatoes.

Today, you can find a wide variety of whole grain bread and cereals and many made from grains other than wheat. Other whole grains include oats, spelt, bulgur wheat, quinoa, amaranth, barley, or wild rice. If you are uncertain about whether a product contains whole grains look at the ingredient list ... the first word of the first ingredient should be WHOLE (as in WHOLE wheat, WHOLE oats, and so on). Look also at the amount of fiber per serving. A bread made with whole wheat will have at least 3 to 4 grams of fiber per slice (1 slice = 1 serving). Breads made from refined grains (white breads and some wheat breads) have a gram or less. The more fiber in the product, the closer it is to its natural state and the less processing it has undergone. In other words, it is closer to its natural state in God's garden than is a product that has been stripped of nearly everything that makes it worth eating. Whole grains reduce the risk of heart disease,[138] [139] [140] [141] and some whole grains, such as oatmeal, actually can lower your blood cholesterol level when eaten regularly.

- Start every day with a healthy breakfast. This is essential to long-term weight management. Build your daily breakfast around a fruit, non-fat or low-fat dairy or soy beverages, and heart healthy whole grain breads and cereals. Good options are old-fashioned or quick cooking oatmeal (from the cylindrical packages, not the sugar-laden pouches); good quality cold cereals, such as Quaker Oat Squares, plain Cheerios, Kashi products, and others that supply about 150 calories per serving, are low in sodium and fat, and supply at least 3 grams of fiber and 6 or more grams of protein. If you eat on the run or snack at work, the cold cereals are a great option. You may find it helpful over the course of a day to eat several small, well-balanced meals (essentially large snacks). This may help keep your hunger at bay.

153

- Fat matters ... in a good way. Fat is essential for life. Fats are critical to the makeup of cell membranes, the functioning of your nervous and endocrine systems, your cardiovascular system, and they are a source of fuel, particularly for long-term endurance exercise. While no one's diet should derive more than 20% to 30% of total daily calories from fat, what matters more is what kind of fat you eat.

    a. Saturated fats will kill you. The easiest way to tell if a fat is saturated or not is whether it is solid at room temperature ... think of butter and beef, chicken, or pork fat. Whole milk products also contain significant saturated fat, as do coconut milk and palm oil. When you eat saturated fats, you contribute to your risk of heart disease because you raise your LDL (bad) cholesterol. You should limit your saturated fat intake to no more than 5% to 7% of your total daily caloric intake; the less the better. While saturated fats also raise your HDL (good) cholesterol, eating them is not a particularly savvy way to elevate HDL.

        For many people, this means making a big shift in eating habits, moving away from beef, pork, and dark meat poultry to fish, or lean skinless white poultry and using different ingredients in cooking — switching, for example, from butter to olive oil to sauté vegetables. You literally can live without both saturated fats and trans fats (see p. 155). Fried foods are typically very high in saturated fats and we strongly encourage that people reduce their intake of fried foods to zero, or as close to that as they can get.

    b. Monounsaturated fats are good for you. Monounsaturated fats help manage the fats and cholesterol in your blood which, in turn, helps reduce your risk of heart disease. You can find monounsaturated fats in avocados; olive, canola, and peanut oils; peanuts and peanut butter; almonds; and walnuts. These fats are liquid at room temperature (obviously, the monounsaturated fats in nuts are bound inside the nut). More importantly, they do two good things when you eat them. They help lower LDL cholesterol and raise HDL. Olive oil does this particularly well. It even exerts a protective antioxidant effect in your bloodstream, helping to lower the amount of oxidized LDL cholesterol in your blood.[142] (Oxidized cholesterol is cholesterol that has reacted with oxygen and become more likely to contribute to a blockage of an artery than cholesterol that is not oxidized. Thus, it is a key culprit in heart disease.)

c. Polyunsaturated fats are also good for you. You can find these in safflower, corn, flaxseed and flaxseed oil, and soybean oils as well as fish. These, too, help raise HDL and lower LDL. Especially important are omega-3 and omega-6 fatty acids, which you must get from food, because your body cannot otherwise produce them.

d. Trans fats are more artery clogging junk. Trans fats are unsaturated fats that have been chemically modified ("partially hydrogenated" is what the label says) to make them more stable and suitable for use in a wide variety of products from many readily available margarines, to Crisco shortening, chips, and fried foods. As we noted above, fried foods are terrible for you, and we urge you to avoid them altogether. These fats add to the heart disease burden, because relative to unsaturated fats, they raise your LDL.

The trans fat issue has recently been improved because, in a moment of rare inspiration and common sense, the US Food and Drug Administration changed food labeling requirements to compel disclosure of the trans fat content in packaged foods. Now, as consumer awareness of the issue rises, companies are running to reformulate their foods to get the trans fats out so that they can list "0" trans fats on the label.[143] It's amazing

155

the effect that mandatory disclosure can have on corporate behavior. Too bad they did not do this simply because it was the right thing to do. We don't think people are stupid ... it may take some getting used to the "new" taste of your favorite cookie, but we suspect most thoughtful people would rather make that adjustment than the one that comes with dealing with the consequences of a premature heart attack.

- Use protein to your advantage. Protein is the essential nutrient for building strong, healthy muscles. Most Americans get more than enough protein in their diets to meet all their daily needs, including more than enough to build healthy muscle from strength training. Good sources of protein include seafood, skinless white meat poultry, non-fat or low-fat diet dairy products, soy products, eggs and egg substitutes (such as Egg Beaters), nuts and nut butters (but, remember they also have a high fat content so use sparingly), lentils, chick peas, beans of all varieties, and even whole grains.[144] You should get about 15% of your daily calories from protein, but be aware that you can safely increase that to 20%, according to the Institute of Medicine. You should not, however, increase your protein intake if you have kidney disease or another ailment that may affect your kidneys, such as diabetes. Increased protein in your diet can stress your kidneys and you should not increase protein intake without first discussing such a step with your doctor or a registered dietitian.

  A final note about protein. Recent research indicates that it may be a very useful tool for weight loss. If you slightly increase your protein intake, and reduce your saturated fat and refined carbohydrate consumption, you may find that you will spontaneously eat somewhat fewer calories, and, thus, lose weight or keep it off.[145] [146] Protein is filling and takes longer to digest, which is why it may help blunt your appetite.

Step Four: Supplement sparingly.

Our culture is fascinated with supplements ... from children who think they need protein supplements to succeed at sports to middle-aged adults who will unthinkingly swallow every pill, powder, potion, or gel that claims health benefits ... and most of it is useless swill.

- Let's start with a clear understanding of the difference between the supplements industry and other manufacturers. Thanks to a powerful lobby and a complicit US Congress, in 1994 the supplements industry was almost completely deregulated, which is the polar opposite of the regulatory authority that the Food & Drug Administration exerts over food producers and how they label their products. Thus, supplement manufacturers can say virtually anything they want about a product, as long as they do not claim that it prevents, cures, or treats a disease. This leaves a lot of wiggle room, and, within this context, supplement manufacturers often dance tantalizingly close to making health claims. For example, pick up a bottle of vitamin E capsules at any grocery store and you will often see a claim that the product "supports heart health" or something quite similar. It is a statement so vague that it is substantively meaningless, but it is also so appealing that it virtually beseeches you to buy the product. The claim is not backed by studies or a consensus of expert opinion. In fact, quite the opposite, as studies of the value of vitamin E supplementation to prevent heart disease conflict, and there is not a shred of evidence that supplementation will reverse heart disease.

  Over the past several months, there have been several studies showing that vitamin E supplementation — for both athletes and non-athletes — is useless.[147] Despite this, supplement manufacturers want consumers to believe that vitamin E supplements still have prospects as disease prevention tools ... even though they have *no evidence* to support their view. More to the point, they often

157

criticize studies done in people who already have a chronic disease, such as heart disease, saying that researchers need to evaluate the effect of vitamin E in people who are healthy ... this is an illogical position. In a population of healthy adults, who are otherwise at low risk of heart disease, it would take an extremely large and lengthy study to show any benefit. Indeed, in a broadly healthy population, we would not expect to see much risk reduction at all from something such as pedestrian as vitamin supplementation.

• Contrast the vitamin E claim with the labeling for two important foods with proven health benefits — oats and plant sterols. A wide variety of products made with whole oats — such as the popular Quaker Oats and Cheerios cereals — carry a health claim on their labels that oats can reduce cholesterol. Likewise, two relatively new butter substitutes — Take Control® and Benecol® — carry a health claim that their noteworthy ingredient, plant sterols, can also reduce blood cholesterol levels.[148] In both these cases, the claims are backed by real science: clinical studies completed in a rigorous fashion, published in credible scientific journals, and reviewed and approved by the nutrition scientists at the FDA. Barley has recently also received FDA permission for a health claim, and it is shown in studies to reduce cholesterol.[149] The difference between the two approaches should be clear ... supplements that claim a vast array of unproven, and often scientifically implausible benefits versus real, whole foods that can actually make a difference in your health. Whole foods, eaten in modest, carefully considered quantities are the surest path to a healthy weight, heart health, and sufficient fuel for plenty of physical activity.

• Unless you have a documented nutrient deficiency, it is highly unlikely that you need, or will benefit from, anything supplemental other than a simple daily multivitamin. Many people who want to lose or manage their weight by eating a somewhat calorie restricted diet (which, by the way, includes both of us), can provide themselves with a bit of nutritional insurance by taking a daily multivitamin. You should look for the least expensive generic vitamin you can find, typically a store brand rather than a name brand, which provides 100% of the recommended value of most of vitamins and minerals you need daily in a single pill. A typical, healthy active adult does not need "mega" or "super" doses of any nutrient, especially given that there is no research to support their use. Beware, however, that even a simple daily vitamin is not a panacea. There is little or no compelling evidence that taking vitamins actually prevents disease.[150] [151] While current or future clinical trials may shift this thinking, the present data are insufficient to make solid recommendations about vitamin consumption. Our recommendation to take a simple multivitamin is based on the rationale that by eating a calorie restricted diet, you may limit your intake of some nutrients; a vitamin can help compensate to ensure that you do not develop a deficiency.

Also, make sure that the label contains the letters USP. USP stands for United States Pharmacopeia, which is a not-for-profit organization in Rockville, Maryland. The USP sets standards for the drug and supplements industry. When a label shows USP, the manufacturers is certifying that the vitamin meets USP standards for purity of ingredients and for its ability to disintegrate in your stomach. After all, if the pill or tablet does not dissolve properly, it is not going to do much good for you. A surprising number of vitamins do not say USP on the label. Generally speaking, you can help facilitate absorption of the vitamins and minerals if you take the tablet after a meal.

If you do not eat dairy, soy, or fortified grains, you may need an additional supplement to ensure that you get about 1,000 milligrams of calcium daily to support both bone and muscle health. If you use a calcium supplement, remember that there are two predominant kinds: calcium citrate and calcium carbonate (such as is found in the Tums or calcium-rich Rolaids). Calcium citrate is more readily absorbed, but you need to consume more of them to meet your supplement needs. Calcium carbonate is less well absorbed, but you can boost its uptake by using it after meals. Talk to your physician or a registered dietitian for more guidance on your specific calcium needs, especially if you are a woman who has, or is at-risk for, osteoporosis.

Step Five: Cultivate your love of reading ... food labels, that is.

Today, nothing is more essential to good nutrition than knowing how to read a food label. All packaged foods sold in the US have a nutrition facts label that discloses calorie content, as well as information about the protein, carbohydrate, fat, and vitamin and mineral content. Below is a sample food label, downloaded from the website of the US FDA, the federal agency that oversees product labeling.

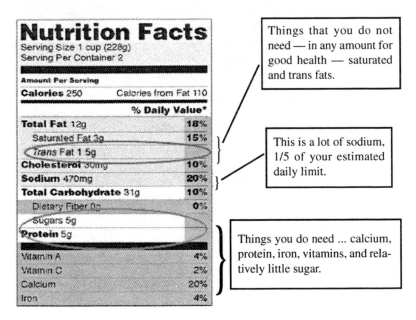

Source: US FDA at http://vm.cfsan.fda.gov/~dms/foodlab.html. Downloaded via Yahoo on 3/28/2006.

As you can see, this label tells you a great deal about the food that you are about to eat, but not everything. In particular, it tells you that if you eat this product, you will have eaten about 18% of your total intake of fat calories for the day.[152] To learn how many fat calories there are in this product, however, you must do some math. At 12 grams of fat, with 9 calories per gram, this product has 108 calories from fat, 43% of the total calories in the product. Further, one-quarter of the fat calories come from saturated fat and half of those come from worthless and dangerous trans fats. In addition, this product has 31 grams of carbohydrates (124 calories at 4 calories per gram), 5 grams of protein (20 calories at 4 calories per gram), but no fiber, so we know that the carbohydrates are NOT whole grain. Finally, it has 20% of the recommended amount of sodium you should eat ... a critical factor if you have high blood pressure, because most people get more sodium than they need.

So, as you can see, a food label does not tell the whole story ... in order to get a full understanding of the nutritional makeup of a food, you need to do some of the math yourself. Despite this limitation, knowing how to read and interpret a food label will go a long way toward helping you become a wiser food consumer. Build your food label reading skills by looking at different product labels when you shop and comparing them. You will rapidly learn to discern important differences in things such as sugar, protein, fat, trans fat, and calcium content. We do not know what this product is, but we are not impressed with it from a nutritional perspective ... lots of fat and sodium and no fiber for a relatively paltry amount of protein and calcium.

Step Six: Drink merrily and moderately.

If you do not drink alcohol, this diet is NOT a reason to start. If you do drink alcohol, we want you to make sure that you drink moderately, which is defined as one or two drinks daily for a man or one drink daily for a woman (a drink is a 12-ounce beer, a 4- to 5-ounce glass of wine, or about 1.5 ounces of distilled spirits, such as scotch or gin). Pregnant women should NEVER drink. The wine industry wants you to believe that there is something special in their product that can prevent heart disease. There is, as yet, no consensus on this issue. It may be that it is simply the alcohol itself that offers a benefit, by helping to reduce inflammation in your blood vessels and lower the likelihood that your blood will clot and block a coronary artery.[153] Alcohol may also help increase HDL. If you drink now and cannot limit your intake to the amounts articulated above, get professional help.

Step Seven: Enjoy your food.

Food should be fun. Nothing is more reflective of our success as a species than the incredible array of foods that we produce. However, with our persistent search for the perfect diet, the widespread dissemination of countless myths, half-truths, and gimmicks, and our use of food as a means to self-medicate, we have made eating into a kind of personal torture. We have forgotten how to savor what we eat, and, simultaneously, be grateful for both the food and the good company of family, friends, coworkers, or even strangers. Make time to eat with family and friends at least once a day and do it without the blather of the television or the hum of a hard drive.

Make it a point to try new foods regularly, even revisiting something that you may not have enjoyed so much at an earlier time; do this especially for fruits, vegetables, and whole-grain products. Be an adventurous cook and take advantage of the internet to research creative ways to prepare foods that can build health at the same time, such as finding recipes that use olive oil instead of butter, fresh seafood instead of beef or pork, and whole rather than refined grains.

Most importantly, take time to eat the things you really like, but learn to use moderation and control as your guides. Don't be an automaton — think about what you are eating and why. A beer is not a bad thing ... a six pack in one sitting is. A slice of pizza is not a bad thing ... three slices might be ... an occasional soda is not going to unravel your diet ... three cans daily surely will. Balance, moderation, and good decision-making are the foundations of a wise, healthy, lifelong approach to good diet.

Recognize also that we all eat in patterns or constellations. We may like to eat chips while drinking beer, munch nuts with soda, or always have a baked potato when eating a steak. Thus, in many instances throughout the course of a day, it is not only solitary foods that cause problems, but the eating patterns that they drive. This is why it is so important not to think about being on a diet, but to really, fundamentally, alter the way you think about food. Our eating patterns, perhaps traditions passed to us by family and friends, are comfortable and familiar, but over the long term, can prove harmful. The challenge is to learn how to reconfigure your approach to meals, and to use strategic thinking — the same thing that helps you succeed in other facets of your life — to help leverage nutrition as a tool that can alter your health-risk factors. Your diet diary, Dr. Willett's book, and staying on top of good nutrition research, not marketing claims, will go a long way in helping you reach this goal.

To summarize this section, then, we offer the following table on the evidence to support a Mediterranean-style diet versus the other commercial diet programs whose costs we highlighted earlier. We think that, between costs and benefits, your choice is evident in black and white.

Diet name	Lowers your oxidized LDL (bad) cholesterol	Lowers your risk of heart disease	Improves longevity	Helps with weight loss	Lowers blood pressure
The Mediterranean Diet	YES	YES	YES	YES	YES
Atkins	?	?	?	?	?
Jenny Craig	?	?	?	?	?
NutriSystem	?	?	?	?	?
Ornish	?	?	?	?	?
Slim Fast	?	?	?	?	?
South Beach	?	?	?	?	?
Subway	?	?	?	?	?
Sugar Busters	?	?	?	?	?
Weight Watchers	?	?	?	?	?
Zone	?	?	?	?	?

The Spiritual Value Of Slow Food

The story is told of the day the pope received a call from a McDonald's executive. The fast-food giant wanted to make a gift of $1 billion to the church, in exchange for one small concession.

From now on, the Lord's Prayer would have to read, "Give us this day our daily hamburger."

Naturally, the pope was horrified, and refused to accept this offer. But the executive was persistent, the amount of the gift was increased, and finally the pope reluctantly agreed. Calling together the College of Cardinals, the pope announced, "I've got some good news and some bad news. The good news is that McDonald's is giving us a gift of $5 billion. The bad news is that we've lost the Wonder Bread account."

Sure, we laugh at "daily hamburgers" and "Wonder Bread accounts" — but Big Macs are no joke. At least, not in Italy these days, where one theologian is asking the very serious question: Are hamburgers a sin?

A Roman Catholic priest from Tuscany has added fuel to the fires of Italy's debate over fast food by condemning the hamburger, French fries, and cola as "the fruit of a Protestant culture."

"Fast food reflects the individualistic relation between man and God introduced by Luther," the Reverend Massimo Salani said in a full-page interview published in a Catholic daily newspaper. In addition, he insisted that fast food lacks "the community aspect of sharing." With Italians deeply divided over the arrival of McDonald's and other fast-food chains in a country that takes its three-hour lunches almost as seriously as soccer, other newspapers leapt on the story with obvious glee.

"Theologian Excommunicates the Hamburger," proclaimed a headline in a Rome paper. "The individualistic relation between man and God, started by Luther, is also reflected in the world of eating," said the priest. But his venom was not directed only toward Protestants — the Father also criticized Catholics who eat too much, and Muslims who do not have "a balanced diet."[154]

Perhaps the priest is right: We have a preference for the wrong style of eating, wolfing down super-sized quarter-pounders, fries, and colas in an effort to quickly gratify the desires of the flesh. In his letter to the Galatians, the apostle Paul warns us about those actions which simply make our earthly flesh feel good, and he gives us a menu of tasty and tempting vices that he knows are hard to

resist: fornication, impurity, licentiousness, idolatry, sorcery, enmities, strife, jealousy, anger, quarrels, dissensions, factions, envy,
drunkenness, and carousing (Galatians 5:19-21). Quite a selection.
Would you like fries with that?

This is not the nourishment that God wants us to take in. "Live
by the Spirit," says Paul, "and do not gratify the desires of the
flesh" (v. 16). Resist the fleeting feelings of satisfaction that come
from gulping down a meal made up of one or more of these vices:
fornication, licentiousness, drunkenness, and carousing. Just say
"no thanks" to sorcery, strife, quarrels, dissensions, and envy. Stay
away from the temptations of impurity, idolatry, enmities, factions,
jealousy, and anger.

Admit it. You know that even *anger* can be tempting and can
satisfy our human hunger for a moment or two. In fact, observes
author Frederick Buechner, anger is possibly the most fun of the 7
deadly sins. Yes, the most fun. "To lick your wounds, to smack
your lips over grievances long past, to roll over your tongue the
prospect of bitter confrontations still to come, to savor to the last
toothsome morsel both the pain you are given and the pain you are
giving back — in many ways it is a feast fit for a king."

But anger is not very nutritious. The chief drawback, says
Buechner, is that what you are wolfing down is yourself.[155]

So let's resist these cheap and easy fast-food vices, and focus
instead on the fruit of the Spirit. Paul wants us to fill ourselves with
qualities that can truly nourish us and help us to grow into the
spiritually healthy and vigorous people that God wants us to be.
The fruits we are invited to feast on are "love, joy, peace, patience,
kindness, generosity, faithfulness, gentleness, and self-control" (vv.
22-23). These qualities can fill us, satisfy us, and strengthen us —
and best of all, no spiritual dietitian or gastronomic theologian will
say that such fruit is bad for you. Go ahead, eat all you want. Stuff
yourself to the bursting point. Paul insists that there "is no law
against such things" (v. 23).

The fruit of the Spirit is good food, not fast food. The fruit of
the Spirit is never going to be a hamburger — if, by a hamburger,
we mean an entree that is cooked, wrapped, and rushed to a raven-
ous customer in a matter of minutes. No, the fruit we should be

166

interested in is slow food, food that takes time to cultivate and develop, food that is not going to be available at a quick and convenient drive-through window.

If the fruit of the Spirit is good food, then yes — a hamburger *is* a sin. And maybe it deserves to be excommunicated.

In our ever-accelerating world, we should take the time to focus on the slow and careful growth of spiritual fruit. The art of living — especially Christian living — is about learning how to give time to each and every thing — love, joy, peace, patience, kindness, generosity, faithfulness, gentleness, and self-control. These things take time, but they are the best possible investment of the time we are given.

They also require community. Christianity is based on a shared communion meal and life together in the body of Christ — not on fast-food pit stops and individualistic approaches to the faith. It is within the community that Paul challenges us to become "slaves to one another" through love, resisting the temptation to use our Christian freedom "as an opportunity for self-indulgence" (v. 13).

It's like the Italian theologian said: Fast food lacks "the community aspect of sharing." Fast food is as deficient as "fast faith" — an approach to Christianity that is rushed, individualistic, and overly simplified.

Let's spend our time wisely, and spend it together, cultivating the fruit of the Spirit and creating a healthy rhythm for our lives. Give time to each and every thing that matters, and stop wasting time on activities that consume us, and add little value to life.

Fast food approaches have got to go, at least in a life of faith and fitness that is good and slow.

Your Action Steps From Commandment Five

1. Take a family field trip to the grocery store, and compare the produce section to the meat aisle.

2. Calculate your estimated daily caloric needs and start planning this week's meals with our face-of-a-clock strategy.

3. Make a list of the foods you presently eat that you can reduce or eliminate from your diet. These include refined grains, red meat, or products high in saturated or trans fats.

4. Have a slow family meal together, one that reflects the gifts of the Spirit, "love, joy, peace, patience, and kindness." Turn off the television, radio, iPod, BlackBerry, and enjoy a quiet meal together.

Commandment Six

Thou Shalt Raise The Bar

Overcoming Emotional And Intellectual Limitations

It is inevitable. No matter how closely you hew to the guidelines we offer for both faith and fitness, you will eventually make mistakes, become complacent, or find yourself frustrated with your progress. These things are natural and happen to even the most experienced, determined, and diligent people. Can you imagine that Lance Armstrong never had a bad day on his bike? Or, that Vince Lombardi never made a bad decision while patrolling the sidelines of his beloved Green Bay Packers? Of course not. The issue is not that bad days, mistakes, and lapses in judgment happen; rather it is to place them in proper perspective, learn from them, repair damage done, and, finally, strategize ways to prevent repeating them. Ultimately, that is the challenge in all life's pursuits ... how do you get better at repeating the things that are good for you and not repeating the things that you know set you back or cause problems?

Even the people most committed to faith and fitness find that their disciplines do not guarantee a series of mountaintop experiences. "I do not 'enjoy' exercising," admits Tom Larsen, an aerospace engineer who has been a member of Vik and Henry's faith and fitness class at Fairfax Presbyterian Church. "I probably never exercise hard enough to get a rush of endorphins. Unless someone else who got to the exercise room ahead of me has already set the television station, I always turn to CNBC and watch the financial news, hoping to learn something. As a result, I can't say that exercising is a spiritual experience for me, other than based on my belief that our body is God's temple, so we should take good care of it."

Tom may not get a great deal of pleasure out of his workouts, but he is committed to them, and his physical fitness is clearly improving through his regular endurance exercise, especially his

169

newfound interest in strength training. Tom's exercise routine has not led to any surprising spiritual insights, but it has been a faithful expression of his belief that his body is God's temple — a structure deserving care and respect. Although Tom may be disappointed that his exercising has not felt like a "spiritual experience" to him, in fact it has been a profound experience of devoted, daily care for God's gift of the human body. Faithful living is really all about performing quiet, low-key, health-improving routines, rather than experiencing loud and dramatic "quick-fix" transformations.

In this relatively brief chapter, we will ask you to deepen your understanding of the psychological and emotional aspects of exercise and nutrition, as well as to challenge yourself to overcome your emotional and intellectual limitations — because doing so is essential to eventually achieving your fitness goals. We take this approach because we believe firmly that in order to make good choices you must undertake a rational, analytic process that allows you to differentiate from among the options before you. Useful, health-giving choices come, first and foremost, from useful, critical, health-seeking thoughts.

This is not an approach for the weak, because it requires considerable introspection, an ability to admit — to yourself and God — your shortcomings and mistakes, and, consequently, a commitment to overcoming them through work. Consistent with our approach elsewhere in this book, we will not offer you a quick fix of any kind ... rather, we can only help guide you along a difficult, challenging, but finally rewarding path to personal betterment.

The Stages Of Exercise Adoption

There is no universal truth about the people who succeed at exercise, other than being physically active is remarkably good for you. Some are born to it and love the feelings and physical changes that come from moving, sweating, and persistently chasing one goal after another. Others of us, such as Tom Larsen — probably the majority, but we cannot quantify this belief — have to work at it. We struggle to find the right combination of activities, work hard at learning new things and improving our skills, and go through the roller coaster process of lurching from complete fealty to our

170

exercise program on the one hand to feeling miserable about every workout we miss on the other.

We (the two authors of this book) probably fall somewhere in the middle of this spectrum. Neither of us claims any athletic prowess at all, and we readily admit to being virtually incompetent at the kinds of competitive team sports that captivate our national consciousness. We are, however, both highly fit. Henry is a marathon runner, while Vik is a weight lifter of 30 years standing, an avid road cyclist, and runner. Both of us have fitness levels that put us in the 80th to 90th percentile for men our age, meaning that, based on normative data, we are more fit than 80% to 90% of men in our age group (forty to fifty). In turn, this also dramatically cuts our risk for a wide range of potentially deadly or disabling diseases. We got to this point not because of any particular abundance of physical gifts, but largely by dint of planning, hard work, and lots of trial and error.

Fitness is not a realm only for the athletically charmed; it is a place with room for everyone who is willing to dedicate himself or herself to the hard work it takes to get there. In this way, we find that faith and fitness are perfect metaphors for one another. In fact, you can likely take comfort from the fact that by the time you finish with this program, you will probably be better versed about *fitness* than most people who come out of the culture of competitive athletics. Training for competition is different from learning how to be fit, strong, and make good nutritional choices. Indeed, studies of competitive athletes show that upon leaving sports, they regress to the mean in terms of body weight (they get fat, too), because no one teaches them how to translate their years of regimented training into a sensible eating and exercise plan that fits with living a normal working life.

In too many churches today, young people prepare for their confirmations as though they were training for competition. They work hard, pass their required classes, become adult members of the congregation — and then fall into religious inactivity. This is not a good program for lifelong faith development, and it does little to prepare young people to be spiritually healthy and active as adults.

It is far better for churches to offer confirmation classes that include the mentoring of young people by older, spiritually mature members of the congregation. Following a program developed by William Willimon, the former campus minister at Duke University, many churches across the country have paired young people with adults who are particularly active members of the congregation, and asked these teams to talk, study, worship, and perform service projects together. Churches encourage these pairs to move beyond theological book work to gain an understanding of what it means to be a committed, faithful Christian today. Significant relationships develop, and then young people move forward alongside a person who can continue to help them to be spiritually fit, strong, and able to make good choices.

In exercise science literature, there are several psychological theories in play about how people develop successful, long-term exercise habits. If you wish to read a detailed review of them, we strongly recommend a chapter in the American College of Sports Medicine's *Resource Manual for Guidelines for Exercise Testing and Prescription*.[156] However, for the purposes of this chapter, we want to concentrate on one specific theory, because to us it exemplifies the way that people move through many aspects of life: considering options, making mistakes, and suffering relapses into undesirable behaviors, and then, ultimately, shifting strategies and finding success. This theory is called the transtheoretical model (TTM) and has five stages:

1. Precontemplation
2. Contemplation
3. Preparation
4. Action
5. Maintenance

Stage One: Precontemplation

If you are in this stage, exercise is not yet on your radar screen. And, perhaps you are reading this book to figure whether it should be or how to put it there. In that case, we applaud you. A precontemplator is, as people say, someone who does not yet "get it." If you have not started to consider exercise's importance to your quality of life, we recommend that you go back and re-read the introduction and First Commandment to help put its benefits and the risks of not exercising in proper perspective. Throughout Christian history, there have been precontemplators who have been challenged to abandon an old way of life and embark on a new style of living. "Put away your former way of life, your old self, corrupt and deluded by its lusts," says Paul to the Ephesians. "Put away from you all bitterness and wrath and anger and wrangling and slander, together with all malice, and be kind to one another, tenderhearted, forgiving one another as God in Christ has forgiven you" (Ephesians 4:22, 31-32). Whether we are focusing on faith or fitness, precontemplation is what helps us to make the decision to turn from one style of life to another.

One way to help move out of this stage and into the next one is to start the process of identifying small, achievable goals, which does not necessarily mean abruptly starting physical activity. Rather, you will benefit the most from taking the time to learn, question, research, and then consider what you have learned. A person who is in the precontemplation phase is often someone who still needs to gather useful information about exercise and good diet and process it thoroughly. This is easier said than done in an environment where our media and popular culture often mistake celebrity for credibility. We really do not care about how Brad Pitt works out, nor should you. What you should care about is that there is a growing — and highly credible — body of scientific evidence about why exercise matters, as well as the good, better, best, and worse ways to do it.

So, a good initial goal for a precontemplator is to finish this book. After doing so, we urge you to challenge yourself, raise the bar, and push your learning plateau a little higher. Then, it is time to get out (or start) the exercise and diet diary that we urge everyone to keep. Start your diary with a series of observations ... about yourself. Here is our recommended approach:

- List the 10 most important things you believe you have learned by reading this book. How have we stimulated or changed your thinking about faith and fitness? What have you learned about exercise science that you did not know? About diet? About faith? How have we challenged your thinking and caused you reconsider a previously long-held belief (does lifting weights to a 10-count really do anything for you and are diets that urge eating no fats or no carbs anything other than hype intended to get you to buy something)?

- Now, list out how you think exercise might help you. Be as specific as you can ... for example, exercise might help you manage your day-to-day stress better; it may help you lose weight, improve your cholesterol levels, and avoid going on prescription medications; or, it might give you the physical resources you need to accomplish a long-desired goal, such as running a 10k.

- Next — and this is where the writing gets tough — make a list of the things that you believe impede you from exercising and eating properly. We say that this is tough because it requires a great deal of introspection and honesty. The reasons that people do not adopt exercise are legion ... failure to understand and appreciate its importance, poor guidance on how to exercise properly, disorganized planning and time-management skills, challenges in decision-making and prioritization, and more. What are your reasons for not exercising? The more honest you can be with yourself, the more likely you are to eventually find a way out of this stage. Once you identify your obstacles, you can start to actually conceptualize ways to handle them. Then, you can begin visualizing how to reach your goals. The key to move from this stage to the next one is to start the process of learning and analysis because you will need it not only now, but in the future, even when you finally reach the maintenance stage.

Stage Two: Contemplation

This is the "thinking about it" stage. If you get here, it means that you have absorbed some of the lessons learned in

174

precontemplation, but you are not yet actually moving. This is still a learning stage, but it is a bit more challenging and sophisticated. Contemplation requires that you sort and sift through the information in this book, as well as what you learn from other media, and place it in a context that you can understand. What are the relative advantages and disadvantages of the different exercise options you have before you? What activities do you enjoy or not enjoy? And, if something you don't enjoy is nonetheless necessary and useful, how can you craft a way to do it regardless of your lack of enthusiasm for it? What have you done in the past and really liked? What do friends, family, and coworkers do and seemingly enjoy that might yield an opportunity for you to participate?

Get that diary out again. This time you can make a small table where you can outline the issues and factors that we discuss above. Your table might look something like this:

Activity	Advantages	Disadvantages	Incentives	Notes
Running	Burns calories efficiently; builds heart health and strong bones	Requires good ($$) running shoes; tough to do outdoors in inclement weather	Get to run with friends before work every morning	Can alternate with cycling and hiking for variety
Strength training	Essential to long-term muscle and bone health	Need access to gym or buy weights to keep at home	More self-confidence, energy, and muscular strength	There is no substitute for muscle health

Make your table as long or as short as you need. You can always add to it as you learn about new options. Laying things out in writing this way gives you the baseline you need to start taking an analytical approach to your activity options. Building your comprehension of the relative pluses/minuses of different activities increases the likelihood that you will make rational choices and also find ways to balance your approach. For example, while you may not find the idea of strength training particularly appealing, there really is no substitute for it when it comes to maintaining healthy muscles and bones. Thus, even if it is not your main activity, you can make a rational decision to do it twice weekly, for a brief period, to ensure that you get the benefits. This helps support your devotion to other things that you may enjoy more, such as running, cycling, and walking.

A contemplator needs to absorb an important lesson that all successful exercisers must learn. The quality of life derived from diligent, persistent exercise is not just about doing only the things that you like, but it is also about doing what is necessary. This is anything but the message that our culture sends. In a popular environment suffused with messages about pursuing immediate sensory and sensual gratification — regardless or whether it is right or wrong in any meaningful ethical or moral construct — we all get a warped sense of what the words responsibility and obligation mean. We are a little too taken with the need to "just have fun" or worse still, to "just have fun" and then yak about it endlessly, and we do not sufficiently focus on doing the right thing because it is necessary and appropriate.

There is a wonderful line in one of the Harry Potter movies in which Dumbeldore, the Hogwarts' School headmaster, tells the young wizards that difficult times lie ahead and that each must choose between doing what is right and what is easy. How true. You can take the easy way out and say, for example, "Well, I did not work out today because I was too busy" or you can take the right approach and say to yourself, "I missed my workout today because I did not manage my time well, and I need to learn from today in order to avoid that mistake in the future." One approach lets you duck responsibility while the other requires you to analyze, critique, and change. With the global health care system headed for a likely epidemic of heart disease — driven by the rise in physical inactivity and calorie-rich diets — ducking personal responsibility is an inopportune path to take. You can probably guess which approach we advocate.

176

Stage Three: Preparation

This stage is, quite literally, where you take your first steps. Someone who is in the preparation stage is starting to become active. They may not be very regular about it and may not even be sure exactly what they want to do, but they are taking their first stabs at exercise. The major focus of this stage is to stabilize your approach to exercise from those tentative and perhaps inconsistent first steps to a sound baseline on which you can build. For example, the American College of Sports Medicine recommends that for good health (not necessarily for weight loss or weight management), everyone should be physically active for 30 minutes most or all days of the week.

For someone just moving from contemplation to preparation, this goal might be too aggressive at first. So, you have to be prepared to start small, with an eye toward eventually reaching the ACSM recommended plateau or even exceeding it. This is where your exercise and diet diary once again takes an important place. You can plan your activity here, as well as make notes about how things went when you exercised.

This is the time to also start developing strategies that will help keep you on track. And, they are often very simple. For example, if you exercise at a gym near your office, but find that you frequently forget your gear in the rush out the door each morning, try assembling your workout gear the night before and leaving your pack near your briefcase or in your car, so that you do not even have to think about it the next day. Likewise, if getting in a healthy breakfast is a challenge, try keeping a box or two of good, high-quality whole grain cereals (such as Quaker Oat Squares or plain Cheerios) at your desk; make them and a piece of fruit or low-fat yogurt into your at-work breakfast. The cereals also make great, crunchy snacks and they deliver good nutrition to boot.

When you meet one particular challenge, note that in your exercise and diet diary, and then set a new goal or focus on overcoming the next obstacle. As you reach goals and cross obstacles off your list, you will find yourself — naturally and without even noticing it — coming ever closer to reaching your ultimate, desired exercise and nutrition goals.

177

Stage Four: Action

Now things are getting really physical. For someone at the action stage, regular exercise is now a reality, albeit a short-term one. People at this stage have stuck to their exercise habit for up to six months, and this is a classic good news/bad news scenario. The good news is that you have been regularly active (at your target level) for six months; that also happens to be the bad news because this is probably the point at which you are most at risk for a relapse into inactivity. It can happen because of work pressures, an illness, an injury, or other reasons. And, we assure you, this has happened to the best of us.

One way to minimize the potential disruption from these inevitable events is to plan for them. Developing mini-intervention plans will help give you peace of mind, so that when family, work, or other problems erupt, you will have the resources to stick with your exercise and diet plan, at least for the most part. For example, let's say you try to get out for a 3-mile run three times a week before work, but you know that with a small child at home, some mornings will be just too hectic for you to do so. Beyond the obvious, but difficult, solution (get up before your child does), you might consider running *to* work (if feasible). Or, consider joining a gym near your office and running on a treadmill there on days when your morning plans are foiled, or heading to a park with your family after work every day, where the children can play and you can run or walk. Because the list of potential complications is endless, we cannot envision or write about all of them here. However, we do believe that you can profit by thinking about the few things that are most likely to disrupt your exercise schedule, and then thinking about two strategic approaches to each obstacle. For most people, the complications will boil down, broadly speaking, to work, family, school, illness, and the weather.

Last but not least, at this stage it is important to start setting new, small goals for yourself. The goals can relate to any of the three areas that matter most to your exercise plan: frequency (how often you exercise), intensity (how hard you exercise), or duration (how long you exercise). To prevent lapses, particularly those related to injury or illness, you should ensure that each goal advances

178

your program in small increments and that it is achievable. So, for someone at the action stage who is consistently lifting weights for 30 minutes twice a week, it is inappropriate to set a goal of doubling that lifting time to 60 minutes. A more appropriate and achievable goal is to learn one or two new exercises each week. This expands your strength training repertoire in a manageable way, helps prevent boredom, and keeps workouts fresh and challenging.

With regard to diet, goal setting is also important. But, again, caution is the order of the day. We want you to keep pushing toward adoption of a Mediterranean-style diet, but to do so in small steps. If you have succeeded in reducing saturated fat to less than 7% of your total calorie intake, an appropriate next goal might be to start shifting your carbohydrate consumption from refined products to whole grains. A safe and achievable way to go is to try to ensure that you have a serving of whole grains (such as oatmeal) for breakfast at least 5 days per week.

Stage Five: Maintenance

When you reach this stage, the first thing you should do is pat yourself on the back. You are at the cusp of what it takes to succeed at a healthy, lifelong exercise and nutrition habit. The maintenance stage means that you have sustained your fitness plan for at least six months. If you can do this, you have a much higher chance of lifetime success than someone who bounces back and forth between preparation and action.

For people at the maintenance stage, future success really means remembering the lessons learned at all the other stages and continuing to do these things:

- *Active learning.* Be an active rather than passive consumer of exercise and nutrition information. Assert yourself, ask questions, challenge claims (especially the most outlandish ones), and be a polite but persistent skeptic when someone tells you that they have found (and want you to buy) the magic fitness bullet. You, too, have found the magic bullet ... it is called hard work, with a pinch of planning and a large dose of humility and honesty. In both faith and fitness, personal growth comes from regular, disciplined activity over the course of weeks, months, and years.

- *Relapse prevention.* Life throws curve balls at all of us, and no doubt, one day something will happen for which you do not have a plan of action to preserve your exercise program. That is okay. When the crisis subsides, take time to consider what went wrong and why, learn from it, and move on, making the lessons learned part of your personal strategy going forward. This is a good time to turn to your Covenant Partner for feedback and support.

- *Enjoyment.* People enjoy exercise in vastly different ways. Some love the social aspects, while others (including the two of us) revel in the solitude of a long run, bike ride, or an hour of lifting with no disturbances. Regardless of whether you enjoy activity with friends or on your own, take time during your activity to be present in the moment. Be conscious of what you have accomplished, be grateful for the skills and reason necessary to identify and reach your exercise and nutrition goals, and thank God for giving you the wisdom to take the time to learn how to do things well.

- *Getting better.* Don't be afraid of getting stronger, faster, and better at whatever activity you choose to do. Just remember that the more you push yourself, the closer you come to risking injury. So, you will need to find a balance that lets you get all the enjoyment and performance that you want from your exercise program, but not push yourself to the point where you suffer an injury or get sick. While exercise can boost your immune system, too much can actually depress it and make you more likely to get sick. Discovering and respecting your personal boundaries is a critical part of both physical and spiritual fitness.

Raising The Bar Spiritually

Do you know what rock-climbers love? An "on-sight" ascent.

This term describes your very first attempt to climb a particular rock face. It means that you are the one to lead the climb, and you haven't been given any information about the moves you need to make. No advice, no hints, no tips, and no warnings. "You get one chance for an on-sight," says Jim Collins, an avid rock climber for more than 30 years. "Once you start to climb, if you blow it and fall onto the rope, you've lost the chance forever."[157]

An on-sight ascent. It's thrilling for rock climbers. But it's deadly for those who are trying to reach the next level in their spiritual growth.

Jesus doesn't want any of his followers to have to climb without guidance, so he gives them explicit instructions in Luke 10:1-20. Appointing 70 followers, he divides them into teams of two and sends them on ahead of him into every town and place where he himself intends to go (v. 1). He tells them what to carry, what to say, what to do, and how to respond to various challenges ... including the rude shock of personal rejection. Jesus is sending the 70 on a mission as daunting and as dangerous as a trip up a sheer rock cliff, and he wants them to be extremely well prepared.

Rock climbing "is a sport from which you do not always get a second chance to learn from your mistakes," writes Jim Collins; "death tends to stop the learning process." The very same thing could be said of the spiritual sport that the disciples were playing, since their eventual destination was Jerusalem, a city that "kills the prophets and stones those who are sent to it" (13:34). Because the 70 were well trained by Jesus, they not only survived but actually thrived on their first trip up the mountain. They were well-prepared as they raised the bar in their growth as disciples of Christ.

The words of Jesus are terse and to the point, much like the lessons that Jim Collins gives to would-be rock climbers. We can learn from both Jim Collins and Jesus Christ as we ponder the rock-climbing mission of the 70 and discover what it says to us today. There is wisdom here about raising the bar, and also about discovering and respecting our personal boundaries.

Lesson One: Climb to fallure, not failure. This lesson makes a distinction between "fallure," in which you fall onto your safety rope after using up every mental, physical, and spiritual resource you have, and "failure," in which you give up and let go. The difference is subtle, says Jim Collins, but it is all the difference in the world: "In fallure you fall; in failure, you let go."

181

Jim tells the story of climbing a beautiful sheet of rock called the Crystal Ball, a silver granite wall with a baseball-sized handhold about 50 feet up. Jim attacked the rock and made it to a point about 10 feet below the handhold. There he ran into trouble and made a bad move that lowered his chances of success. He became stressed out and decided to quit, dropping onto his rope in a safe, controlled fall.

Problem is, Jim ended up feeling that he had failed. Not that he failed on the climb, which he later went back to complete, but failed in his mind. When confronted with the moment of commitment, the moment of decision, the moment of intense challenge, he chose failure instead of fallure. He gave up and dropped, instead of pushing on with full commitment.

Jesus challenges his followers to climb to fallure, not failure. He asks them to put their full heart, soul, mind, and strength into the mission that lies before them. He doesn't expect them to be seen as winners in every town they enter — in fact, he predicts that some people will welcome them and some will reject them. There are limits and boundaries to what any of us can achieve. Whether they are welcomed or not, Jesus expects his followers to proclaim the kingdom of God. All that matters is total commitment, whether the odds of success are high ... or low.

Where is it that you are accepting failure, instead of fallure? Where in your life are you giving up and dropping without using all of your mental, physical, and spiritual resources? If you push to fallure, you will find that you can be successful even if you never reach the top. If you stretch toward fallure, you will find that you have power you never dreamed of, and opportunities you never envisioned. You might even find, as the 70 did, that you are successful beyond your wildest expectations. "Lord," they shout as they run joyfully back from their mission, "in your name even the demons submit to us!" (10:17).

Climbing to fallure might mean accepting a project at work that will really stretch you, mentally and emotionally.

Climbing to fallure might mean working hard at a difficult relationship, and being willing to learn and grow and make some changes in your own life.

Climbing to failure might mean responding to some troubling developments in your denomination, and being willing to stand up, speak out, and help shape the future of the church.

Climbing to failure might mean traveling to a foreign country to do some mission work, or staying home and repairing the homes of low-income residents in your own neighborhood. Spiritual growth comes through focusing on the needs of others and taking a risk to meet those needs. We raise the bar whenever we step out in faith and follow God into a challenging new opportunity.

Disciples of Jesus know that it's important to climb to failure, using all of their mental, physical, and spiritual resources. When they do, they experience tremendous growth ... and, very often, success.

Lesson Two: Climb in the future, today. This means that we change our frame of mind, and imagine how today's challenges will be faced in the future.

Back in 1979, Jim Collins faced a smooth, slightly overhanging 100-foot slab of red rock in Colorado's Eldorado Canyon. No one had ever free-climbed it before, which meant ascending the rock entirely under the climber's personal power, using ropes only for safety.

It was considered to be an impossible challenge, until Jim realized that the next generation of climbers would undoubtedly conquer it and come to consider it a routine climb. So what did he do? He imagined that the year was 1994 instead of 1979, and he walked into the canyon and tried to picture the rock as a 1990s climber would look at it. With that change in psychology, he managed to climb to the top of the route, amazing many of the best climbers of the day.

Jim succeeded by changing his frame of mind, and so did the disciples who agreed to cure the sick and proclaim the kingdom of God. As run-of-the-mill residents of Galilee, they had no chance of succeeding in this mission, but as followers of Christ there was literally no limit to what they could do. After they returned to Jesus with joy, he said, "I watched Satan fall from heaven like a flash of lightning" — or like an incompetent climber tumbling off a cliff

(v. 18). Clearly, the people who are going to make it to the top are those who conform their minds to the climbing techniques of Jesus.

What does it mean for us to climb in the future, today? It is important for us to change our frame of mind, and imagine how today's challenges will be faced in the future. As followers of Jesus Christ, there is literally no limit to what we can do. When God is with us, as he was with the first 70 disciples, we can have faith that our mission will be successful.

Imagine what your church will look like a quarter-of-a-century from now. That's not too far into the future — only 25 years. The internet will be a constant presence in your life, even more than it is now, and it will be accessible through all kinds of portable devices. The church will use the worldwide web to keep members connected to one another every day of the week, in conversation and in prayer. Community mission will expand as you reach out to the waves of immigrants that will continue to transform your community. Styles of worship will continue to evolve, and some services in 25 years will involve high-tech sights and sounds that you can only dream of at this point. But at the same time, you will be challenged to preserve tradition in your worship services, so that you can provide members with a quiet place to hear the still, small voice of God.

The challenge for each of us, as individuals and as church members, is to climb to fallure — not failure. Our goal is to climb in the future instead of in the present, always focusing our hearts and minds on where Jesus is leading us. If we take these steps, repeatedly raising the bar for ourselves and our congregations, we'll be amazed at the mountains we can conquer.

Your Action Steps From Commandment Six

1. Identify an obstacle to personal fitness that you must overcome, and develop a strategy to surmount it.

2. Lay out a plan for enhancing your performance in an activity you already enjoy.

3. Discuss with your Covenant Partner the difference between "fallure" and "failure" in your spiritual life. Where are you giving God everything you have, and where are you giving up?

4. Imagine what you would like to be like, physically and spiritually, one year from now. Set some goals for endurance exercise, strength training, and nutrition ... as well as for prayer, Bible study, and service to others. Then "climb in the future, today."

Commandment Seven

Thou Shalt Periodize

The Periodization Process

As we get older, we can typically look back on our lives and identify distinct periods that were often characterized by particular events, people, or milestones. Your exercise life should have periods, too. More to the point, the periods in your exercise life are things that you will not only consider in retrospect, but actually plan for in advance. Exercise planning of this sort is known as periodization. Put simply, periodization is the process of planning exercise in a way that makes it as productive as it can be while recognizing the need to allow time for rest and recuperation which, in turn, helps improve your fitness, and reduces the risk of illness and injury. In a periodized approach, there are times when you will work harder and other times when you work less intensely. It is a process of managing key physical activity variables: frequency, intensity, and duration.

The goals of periodization are to not only build fitness, but to also keep your exercise routine fresh through a thoughtful and planned-for infusion of variety. A monotonous exercise routine can wear down and demoralize even the most dedicated person. Periodization is a key way to avoid exercise fatigue, get you more deeply involved in planning and understanding your exercise efforts, and also let you have a taste of how highly accomplished athletes train.

There are many books and scientific papers written about periodization and how to apply it to nearly every conceivable kind of athletic training, from cycling, running, and rowing to weight lifting. Even professional athletes playing team sports use periodization in their training, as surveys of the strength coaches for pro basketball and baseball players show.[158] [159]

Our approach to periodization is "Periodization for everyone." Periodizing an exercise program can become incredibly complex,

187

calling for a detailed understanding of physiology, nutrition, biomechanics, and other esoterica. When you enter that realm, the periodization process is best left for competitive athletes and their coaches. By contrast, however, we believe that periodization is also appropriate for everyone who exercises regularly and has cemented an exercise habit. In most cases, this will include anyone who has stuck with his or her exercise program for at least a year. So, when you can exercise regularly for a period of a year, it is time to periodize your plan going forward. The book that we recommended in Commandment Four, *Optimizing Strength Training* by Kraemer and Fleck, is a lucid and insightful discussion of periodization for strength work. You can also apply the broad principles of varying intensity, frequency, and duration to nearly any physical activity.

To get the most from this process, you must dispense with mythology (such as "no pain, no gain" or "go all out all the time") and be willing to put a bit of time each week into analyzing previous workouts, as well as planning upcoming ones. The periodization process will help you learn about exercise science and understand better how your body adapts to the demands imposed upon it by regular activity. In doing so, we believe that you will discover, among other things, that building strength does not come from trying to lift as much as you can every time you go to the gym. Rather, it comes from gradually increasing the amounts you lift in small increments, occasionally lifting more than you have tried to lift in the past, and then backing off for periods of rest, recuperation, and lighter training. By training in this way, you can learn how to manage the stress of exercise by manipulating four key components of activity:

- Frequency — how often do you exercise
- Duration — how long is each workout (number of minutes)
- Intensity — how hard is the workout
- Rest — how much rest do you get between exercise sessions

A periodized approach will help you manage these components. The key to a successful long-term periodized exercise strategy is to do the majority of your workouts at a relatively modest

188

intensity. This issue gets particularly acute as people age, because older exercisers recover from their workouts more slowly than do younger people. Thus, while a young person may be able to pile high intensity workouts upon one another (regardless of the wisdom of doing so), an older (and, hopefully, more mature) person will not. For the older athlete, high-intensity workouts will be less frequent, but that does not mean that they will be less rewarding. Rather, with the additional rest and low-intensity work, he or she should be able to make each high-intensity workout even more productive.

One way to visualize how your exercise plan may look when you take a periodized approach is to use a bell curve. As you may remember from high school or college statistics, a bell curve shows the normal distribution of data. Most of the data in a bell curve falls under the largest part of the area under the curve. Smaller amounts of data appear at the right or left end of the curve. These extreme areas are typically referred to as outliers.

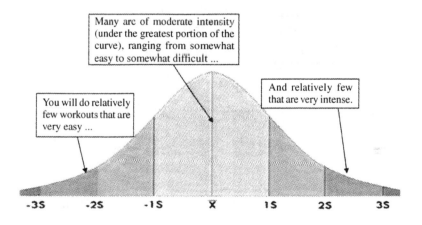

Source for this image of a bell curve: http://www.ap.buffalo.edu/ idea/udny/Sec1images/1-12.jpg. Downloaded 4/26/06.

189

The chart on the previous page is a useful way to visualize the periodization for everyone. Most of your workouts would fall into the shaded areas from -2S to 2S. A few would be very easy, from -2S to -3S and a few would be very hard, from 2S to 3S. Thus, on a day-to-day basis, your exercise would vary around X, which represents, for our purposes, an average or moderate level of intensity. Using the RPE scale of 0 to 11, most of your workouts should be in the range of 3 to 6, with occasional forays into greater intensity levels.

To demonstrate our points, let's create a hypothetical aspiring exerciser, a fifty-year old man ("Sam"), who wants to do 45-minute walks or walk/jogs 4 times every week and will also lift weights twice weekly.[160] For endurance exercise, he should start by understanding what his theoretical maximum heart rate (MHR) is — it is 170 (220 - 50 = 170). Following the recommendations of the ACSM, he should exercise at about 70% of his MHR in most workouts or about 119 beats per minute (bpm). As we have already discussed, he can judge the intensity of his workouts by either using a heart-rate monitor or the Talk Test. At this point, he now knows all of the key components of a periodized program — frequency (4 times weekly), duration (45 minutes), and intensity (an average heart rate of 119 bpm). By design, he also knows that he will have three days of rest from endurance work each week; he will lift weights two of those days.

To periodize this program, then, requires understanding how to vary the workouts successfully so that our exerciser can get the most out of them to lose weight and build long-term heart health. His target heart rate of 119 bpm is an average heart rate for a walk or walk/jog because, in reality, his heart rate will vary during any walk, due to changes in terrain, pace, and stride length, among other things. His heart rate will rise when he walks up a hill and drop when he walks downhill. Likewise, if he quickens his pace or lengthens his stride, it will impose a greater demand on his cardiovascular system and also raise his heart rate. His heart rate will also go up if he leaves pavement and decides to do a hike on a wooded trail where the terrain is more challenging and may require climbing over logs, rocks, or other obstacles.

190

In a typical week, he should shoot for an average heart rate of about 70% to 75% of his maximum heart rate (about 120 to 128 bpm) across all of his walks. However, in order to build heart health, it is important to spend some time working harder. In addition, more intense exercise burns a greater number of calories, which will help Sam lose weight. On his "hard" days, he may want to shoot for spending some time at 80% or 85% of his maximum heart rate (136 bpm and 145 bpm, respectively), translating to an RPE of perhaps 6 or 7. How much time he can spend at the higher heart rates will depend on his fitness level. A more fit person will be able to exercise at the higher intensity level for a longer period of time, while a novice or less fit person will have to start out with modest periods of high-intensity exercise (a couple of minutes at most) and build up gradually.

One way to periodize this program is for Sam to try to do his first and third walks of each week at higher intensity and his second and fourth ones at slightly lower intensity, giving him the chance to intersperse relatively hard and easy endurance exercise days. This is a *daily* approach to periodization. He can vary workout intensity at his own pace, and, as he builds fitness, further increase time or distance to accommodate his newfound strength and capacity. Thus, he may ultimately reach the point where he is able to do most of his exercise at 75% (128 bpm) to 80% (136 bpm) of his maximum heart rate and, on a hard day, reach 90% of maximum (153 bpm) even if it is only for a brief time. An alternative approach is to periodize on a weekly basis; in a weekly periodization approach, Sam would work at each intensity for a week at a time, moving from light to moderate to difficult over three weeks and then perhaps taking a few days off before starting the cycle over again. Over time, when Sam returns to baseline to start the cycle over again, he will eventually find that he can increase the intensity of each level of activity. That is, his low-intensity training may now take place at 60% of MHR rather than 50%, moderate intensity is 75% instead of 70%, and difficult training lets him push his heart rate to 90% of MHR for brief periods.

You will notice that we built a rest period into Sam's program. Rest is critically important to general health and fitness. We will talk more about it in the next chapter. Rest has an important place in any periodization discussion, because rest is one of your body's most important tools for adapting to the stress of exercise and gradually getting stronger and more fit. Thus, you must plan for it, just as you would any activity that you intend to do.

A note to those who aspire to athletic competition: We strongly suggest that you find books that specifically discuss how to apply the principles of periodization to your sport. Because the physical requirements of different sports vary so much, it is essential that you focus on proven training methods in order to both maximize your chances of success and minimize your chances of injury or burnout. Exercise science journals are also replete with studies about periodization. These papers are worth reviewing if you want to delve into this in greater detail.

Periodization And Spiritual Growth

Remember Richard Hatch who was on the summer of 2000 television show, *Survivor* — the fat, naked "snake" Richard Hatch — the sole survivor of the show's first season, the one who walked off the island with a million dollars?

How soon we forget.

Not that our amnesia is related only to Rich. Do you know anyone who can still name all five Spice Girls? How about last year's Academy Award winners for Best Actor and Best Actress? Can you remember more than a handful of gold medal winners from the last Olympics?

The bottom line is this, writes Jay Martel in *Rolling Stone* magazine: "Everything's a flash in the pan, so why not get the most out of your flash?" Richard Hatch had his moment in the sun, and he milked it for all it was worth ... even appearing in those ever-present "Got Milk?" ads. As far as the future goes, all bets are off: The Nasdaq creates and wipes out fortunes in a single day, fashions inspired by hip-hop are completely unpredictable, and all we know for sure about next year is that we'll all need new computers. So many people today pursue the flash by trying to get *whatever* they can, *while* they can, *however* they can, as *fast* as they can.[161]

192

This flash-in-the-pan mentality is dangerous for our bodies and our souls. When we focus on instant gratification, we run the risk of injury and burnout, and undermine our physical and spiritual wellness. It is far more healthy to build periodization into the practice of fitness and faith, realizing that there is a benefit to working hard at one point, less intensely at another, and always allowing time for rest and recuperation.

Instant gratification was part of the temptation Jesus faced when he spent his 40 days in the wilderness. At that time, the devil suggested he turn a stone into bread, saying, in effect, "Go ahead, Jesus — get it *while* you can!" And he offered him all the kingdoms of the world, "Go ahead, Jesus — get them *however* you can!" And he tested him by challenging him to throw himself off the temple and into the hands of God, "Go ahead, Jesus — grab hold of the Lord's protection as *fast* as you can!"

What's interesting is that God was *already* working to provide Jesus with all these attractive things, all in good time. They would come to him eventually ... at the right time, in the right place, according to the divine plan. Jesus would certainly be fed with nourishing bread. He would definitely become the cosmic King of kings and Lord of lords. Jesus would even be rescued from the finality of death by the power of God.

But not yet. Jesus would receive these things only after entering into the day-to-day practice of his ministry, one that was marked by intense activity, as well as by periodic breaks for prayer, rest, and recuperation.

Jesus knew how to periodize.

This is important for us to remember, because temptation is so often connected to impatience. We want something that is really quite innocent in itself — a piece of bread, a chance to be a leader, a sign from God — but we get into trouble because we want it *now*. We're unwilling either to wait for it or to work for it, so we take shortcuts — and end up getting into trouble.

Picture this: You're hungry, you crave an elegant meal, you walk into a 5-star restaurant. You order up a feast — one you really can't afford — enjoy it immensely, and then charge the whole thing on your credit card. Then, because you can manage only to make the minimum payment on your monthly balance, you pay for this dinner for years, and your $100 meal ends up costing you thousands.

The problem is wanting it *now*. The temptation is instant gratification. The solution is to resist the lure of the moment, periodize your trips to fancy restaurants, and trust that God will satisfy you in the fullness of his own divinely appointed time.

Not that food is our only problem. Think of money ... sex ... success. All can be good or bad, depending on the timing and circumstances. All are wonderful gifts of a loving and life-giving Lord, designed to bring us nourishment, opportunity, pleasure, and well-being, but not if we gobble them, grab them, force them, or rush them.

Bread can satisfy our deep hunger, except when God says, "No, not now." World-class leadership is a goal worth pursuing, but not at the expense of making a deal with the devil. Being a child of God is a cherished blessing, except when you challenge the Lord to a fast and dirty test of his love. The devil so often takes good and graceful gifts and corrupts them — luring us into wanting them now, grabbing them however we can, and getting them fast.

As people of faith, we don't have to join the rush. We don't have to fall into the trap of feeling that we need to grab everything we can in our flash-in-the-pan world. In the face of our society's fleeting, superficial, and increasingly sinister and seductive style of success, Christianity challenges us to take the long view and focus on eternity. Resisting temptation, balancing activity and rest, and taking things slowly are important parts of what it means to follow Jesus faithfully.

Truly good things take *time* to develop, and we cannot expect a harvest overnight. For everything there is a season, including working and resting, praying and playing. Like a farmer who works the soil, cultivates, waters, and weeds, we need to take time to invest ourselves in activities that will bear a good and lasting fruit. If we resist the lure of the quick buck, the flashy image, the easy answer, and the tempting moment, God will satisfy us in the fullness of his own divinely appointed time.

No doubt, the world will continue to sing the old Janis Joplin hit "Get It While You Can." Society's stars will burn brightly, as Janis did, and then quickly fade away. Celebrities will experience their own flash-in-the-pan, and many will simply make the most of their momentary glory.

We followers of Christ have our eyes on a different star — one that burns brightly, but never fades away. We're willing to watch, wait, work, and rest, in a discipline of spiritual periodization, always trusting that our Lord will bring us nourishment, opportunity, pleasure, and well-being. All in his good time. All according to his divine plan.

We may not experience instant gratification, but we can enjoy a life of physical and spiritual fitness, one that endures.

Periodizing Endurance Exercise

So, how do we build periodization into our daily exercise routines? Successful periodization of endurance exercise does not require use of a heart-rate monitor, although that is fine. The advantages of using a heart-rate monitor are that it gives you immediate, precise feedback about your heart rate and allows you to quantify your progress quite precisely. The downsides are that some heart-rate monitors are quite complicated to program and most require that you wear a chest strap that senses your heart rate, as well as a wristwatch with a readout that lets you see what it is during exercise. Many of these connect to computers and allow you to download workout data automatically. As we already noted, a heart-rate monitor from Reebok (Reebok Strapless) eliminates the chest strap. You wear the small wristwatch on your wrist and anytime you want to see your heart rate, you simply put two fingers on the touch points around the watch face, and it takes your pulse. This is more than adequate for most people to use during runs, walks, and hikes.

One problem with the heart-rate approach is that it does not take into account the problem of cardiovascular drift. This is the phenomenon in which your heart rate naturally rises during endurance exercise for two reasons that are tangential to your work intensity — dehydration and heat. As you exercise, you gradually lose fluid from your body, through sweat and respiration. This gradual reduction in fluids causes your heart to pump faster in order to maintain a constant flow of blood (with its vital nutrients and oxygen) to working muscles. To this you must add consideration of accumulating heat.

The primary byproduct of metabolism is heat. When you exercise, you generate a great deal of it, which you dissipate, in part, through sweating. Your body also gets rid of some of the heat by having the blood vessels closest to your skin dilate and there is an increase in blood flow through those vessels. As an endurance workout lengthens or gets more intense, your heart pumps faster to get blood through those dilated sub-dermal blood vessels to dissipate the heat. The net effect of these factors is that your heart rate will rise during exercise on a hot day, simply because it is hot, and not just because you are working harder. To reduce the impact of cardiovascular drift during exercise, you should drink both before and during activity and exercise extreme caution (perhaps even skipping a workout) on excessively hot or humid days (heat index >90 degrees or Code Orange or Code Red air quality). Adequate fluid intake on a warm day is essential to lessen the impact of cardiovascular drift, thus helping to prevent illness or injury and give you the liquids you need to get the most from your physical activity.[162]

To gauge and plan your endurance work, we believe that there are alternatives worth exploring. There are two in particular that we encourage you to try. The first is a Training Impulse Score or TRIMP Score. The second is to use the Foster Index.

TRIMP Scoring And Foster Index

TRIMP scoring is a credible, valuable, and valid means of understanding the relative intensity of any kind of aerobic exercise.[163] [164] [165] Its chief drawback is that it does require use of a programmable heart-rate monitor. Specifically, you need a monitor that will let you track how much time in every workout is spent in each of four heart-rate training zones (Zone 1, Zone 2, Zone 3, and Zone 4). To demonstrate how TRIMP scoring works, and help with workout planning as well as analysis, let's revisit our hypothetical exerciser, Sam. Here are the key steps in TRIMP scoring.

1. Establish your estimated maximum heart rate (MHR) during exercise. Although there are numerous ways of doing this, each with its own advantages and limitations, the easiest approach is to subtract your age from 220. For Sam, this yields 170 (220-50=170 beats per minute).
2. Now calculate your heart-rate training zones. Each zone represents a percentage range of your estimated maximum heart rate.
    a. Zone 1 is a low training intensity. This is the zone in which you will most often warm up and cool down. It is also the training zone for people with serious chronic illnesses (such as severe heart or lung disease), or those who are extremely deconditioned or overweight. Zone 1 is approximately 35% to 54% of your MHR. In Sam's case this is 60 bpm to 92 bpm. Program this into your heart-rate monitor as Zone 1.
    b. Zone 2 is a moderate-intensity workout zone. This is the zone where many people will spend a large proportion of their exercise time. Zone 2 is approximately 55% to 69% of MHR. In Sam's case, Zone 2 is 94 bpm to 117 bpm.
    c. Zone 3 is a moderate-high workout zone. This is where you will get the biggest bang for the buck. Spending some time in Zone 3 every week will not only help you burn more calories (relatively harder exercise burns more calories in a given period than does relatively easier exercise), but it also builds heart health. For Sam, Zone 3 is 70% to 89% of MHR or 119 to 151 bpm.
    d. Zone 4 is the hardest level of intensity. Zone 4 is not appropriate for people other than the most experienced and fit athletes. It is a training zone that is largely reserved for improving performance in endurance activity, often for competitive purposes. Zone 4 is 90% to 100% of MHR. Sam's Zone 4 is 153 bpm to 170 bpm.

197

Here, then, are Sam's four heart-rate training zones:

	Zone 1	Zone 2	Zone 3	Zone 4
% of MHR	35%-54%	55%-69%	70%-89%	90%-100%
Beats per minute	60-92	94-117	119-151	153-170

From this point forward, TRIMP scoring for Sam is easy. To calculate Sam's TRIMP for a 40-minute run, for example, he would look at his heart-rate monitor after the run to see how much time he spent in each of the four training zones. Then, he would multiply the number of minutes in each zone times the zone number (1, 2, 3, or 4). Thus, 10 minutes in Zone 1 is 10 (10 x 1), 20 minutes in Zone 2 is 40 (20 x 2), and, 10 minutes in Zone 3 would be 30 (10 x 3). Add the scores together and the sum is 80 (10+40+30). This is Sam's TRIMP score for this run.

By using this process consistently (you can build a simple spreadsheet in Excel to do it), Sam has all the data he needs to understand how hard each workout should be compared to those that preceded it, as well as those that will come afterward. The TRIMP scores provide an indicator of the relative intensity of workouts by instantly encapsulating both time and intensity in one number. It also offers an upper and lower limit for exercise intensity. If Sam consistently runs for 40 minutes and he spent it all in Zone 1, his TRIMP would be 40 (40 x 1); for Sam, this is likely a very easy workout. Conversely, if he spends all 40 minutes in Zone 4, his TRIMP is 160 (40 x 4), which is an extremely intense workout. By using the TRIMP scores, Sam can adjust his workout plan to ensure that, for example, he does not do two consecutive days of hard runs (a TRIMP of >120), which can lead to injury or excessive fatigue and also intersperses relatively easy days (TRIMP 80 to 100) in his routine to help him stay fresh.

TRIMP scoring can help overcome some of the limitations of heart-rate training alone, especially if Sam considers the distance he covers as well as his TRIMP score. If, after a period of consistent activity, Sam finds that he is able to cover more ground at a lower TRIMP score, then he will see — in black and white — how his fitness is improving. Were Sam a cyclist, he would look for increasing speed at a consistent or lower TRIMP score, which would, by proxy, tell him he has become a more powerful cyclist who is able to cover more ground in less time with lower work effort.

Vik uses TRIMP scoring to track and plan his bike rides, and his spreadsheet entries for three rides in April 2006 look like this:

Date	Total TRIMP	Ride Time	Foster Index	Time RPE	Time in Z1	Time in Z2	Time in Z3	Time in Z4
4/11/06	200	85	340	4	17	26	37	5
4/13/06	383	135	1080	8	12	21	79	23
4/16/06	167	69	414	6	13	19	32	5

Thus, the ride on 4/13/2006 was the most intense ride, being substantially longer and at a higher heart than the rides surrounding it. You will also notice entries for the "Foster Index" and RPE. These are valuable and valid tools for tracking endurance activity if you do not use a heart-rate monitor. Here is how to use the Foster Index, which does not even require making a spreadsheet.

1. As we have already taught you, you should assign to every workout (whether endurance or strength training), a numerical score of 0 to 11, representing the Rating of Perceived Exertion or RPE for that exercise session.
2. When you make your workout entry in your exercise and diet diary, note the RPE and the time (in minutes) of the walk, run, jog, or bike ride. Multiply the two entries to get a Foster Index. In Vik's bike ride entries, notice that all he

had to do was multiply the time by RPE to get the Foster Index scores of 340, 1080, and 414 for these three rides. Your entries could look simply like this: "Walk, 30 min @ 6 RPE. FI = 180." Because the RPE is a scientifically valid means of scoring exercise, you can use your Foster Index calculation to both understand and plan your exercise progress.

To maximize your opportunities for success, and to prevent burnout, we urge you to seek to do most of your workouts at a moderate intensity, around 3 to 6 on the RPE scale, or in mid-Zone 2 to low-Zone 3 of your heart-rate training zones. You should, however, vary workouts sufficiently to challenge yourself and, thus, build fitness. You will know when you are making progress when you notice both subjective and quantifiable changes in your performance. First and foremost, increasing fitness means that a given exercise workload will start to feel easier. This is true for both endurance and strength work. You will start to cover more ground in your walks, runs, or bike rides with less effort and the exercise will feel less taxing to you, translating into a lower RPE. Likewise in strength work, where (barring injury) you will make rapid progress in both the efficiency of your movements in the gym as well as in the amount of weight that you can lift.

Periodization For Strength Work
Periodizing strength work is similar to the approach outlined above for endurance exercise. First, you will need to establish a baseline of information on how strong you are now, which we teach you in "Thou Shalt Be Strong." Once you know how strong you are in at least one exercise for every major muscle group (legs/lower body, chest, back, shoulders, biceps, triceps, and calves), you can take time to invest in workout planning following the guidelines laid out in chapter 4. The simplest approach to periodizing strength work for overall muscle and bone health is to do so on a daily basis.

If you are a beginner to strength training (less than one year's experience) and follow our prescription, you will lift 3 times weekly, using about 60% to 70% of your 1 rep maximum (1RM) weight. An intermediate lifter (1 to 2 years of experience) should lift twice weekly at about 75% of 1RM; finally, an advanced lifter (> 2 years of experience) needs to lift the most to both continue gaining strength and preserving what he or she has already accomplished. This person needs to also lift only twice weekly, but at a much higher intensity, about 80% to 85% of 1RM.

As with periodized endurance exercise, you can periodize your strength training on either a daily or weekly basis; do most of your workouts in the midrange of intensity (around 3 to 5 on the RPE scale). However, in order to improve, you will need to do some work at a higher load, which is what will help your muscles continue to improve. So, no matter where you are on the strength training spectrum, you will get the most from your efforts by spending most of your time lifting in the percentage ranges that we recommend. Improvement, however, will come from occasionally challenging yourself by doing a workout or two at a higher intensity (75% of 1RM for a beginner, 80% of 1RM for an intermediate lifter, and 90% of 1RM for an advanced lifter). As with endurance exercise, however, ensure adequate rest and never work the same muscles on two consecutive days. Also, avoid doing two intense workouts in a row.

To use another example from Vik's exercise records, he also notes the progress of his strength work. Here are three recent entries:

Date	Activity	Muscle group	Muscle group	Period	Number of sets	RPE	Time
8/24/07	Lift	Torso		STR	20	5	50
8/25/07	Lift	Legs	Arms	POWER	16	6	30
8/28/07	Lift	Torso		HYPER	18	4	30

Note that Vik characterizes his workouts by muscle group. Torso includes the chest, upper back, and shoulder muscles; legs include thighs, calves, and lower back; arms are biceps and triceps. He also varies his periodization phases. A strength workout ("STR") is at ≥ 85% of 1RM, at 2 to 6 reps; power work is done explosively at 60% to 70% of 1RM, for 6 to 10 reps; and, hypertrophy ("HYPER" — to build muscle mass) is done at about 70% to 75% of 1RM for 8 to 10 reps. Notice also what he does not do: He does not obsessively track sets, reps, and specific weight lifted. As long as the resistance is appropriate to staying within the prescribed range, it matters little whether or how the reps and weight vary from set to set. As a highly experienced strength trainer, Vik does a lot of sets of work (5 to 8 sets per muscle group), but because he has perfected his technique and planning, he is able to do so free of injury and burnout. He does the majority of his workouts in the moderate intensity range of weight (70% to 80% of 1RM), doing strength work at least once every 10 days to 2 weeks. Despite being nearly fifty, he has seen only a marginal decline in muscular strength since graduate school.

Beginning and intermediate strength trainers should retest their 1RMs every 4 to 6 months, because these upper limits of strength will change very rapidly. Advanced lifters need not do this more than annually because their gains in 1RM strength will be less frequent and less dramatic. When your 1RM goes up, then so too does the amount of weight that you lift in a workout (60% of 100 pounds is 60, but 60% of 120 pounds is 72). And, after all, getting stronger — as strong as you can be — is the whole idea.

If you stick with this approach, you will eventually reach a plateau or increase strength very slowly over a long period. This, believe it or not, is probably your genetic maximum and a great place to be. When you take your place as an advanced strength trainer, with a serious periodized strength-training habit, you will be doing exactly what you need to do to prevent the decline in muscle health that happens to people as they age. Degradation of human muscle tissue starts in your thirties and continues throughout adulthood. The loss of muscle size and strength is critically important to the increased risk of numerous diseases because of a pernicious vicious cycle that it sets in motion: You lose muscle as you get older and consequently feel weaker and tend toward being less active, in part because activity does not feel good. The inactivity leads to further loss of muscle and the spiral begins.

The loss of muscle mass that comes from physical inactivity leads to weight (fat) gain and increased risk for diabetes, arthritis, high blood pressure, heart disease, and stroke. You have probably heard the old saw that as you get older your metabolism slows down. Exercise scientists have yet to determine whether people become less active as they age because they make a conscious decision to become less active, from the progressive loss of muscle mass (making physical activity harder and more uncomfortable), or a down regulation of activity that occurs somewhere in the central nervous system. Whatever the science ultimately establishes, it is true that your muscles account for about 30% of the calories that you burn at rest.[166] Thus, the more of this metabolic engine you allow to disappear, the more you will allow your own daily caloric expenditure to sink and the resultant risk of weight gain to overwhelm you. We all get weaker eventually; you can, however, manage the rate of decline in your muscular health. Strong people get weaker much more slowly than do those who are not as strong; also, muscular strength may even help protect against dangerous disorders such as metabolic syndrome, which places people at significantly increased risk for heart disease.[167]

So, to all of you who seek the Olympic ideals of bigger, faster, stronger — no matter where you start from today — we say, "Bravo!" At the same time, we urge you to periodize your approach to endurance and strength exercise, and to build a rhythm of activity and rest into the practice of your faith. God rewards those who resist the temptation of instant gratification, and instead focus on the long-term goals of physical and spiritual fitness.

Your Action Steps From Commandment Seven

1. Construct a periodized exercise plan for the next week, varying in frequency and intensity of activity.

2. Keep a record of your workouts, using the Foster Index or TRIMP Score. Monitor your progress over the course of one month, at least.

3. Reflect on a flash-in-the-pan gimmick that you have fallen for in the past. What lesson did it teach you?

4. Plan your schedule for the next week with physical activity balanced by meditation and prayer.

Build your annual periodized plan, using the table on the next page. We get you started with hypothetical year-long exercise and nutrition goals. You can change this to suit your needs. After establishing a year-long goal, set a goal for the first quarter, such as learning how to keep an exercise and diet diary. Then, build reasonable, small goals for the first month and then the first week. You do not need to complete all the goal entries now, but can write them as the year goes along, so that they are consistent with where you are in your program to date.

Your year-long goal: lose 10% of bodyweight and build a daily exercise program

	Jan-Feb-Mar			Apr-May-June			July-Aug-Sept			Oct-Nov-Dec		
	Jan	Feb	Mar	Apr	May	June	July	Aug	Sept	Oct	Nov	Dec
Week 1												
Week 2												
Week 3												
Week 4												

Commandment Eight

Thou Shalt Rest

The Physical Value Of Rest

Although this book is, first and foremost, about activity, any experienced exerciser — or competitive athlete for that matter — will tell you that rest is one of the key parts of long-term success. Consider that even your heart muscle rests between beats; just as it cannot remain in a state of constant contraction, neither can you remain in a state of constant motion. Rest is an important interval between bouts of activity, to let emotional, psychological, spiritual, and physical resources recharge.

God knows this, which is why the fourth of his Ten Commandments is "Remember the sabbath day, and keep it holy" (Exodus 20:8). We are instructed to rest on the seventh day of the week, the day on which God rested as he completed the work of creation. Sure, we know that workers today are rewarded financially for putting in overtime, executives are praised for clocking 14-hour days, and parents of young children are "liberated" by working at home via cell phones and BlackBerrys and home computers. Still, refusal to keep a sabbath diminishes our sense of balance. Just because it is easy — even encouraged — to go, go, go, right through a day of rest, we shouldn't just cave in to this temptation. Nonstop activity is not good for us, whether we are working at our jobs or working out in the gym — it threatens our health as individuals and as a society.

Taking a break from our activities and devoting a day per week to reflection and relaxation can benefit us all. Bill Parent, a Roman Catholic priest and long-distance runner, observes that an almost universally recognized training principle is that a runner becomes faster by taking a day off from training each week. "The sabbath principle," he concludes, "is built into our physical bodies." There's also a saying among artists that you must know when to stop painting — if you don't, you'll make one stroke too many

207

and ruin the painting. Overworking can have the same disastrous results as overpainting.

How many times have you come to the end of a particularly grueling workweek and wished for nothing more than a peaceful evening, a good night's sleep and then, having gotten it, awoken on Saturday morning, feeling quite refreshed and ready to resume a full life? For many of us, this is probably a pattern that repeats itself throughout the course of the year, as we juggle the demands of work, family, church, and community. If we are to believe surveys appearing in the popular press, we Americans are an under-rested bunch. We want you to change that, just as we hope that we have encouraged you to embrace activity and better nutritional options.

The concept of rest permeates many of the lessons in this book. In addition to the rest between heartbeats noted previously, we have taught that you need to rest between sets of strength training work and that, indeed, you need to rest between days of strength work so as to avoid overtaxing a particular muscle. In addition, we have asked you to take a conceptual rest from the gimmicky but often baseless buzz that surrounds our contemporary ideas about diet and exercise, and to ground yourself in the *science* of exercise.

Rest's value derives not only from the periodic cessation of motion, but also from the opportunity that it presents for insight, analysis, and problem solving. That process, in turn, lays the foundation for change and adaptation, hopefully leading to new successes down the road. In this sense, we especially like the idea of active rest. Taking a day off from activity (or, yes, eating a meal that deviates from your otherwise very healthy diet), can prove to be very productive and, quite frankly, fun. Rest helps relieve drudgery, provides a welcome and needed interlude from routine, and lets you consider both your progress and your plans. Unfortunately, this is one of the areas of exercise that is least well studied. Consequently, there is a lot less science here and a greater need for you to be intuitive and flexible, aware of your own limits, and good to yourself.

There are few hard and fast guidelines to follow for how much rest you will need, to keep you feeling fresh and energetic every time you exercise. In general, as we have already noted, we hope that you will find a way to be active at least five times weekly, which leaves only two days for rest from physical activity. For some well-conditioned people, taking only one day off each week or every 10 days will work fine. For others, having a day off every week is what works best. For us, Vik takes a day off about every 10 days, while Henry typically takes a day off every 7 days. You may even find that the weather is your friend in rest ... if you tend to exercise outdoors, a day or two of bad weather can be just the impetus you need to take a day or two off.

For people new to exercise, this approach to rest is somewhat counterintuitive. As we noted in an earlier chapter, for beginners who are still establishing an exercise habit, many frequent, low intensity workouts are the ideal. This kind of exercise pattern is actually quite unlikely to result in burnout, overuse injuries, or disappointment. Likewise, because it is low intensity, it is sustainable for a long period without much rest. For example, a man or woman who is building an exercise and weight-loss program by taking 10 to 15 minute walks 3 times a day is off to a good start; because the walks impose a relatively low level of physiologic stress, it is feasible to do them repeatedly without much cause for concern about injury or exhaustion. This is very different from the needs of a moderately or highly conditioned person who exercises intensely several times weekly and then needs time to recover successfully. As beginners make the transition to exercise veterans, and thus, workout more regularly and harder, rest becomes a more important part of developing a personal activity formula that will work for the long term. This is because rest serves several important functions:

- *Recuperation:* Too much or too hard exercise leads to overuse injuries including things such as pulled muscles, sore joints, fatigue, irritability, insomnia, and reduced exercise performance. In other words, doing too much is no fun at all, and it can sap your enthusiasm for activity. Taking the time to build rest intervals into your exercise schedule is actually an important way of helping ensure that you will maintain your momentum.

- *Quality of life:* Studies tell us that people who exercise regularly typically rate themselves as having a better overall quality of life. However, there is another edge to this sword. People who exercise a great deal — or very intensely — may be as prone to a reduced quality of life as people who do not exercise enough.[168] The overdoers may be as likely to have days that they self-report as "unhealthy" as people who underachieve. The folks who strike a balance — 30 to 60 minutes of activity at least five times weekly — report the fewest unhealthy days.

- *Immune system balance:* This is a bit tricky, but exercise is both good and potentially bad for your immune system. Regular, moderate intensity exercise is likely very good for your immune system because of the stimulation that it provides. Recent studies show that even a single workout can prompt the immune system to increase production of some kinds of cells.[169] This is particularly important as we age, because aging blunts the immune system's ability to do its work. This is one reason that older people are so susceptible to both cancer and infection; as aging interferes with immune system function, they are less able than younger people to fight off infections or stem the spread of cancerous cells. Exercise serves a partial antidote to this decline, by helping to prompt increased immune activity.[170]

    However, despite its generally beneficial impact, exercise can also be the factor that tips your immune system function from positive to negative. This is most likely to happen in people who exercise hard and often. Studies show that when the work imposed by physical activity goes from "moderate" to "heavy," the risk of infection goes from "below average" to "above average."[171] This may be one reason that professional athletes, who train frequently and often quite hard, seem to us mere mortals to suffer from relatively frequent bouts of colds or "the flu." To fans, it seems inexplicable how such active and apparently healthy people

210

could get sick so easily, but perhaps not so surprising when you appreciate that their regular schedule of high intensity activity may have their immune systems dancing on the edge more often than not.

Another topic that all physically active people must understand — related to infections and your immune system — is whether to exercise when you don't feel good. This is one place where it is important to use good sense and exercise caution, no pun intended. There are several circumstances in which you should most certainly *not* exercise: a fever, generalized body aches, severe fatigue, nausea or vomiting, diarrhea, or *any* difficulty breathing or chest discomfort. If you have a simple head cold (sinus congestion or a stuff/runny nose), with no fever or body aches, you probably can work out, but should do so less intensely and for a shorter period. If your muscle aches, fever, respiratory symptoms, or fatigue persist for more than a few days, see your doctor. You should be symptom free before resuming your exercise routine or ramping back to your regular intensity level. Above all else, listen to your body. If you are having an off day, as we all do, take a break, rest, eat well, and get back at it tomorrow. Learn to recognize your tolerance limits and respect them. There is no shame in taking a day off.

There is a downside to rest — too much of it is bad for you. A prolonged layoff from physical activity can prompt any exerciser to essentially start over from scratch. The bad effects can be particularly severe if the layoff included a period of bed rest; the deconditioning effect of bed rest is well-documented. The deconditioning that results from a prolonged period of inactivity most often is due to a chronic illness, recovery from a serious injury, or the recuperation from surgery.

A period of prolonged inactivity is called detraining, because many of the beneficial effects of exercise get reversed during this time. The reversal can be sufficiently severe as to render a detrained exerciser the physiologic equivalent of a sedentary person (someone who does not exercise at all). There is typically a loss of musculoskeletal fitness as well as diminution of aerobic capacity (cardiac function). According the American College of Sports Medicine, 8 to 10 weeks of detraining will return a person's VO_2max, a measure of cardiovascular fitness, to pre-exercise levels. The greatest drop happens in the first month of inactivity, marked by a 7% decline in VO_2max in the first 12 days. Detraining causes a decrease in heart size, stroke volume (the amount of blood your heart pumps with each beat), and blood volume. It also results in loss of strength, muscle atrophy (a decrease in both the size and number of muscle fibers), and possibly bone loss.[172]

Recovering from detraining requires a plan and reasonable expectations. Highly conditioned athletes who resume exercise after detraining should understand that they will retain few of their previous physiologic characteristics; and, depending on the underlying medical problem that led to detraining, they may or may not achieve previous aerobic and strength milestones. A retraining plan should include both strength work to rebuild atrophied muscles and endurance exercise to restore aerobic capacity. The initial part of retraining should focus on relatively low intensity (such as 2 to 4 sets of 10 to 12 reps at 60% to 70% of 1 rep maximum for strength work and heart-rate training zone 2 level aerobic work). Add time before increasing intensity for aerobic work. For strength work, add weight in small increments, do not exceed 4 sets per muscle group, and, periodically, do fewer reps (6 to 8) with heavier weights (80% to 85% of 1RM).

If you are recovering from illness, injury, or surgery, make sure you communicate with your physician about when you can resume activity and at what level. Remember, even the smallest steps can help you down the path to recovery. For example, there was a time when the typical post-operative recuperation from open-heart surgery primarily involved bed rest. Now, the standards are different. Barring complications, physicians tell their patients who have had open-heart surgery to walk around their rooms and hospital floors very soon after surgery. This is a tangible reminder of both how standards change with accumulating knowledge and of the need to remain active, even under the difficult conditions of post-operative recuperation.

Be flexible and accepting of your need for rest, because it is not a bad thing. Take the time on rest days to devote some time to perusing your exercise and diet diary. A day off from physical activity is a useful opportunity to do some thinking about what you have been doing and what you would like to change going forward. Some questions that you might find worthy of reflection on a rest day:

1. Am I enjoying my mix of activities?
2. Am I doing a good job keeping track of my workouts?
3. Am I doing too much of one activity at the expense of others?
4. Am I sticking to my diet well enough to reach my bodyweight goals? Is it time to set new goals?
5. What new activities would I like to try, if any?
6. Is it time for me to reduce or increase the intensity of my exercise?
7. What should my next nutrition goal be, and how I will start to move toward it?

The list of potential questions is, quite literally, endless. However, as with many things in life, engaging in a healthy, inquisitive learning process is the first part of changing behavior. Thus, when you take a rest day and spend time thinking about what you are doing and why, you are giving your mind extra exercise that will ultimately benefit you physically.

The Spiritual Value Of Rest

For all the attention paid in recent years to public displays of the Ten Commandments, you'd think people would spend as much energy trying to follow them as they do talking about them. When it comes to the Fourth Commandment — remember the sabbath day — that's certainly not the case. And pastors like Henry, far from being role models, are among the worst offenders, since they work every Sunday.

The problem with ignoring the sabbath is that it hurts us as individuals, families, and communities. Wayne Muller, a therapist and minister, is convinced that modern life has become a violent enterprise — we make war on our bodies by pushing them beyond their limits, war on our children by failing to give them time when they are hurt and afraid, and war on our communities by failing to be kind, generous, and connected to our neighbors. To bring an end to this destruction, we have to establish a healthier balance between work and rest.

Whether religious or not, people know that they need to take a day off in order to maintain their sanity and remain efficient and productive at work. But simple downtime is not enough. We need a formal day of rest, which includes a break from even thinking about work. A true sabbath gives us time to refresh and renew ourselves, regain proper perspective, and redirect our lives to what is good, true, and worthwhile. There is something positive and even creative about allowing ourselves to take a break, as is noted in the Bible when it says that God finishes the work of creation on the seventh day ... by resting (Genesis 2:2). Resting is not a waste of time, but is, instead, an act of creativity.

Unfortunately, our society rewards hard-driving people who are focused on their work 7 days a week, and our technology allows us to be constantly connected to the workplace. "Modern culture's time values often seem enslaving and oppressive," observes Dennis Olson, professor of Old Testament Theology at Princeton Theological Seminary. "Work time seems increasingly to expand and rob us of time with family and friends. Computers and the internet bombard us with a constant flow of data, messages, and information." The number of workdays per year has expanded over the past century, while our sleep has dropped from an average of 9 hours in 1910 to 7.5 today. The result is that we feel harried and hurried, out of balance, and out of sync.

Fifty years ago, blue laws kept businesses closed on Sundays, forcing Americans to focus on church-going, rest, and relaxation. Although many people resented these limitations, and some saw them as a violation of the separation of church and state, these laws did have the beneficial effect of creating a day of rest. But in the 1960s, demand for shopping and entertainment encouraged more

214

and more businesses to remain open on Sundays, and by now almost every mall, theater, and restaurant is operating seven days a week. Even in Europe, where church-going has been in decline for years, Sunday has been — until recently — a day in which most businesses are closed, allowing people to spend time with family members and friends.

Given this history, sabbath-keeping is going to be a countercultural activity, one that requires commitment and creativity. A day of rest does not have to be a Saturday or a Sunday — impossible for pastors and others who have to work on the weekend — but it should be at least one day out of seven, and qualitatively different from the other six (sabbath is related to the Hebrew verb meaning "to cease, stop, interrupt"). The key is to break away from doing and even thinking about work, and take time to enjoy special hobbies or sports or artistic activities — anything that you find to be restful and refreshing. "Spend more time with people in a friendly way, with meals [and] extended conversations," advises Marva Dawn, theologian and author of *Keeping the Sabbath Wholly: Ceasing, Resting, Embracing, Feasting*, "but no talk related to work."

The only non-negotiable requirement is that we cease our work and do something else. Pitcher Pedro Martinez of the New York Mets rests by stopping his throwing and engaging in gardening, but for a professional gardener, sabbath-keeping might involve playing baseball. A computer expert might rest by going to the gym and lifting weights, while Vik might rest by staying home and writing email messages to friends. Henry's practice on Wednesday, his sabbath, always includes a long run, which might seem terribly exhausting to some. But for him, running is restorative because it is so different from the day-to-day work of ministry. His thinking becomes unstructured when he goes for a jog along a beautiful wooded trail, and he is amazed at how his stress melts away and solutions to knotty problems pop into his mind. Although he does not offer formal prayers while he is exercising outside, more often than not he ends up feeling very close to God. This is his way of remembering the sabbath and keeping it holy.

There is a communal dimension to rest as well, one that is important for maintaining healthy relationships in our families and communities. Henry's son is a member of his high school's cross-country team, so he often joins Henry on his long runs. This gives them a chance to talk without time pressures or interruptions, far from the demands of work and school. At the end of life, we'll remember days of rest far more than days of work, and we'll be thankful for the time we spent eating, laughing, and playing with family members, friends, and neighbors. If anything, we'll wish we had devoted more time to sabbath. As the saying goes, no one ever lies on his deathbed and says, "I wish I had spent more time at the office."

One group that desperately needs some sabbath time each week is our children. They need time and attention from us, and they also need time just to be themselves. Days of rest are almost certainly more valuable to them in the long run than additional clubs or classes or teams. Like many parents who are members of our congregations, we worry that we may be giving our children the impression that they are slaves — slaves to school and sports and so many other time-consuming activities. Better sabbath-keeping, we're beginning to discover, could make us better parents. The sabbath is a reminder that we are more than beasts of burden, more than cogs in a wheel, more than students or workers who are valued for our contributions. On our day of rest, we discover we are valuable simply because we exist.

Summers give us another important opportunity for rest: vacation. Taking a week or two away from work is critically important for our personal and family health, but a March-April 2006 survey by the online travel service Expedia.com predicts that each of us, on average, will fail to use four vacation days each year. This refusal to take all the vacation we have earned is going to continue as long as we value labor over leisure, and it will aggravate physical and relational problems caused by stress. Ironically, we can actually be more productive if we take a break from time to time. Marva Dawn, the Christian theologian, is convinced that what we gain is "a greater eagerness to do our work and a better sense of what that work actually is." We can learn from men and women in the European Union, who work hard but still enjoy an average of five weeks of paid vacation per year. They often remark that they don't "live to work," as we do — instead, they "work to live."

So take a vacation every summer, and a weekly sabbath break from your job and your physical fitness routine. You'll be rewarded with not only a more balanced life, but also greater vitality and creativity in your day-to-day activities.

Your Action Steps From Commandment Eight

1. Take a break.

2. Take some time on a rest day to peruse your exercise and diet diary, and answer some of the questions posed in this chapter.

3. Separate yourself from your work for a full 24 hours — no email, cell phone, or computer — and discover that both you and the world benefit from this break.

4. Focus on the communal dimension of rest by planning a relaxing activity with family members or friends.

Commandment Nine

Thou Shalt Reflect

Reflecting On The Past, Planning For The Future

Exercise scientists don't write much about reflection. Why would they? Their purposes are typically to help us learn how and why our bodies work the way that they do, and how we can use physical activity as a tool to reduce health risks, improve our quality of life, and manage the complications of chronic illnesses. However, we believe that there are important reasons for you to reflect on what you have learned, done, or left undone, on this journey through the "Ten Commandments Of Faith And Fitness."

Reflective consideration of past events and planning for the future is not part of our cultural fabric. We are a here and now culture, far more in tune to "What have you done for me lately?" than to "What have you learned and how will you change to ensure that you keep improving?" The difference is unfortunate and problematic — unfortunate because we do not often allow ourselves to take the time to actually think about what we want, what effort and sacrifice we will make to achieve a goal, and then to map out a rational, honorable, and effective means of proceeding, and problematic because we underestimate the cognitive power of reflection, and thus often fail to learn important lessons about ourselves, the world around us, and how we interact with it.

Activity is good, but thoughtful activity is better. Eating is good, but a healthy diet derived from careful research and consideration is even better. Thought, reflection, and critical introspection are the fundamental underpinnings of behavior change. When you think, consider, question, reflect, and research, you are more likely to have confidence in the choices you make, which, in turn, may help you stick to your chosen path.

When we fail to fully appreciate the lessons to be learned from both successes and failures, we miss the opportunity to make ourselves into teachers as well. A parent who does not learn to turn off

219

the television, put down the beer and chips, and take a daily walk is much less likely to raise a child with healthy habits than is the parent who analyzes and works to overcome his or her obstacles to fitness. In fitness, as in many other aspects of life, a child learns first and foremost from his or her parents, not, as much as we would like to believe, from popular culture.[173] [174] Successful, lifelong fitness requires that parents serve as role models. This is important even when the parents themselves do not have a particularly glorious athletic history; indeed, the lessons imparted may be most powerful when parents demonstrate to their children the power of making positive, sound changes that can lead to a better life. Fitness and good health result not from randomness, but from planning and perseverance, and relate only marginally to preternatural or pretentious athletic ability.

You are likely less impressive to a child when regaling her with stories of long-gone athletic exploits than you are when helping teach your child how to hike, bike, run, or lift weights properly — and learning right along with her. With these lessons, your child learns not only the critical elements of maximizing health and opportunity in life, but also that diligence and devotion to health pursuits really matters — a message that is especially corrupted in today's media marketplace.

We all like shortcuts. From salad-in-a-bag to speed-dial to incredibly fast computers, we embrace virtually anything that will save us time or money. Much of the time, these things work to make our lives better or more convenient. We are, however, headed astray when we believe that there are shortcuts to good health. "The reason we have an obesity epidemic in this country is not because we eat too much and exercise too little. It's because we eat what gives us pleasure," writes Rabbi Marc Gellman in *Newsweek*. "Sugar and fat taste better than celery and tofu." He notes that a person can learn to love lettuce, but it takes time — on the other hand, the pleasure of chocolate ice cream is instantaneous. "The reason we have to force kids to exercise is because it is more pleasurable to sit on your tush and play video games than it is to run around and sweat. True happiness, the kind of happiness we ought to wish for our children and for ourselves is almost always the result of doing hard but good things over and over."[175]

A hasty, undisciplined approach to physical, emotional, and spiritual fitness feels good in the short term because it is quite *unde*manding, and allows us to persist in making the choices that are comfortable and familiar, but often unhelpful. Nutrition in a bottle (such as seen in the claims of many supplements), and unproven but highly seductive exercise programs (such as slow weight lifting), are apocrypha at best, and downright subversive at worst, because they distract you from doing things the right and productive way.

This approach is a recipe for frustration and failure, and by any credible measure, today we are wildly successful at collectively failing to do the right things by ourselves and our neighbors. For example, as we noted earlier in this book, a recent study pointed out that a mere 3% of American adults live an objectively healthy life and do all four of these things: they don't smoke, they eat sufficient fruit and vegetables every day, they maintain a normal weight, and exercise for at least 30 minutes most days of the week.[176] Likewise, researchers have also recently calculated that a great deal of the burden of heart disease — *the* leading cause of premature death and disability in our society — comes from modifiable risk factors. These include high blood pressure; too low HDL (good cholesterol); too high LDL (bad cholesterol); smoking, for which there are both prescription drugs and cessation programs; and, finally, poor glucose tolerance. The lifetime risk of heart disease in our country is 50% for men and 33% for women.[177] A woman's risk rises to equal a man's after menopause. More importantly, a great deal of this disease is avoidable by instigating lifestyle changes, the most important of which is a rich selection of physical activities.[178] Clearly, the quick and easy hype, which undoubtedly seizes public awareness periodically, is not getting the job done. Neither is the gym culture, where despite ever rising numbers of gyms and gym memberships, we are the fattest nation in human history.

Throughout this book, we have advocated an approach to exercise and diet that is beyond fashion and fluff. The principles are transportable to any environment or set of circumstances. If you have tried to follow the path we outlined, you have, by definition, tried to take a better approach to something that is critically important — protecting, nurturing, and sustaining God's first and greatest gift to you ... your physical being. "Your body is a temple," says the apostle Paul in his first letter to the Corinthians (6:19) — a temple of the Holy Spirit. Therefore "glorify God in your body" (v. 20).

Reflecting On Fitness And Diet

Two of the dictionary definitions of "reflect" apply here. They are to think seriously and to offer carefully considered thoughts or statements. We want you to embrace both definitions because we want you to engage in both activities.

Think Seriously

The way to begin a reflection on your exercise program is to go back and reconsider where you were when you undertook this process. We urge you to return to the earliest parts of your exercise and diet diary, where you may have made notes about what was important to you and why you wanted to walk this path of faith and fitness with us. Take a look back at your list of medical problems and the medications that you were on.

Critical introspection is hard, but its difficulty is part of what makes it enriching and valuable to you. As you may recall, the diary was intended to serve a couple of purposes. First, it gave you a place to record your exercise information and keep track of your diet. It was also a place for you to note your goals, expectations, and events in your life that may have affected your activity and eating habits. This is the time to revisit those notes. Here are some of the things that we urge you to consider:

- What have you done well? No matter how small or large, you should applaud good decisions because they are the essential elements for future growth and change.
- Have you kept consistent and clear exercise and diet notes, the likes of which will help you make sense of where you

have been and inform the process of setting new goals? What could you do better in your record keeping?

- Did your exercise self-test results surprise you? In what ways? What kind of motivation did that provide for you?
- When you compared the way you ate to how we encouraged you to eat, what differences did you identify and how did you change your eating habits?
- What information from this book and your own experiences was critical to helping you change your attitudes about physical activity and diet? In turn, how did these attitudinal changes help lead you to making better choices?
- What aspects of your diet and exercise choices have you been most happy with?
- In what ways have you not made optimal choices? Why?
- What aspects of exercise and diet have you found most difficult to change?
- What kinds of problems arose for you?
- Did you suffer injuries and physical setbacks?
- How did you communicate your lessons learned to family and friends, and, especially, the children in your life?
- Did you find it difficult to manage external demands on your time, such as work, family, or other obligations? When things went well, what steps were you taking to facilitate your success, and what happened when your carefully laid plans broke down? How hard or easy was it to get back on track?

Because our approach to changing your physical and spiritual life is built around making sound, health-giving, and life-affirming choices, an important question you can ask yourself is, "When I chose unwisely, why did I do so, and how can I support myself to make better choices in the future?" This is the crux of what you must understand about your own limitations and behavior. The more adept you become at making better choices, the more you do to shift the risks of physical inactivity and poor diet away from you and enhance the likelihood that you will benefit from exercise and improved nutrition.

Offer Carefully Considered Thoughts

Once you understand what has gone well for you — and why — as well as what has not gone well, you can move on to the second part of this introspective process and that is to express yourself in a serious manner. Whatever stage of faith and fitness you are in, it is simply the first part of the next phase of work. Even if you have met all your goals, it is now time to set new ones because, as we have pointed out before, the benefits of exercise and diet are like breathing ... to stay alive and continue thriving, you must make the same good choices over and over again. Faith and fitness are not a sprint; they are a marathon.

This is the time to reach out to your spouse, friends, and others who have supported you in your journey. You should include in this process the person whom you identified as your Covenant Partner. Take the time to discuss your successes and failures and ask this person for his or her honest observations about you. You may be surprised at what you will learn from the people who love you, want you to succeed, and have watched or participated in your efforts. Encourage them to be honest — albeit in a kind and generous manner — so that you can learn from their observations. While we all have a certain amount of self-awareness, we can learn a great deal from what others tell us about our behavior and performance (both good and bad). After all, that is what your teachers did all through your years of formal schooling. Even today you may have a boss, pastor, priest, minister, or lay counselor who plays this role in your life. It is a good and useful role and we want you to take advantage of it now.

Revisit And Retest

After you complete the cognitive steps above, it is time to do some physical re-assessment and retesting. Take a look back at how you did your self-tests of physical fitness. It is time to repeat those tests and see if your performance has changed. In addition, you should check your weight, waist size, and hip measurements to see how well you have done with weight loss, if that was a priority for you. Write down the results of your new fitness testing results. For example, if you improved in the 1-mile walk from 16

224

minutes to 14 minutes, your improvement is expressed two ways: 2 minutes, which is also 12.5% ... a terrific change.

Changes in strength work can be calculated a little differently. For example, if you improved in the bench press from 125 pounds to 150 pounds, that 25-pound gain in strength (20%) is quite substantial. It is even more substantial if you lost weight, because data about strength is more rationally discussed in terms related to body weight; as the old sports adage goes, a good big man will always beat a good small one. So, if you are a forty-year-old man who started this process weighing 200 pounds and bench pressing 125, your bench press to bodyweight ratio was 0.625, meaning you were able to lift 62.5% of your body weight. Unfortunately, this put you in the 10th percentile (very poor) for men your age.

If you have lost 25 pounds of fat and gained 25 pounds of bench press strength, your ratio is now 0.85 (you now bench press 85% of your body weight). This is a 36% improvement that also moves you into the 50th percentile for men your age, a much more favorable strength category. By the way, to be in the 90th percentile for upper body strength — stronger than nearly all men your age — you would need to bench press 192.5 pounds or 10% more than your present body weight. If you did 1 rep maximum strength testing in the early stages of this process, redo it now and calculate changes, taking into account shifts in body weight.

se, for many people, nothing will matter as much to ng weight. So, if you have not weighed yourself regu-ow. As important as weight loss is, we want to remind t is not a substitute for physical fitness. In some ways, better to be a bit overweight and very active than very ictive. A recent study from the Cooper Institute also he first time ever, the importance of physical strength of metabolic syndrome, the deadly constellation of signs sems that predispose people to heart disease. Cooper re-llowed over 3,000 men for 7 years and found that the n were 35% less likely to develop metabolic syndrome akest men. This is a huge difference in risk, driven by in muscular strength as measured by 1 rep maximum ng, just as we have taught.[179] You will also understand

225

quite starkly from how your clothes fit whether you are meeting your weight loss goals. Buying new clothes can be fun, especially if it is because you are reaching your targets.

After you complete the physical self-reassessment, it may be time to go check in with your physician. Work with your doctor and health plan to get retested for cholesterol and fasting blood glucose. Ideally, weight loss, better diet, and regular exercise will have helped you move these numbers in your favor. Remember that your goals are to raise your HDL (good) cholesterol to above 60 and lower your LDL (bad) cholesterol. When you raise your HDL, you also favorably change your HDL to total cholesterol ratio. The target for your LDL will depend on your other risk factors; the more risk factors you have, the lower this target needs to be and you may not be able to reach it without prescription medications. Your fasting blood glucose should be below 100. If you are unsure about these targets and what they mean, visit www.nhlbi.nih.gov/guidelines/cholesterol/ where you can find data about the National Cholesterol Education Program, and look at the information for patients. You may wish to print and take some of this information to your doctor for discussion.[180]

Review The Basics

The reassessment process is a perfect opportunity to revisit some of the basic principles that we have tried to impart to ensure that you are sticking with the discipline. Give yourself a tune-up of sorts. Here are the kinds of things that you should review:

- Do you schedule your exercise time at the start of ev week, making these critical health appointments yourself?
- Are you flexible, breaking lengthy workouts into s ones when family and work demands conspire again
- Do you balance endurance exercise with strength Have you mastered these two things well enough as can now consider branching into other activities other learning a sport or participating in yoga, Pilates things?

- Do you rate each of your workouts using the rating of perceived exertion? Do you see patterns in your workout intensity? For example, do highly stressful periods at work correlate with very good or very lackluster workouts ... what does that tell you about yourself and how you use exercise to cope with stress?
- Have you learned to lift weights properly, ensuring that you lift enough (working at between 70% and 85% of your 1 rep maximum, depending on your experience level)?
- What kinds of exercise-related injuries have you suffered, if any? Do you prepare properly for adverse weather conditions, helping to minimize the risk of heat or cold related problems? Do you warm-up before your activity?
- Do you bookend your exercise sessions with proper intake of food and fluids? Do you avoid exercising on an empty stomach, always have water with you for any workout lasting longer than 30 minutes, and eat a light, well-rounded snack within an hour or two of completing your workout?
- What kinds of exercise do you enjoy doing the most and which ones the least? How do you think you can enhance your enthusiasm for the things that capture your attention the least? Would it help to do those activities with a partner?
- Given what you have accomplished so far, what's next for you? Be as specific as possible in setting your new goals. Are you motivated to cultivate a high level of skill and ability (for example in running) and perhaps enter a race or organized running event for the first time? If you are age 50 or older, is the Senior Olympics in your future?
- Last, but not least, look around you and see who it is you can reach out to help. Is there a coworker, family member, neighbor, or parishioner for whom you can be a role model, supporter, or Covenant Partner? This is the essence of Christian love for those around us, that we do not keep our blessings to ourselves, but rather spread them to those around us. Who will you help on his or her own path to faith and fitness?

227

Spiritual Reflection On This Process

Look around our country today, and you can see a terrible division between science and faith, one that we believe is both tragic and unnecessary. Everything we have written in this book is grounded in our conviction that science and religion are critical components of a life of health and wholeness, with both having important contributions to make in a fuller understanding of God's awe-inspiring creation.

As we reflect on this state of affairs, it becomes clear that people need to understand how faith and science can work together to answer the most pressing questions about human life. Whether the questions revolve around physical fitness or the meaning of life, our view is that science and religion answer two different sets of questions about creation, with science answering the "how" questions, and religion answering the "why" ones. Because they approach the truth from different points of view, science and faith can complement rather than contradict each other.

This is the approach that Henry, in particular, has confidently embraced since he studied biology and religion at Duke University in the late 1970s and early 1980s. At that time, he discovered that evolution was a plausible theory for the origin of species, and that religion provided a durable framework for a meaningful relationship with God and neighbor. But the debate between scientists and religious leaders has become increasingly shrill since that time, and today highly educated Christians are taking wildly different positions on evolution and intelligent design. Within Henry's church, one university professor says that he considers evolution to be "mind-boggling and completely illogical," while another says, "I don't see intelligent design fitting into a science class in any way."

While this book is not the place to dig deeply into evolution and intelligent design, this current controversy does give us a hook on which to hang our convictions about faith and science. We believe that the Bible answers the "why" questions of life, providing a faith-based explanation of why life exists, and how humans are to care for it. Science, on the other hand, has never answered the question of why life exists, even through the endless proofs based on observation and replication by multiple sources. Instead, science

228

answers the "how" questions, telling us how things work — whether the things be plants and insects, or human muscles, joints, hearts, and lungs. Science is great at providing information about mechanical matters, but it can never answer questions such as why the Big Bang occurred, or why the first bacterium appeared.

It's fine to learn about different schools of thought, as long as we recognize just that — they're different. Some are religious, and some are scientific. When Henry preaches on the biblical story of creation, he tends to keep his focus narrow. Instead of trying to reconcile scientific and religious ideas about the earth's creation in a 15-minute sermon, he uses the time to preach on what Genesis says about divine creativity, or human sinfulness, or the importance of sabbath rest. In similar fashion, when Vik is helping a client to learn proper weight-lifting technique, he invariably focuses on the mechanics of exercise, and on the importance of grounding a lifting routine in the best available scientific information. Vik cannot use a fitness lesson to explore the mystery of creation; he can, however, use his professional expertise to teach the mechanics of exercise and position that knowledge as a means of honoring a divine gift and as a tool for personal empowerment. Exercise may not tell us much about the meaning of life, but it can certainly imbue life with greater meaning when — done religiously and with reverence — it helps to alleviate the burden of chronic disease and deliver to people the spiritual freedom that can come only from good health.

It's a tenet of Henry's faith that there is divine intelligence at work in every aspect of the universe. Where he differs from some Christians, however, is in his acceptance of evolution as a part of God's creative plan. He thinks natural selection fits very nicely with the Ten Commandments, for instance: Break the rule about adultery, and you will find your longevity threatened by a sexually transmitted disease or a jealous husband. On the positive side, it appears that love and altruistic actions generally enhance a life, rather than diminish it. There's an elegant simplicity to natural selection that fits very well with the concept of a God who is willing to take his time with us, and let us face the logical consequences of our actions, both bad and good. "Natural selection is a study in patience," says Richard Key, a physician in Dothan, Alabama, and a member of an evangelical church. "And God is a patient God."

The same could be said about these ten commandments of faith and fitness. Spiritual and physical fitness is a study in patience, and God is a patient God. Our Lord is willing to take his time with us, and let us face the consequences of our choices, both bad and good, about endurance exercise, strength training, and nutrition. As was said in the introduction to this book, we don't tend to break commandments, we break ourselves *against* them.

Reflecting on these "Ten Commandments of Faith and Fitness," it is clear to us that religion and science are strongest when they are allowed to make their distinctive contributions. Neither of us is insecure about discussing the Christian faith, as long as the conversation remains grounded in religion, and not some religious-scientific hybrid. Equally important, we're not reluctant to speak about the best scientific data available about exercise and nutrition, as long as the discussion remains grounded in facts, and not in wishful thinking or quick fixes. We believe that our faith is strongest when it answers the questions it is prepared to answer, and when it defers the questions it cannot address. For us, a core religious conviction is that God created life and he gives it meaning and purpose. Any questions about the mechanics of life — including endurance exercise, strength training, and nutrition — are best left to science.

Your Action Steps From Commandment Nine

1. Connect with your Covenant Partner and discuss the most significant changes you have made thus far.

2. Do physical reassessment and retesting.

3. Review the basics, from the making of "health appointments" to finding a person to help with faith and fitness.

4. Discuss, with your Covenant Partner, one fitness question that this book has helped you to answer, and one faith question, as well.

Commandment Ten

Thou Shalt Remember

An Endpoint And An Ongoing Process

All journeys eventually reach a point where they must either end or transform into something new. Our last commandment in this program of faith and fitness has elements of both destinations. We are indeed at an endpoint, because we have now reached the last commandment. For you and for us, however, this is also an important point of transformation and transition. Faith and fitness are interesting dualities, in that they are each equally an endpoint and a process.

How is physical fitness an endpoint? We believe that it is an endpoint because it is a definable state, with quantifiable, measurable boundaries. To reach a personal level of fitness is to change your own knowledge base, behaviors, and choices and, in doing so, to reduce the major health risk factors in your life, such as elevated cholesterol and excess weight, that cause so much premature death and disability in our society. Your behavior changes and choices will ultimately help put you within the boundaries of "fitness." Specifically, there are several important characteristics of fitness:

- a healthy body weight and body fat percentage, with special attention to a trim waistline
- not smoking
- healthy blood cholesterol (especially an elevated HDL [good] cholesterol) and fasting glucose levels
- normal blood pressure
- a diet that begins with abundant fruits and vegetables, followed by whole grains, heart-healthy fats, lean protein, and modest amounts of alcohol and sodium, and as little saturated fat as possible

- endurance activity at least 3 times weekly for about 30 to 40 minutes, if you already have a healthy body weight, and up to 5 times weekly for about 60 minutes if you need to lose weight, at an intensity level that will help you ensure the long-term health of your cardiovascular system
- weight lifting at least twice weekly, also at an appropriate intensity, so that you endeavor to become as physically strong as you can be (A disability-free future is within your reach if you appreciate that muscular strength is essential to your long-term health, welfare, and independence.)
- testing and retesting your cardiovascular and muscular fitness, and comparing your performance to normative data from credible organizations, such as the American College of Sports Medicine (Strive to eventually get into the 70th percentile of performance in both fitness categories for your age and gender ... and then stay there as you get older.)

Notice as well what fitness is not. It is not about the size of your chest or biceps or whether you can run a mile faster than your friends. Nor is it about any of the other superficiality that drives so much of the popular fitness culture: It is not about your butt, your bust, or your tan lines. Like faith, fitness is first about what is inside, because when your inner being is happy, healthy, and at peace, you will almost certainly also achieve positive outward manifestations of success, and earn some of the patina that comes with the diligent pursuit of improved health. You are more likely to reach your goals pertaining to outward appearance if you first internalize critical lessons about nutrition and regular physical activity. We all want to look our best, but there is a fine line between the healthy pursuit of self-improvement and the obsession reflected in narcissism that chases one elusive Madison-Avenue-driven ideal after another.

Achieving the fitness milestones noted above means you that you will have moved your physiologic state of affairs into a much more favorable risk category and taught yourself a healthier way of living. You will also benefit from the side effects of having developed better stress management skills and learned to appreciate physical activity and better diet as tools that can tip the scales of risk and reward in your favor. After all, that is why you seek fitness in the first place: to give yourself the opportunity to live a better, happier, stronger life. We cannot promise that you will have completely eliminated the risk of an adverse health event, such as a heart attack. That is a foolhardy claim for anyone to make. Rather, we can only assure you that when you reach a quantifiable state of fitness, you will have done all you can, given the current state of knowledge, to mitigate risk and give yourself the best possible quality of life.

When you reach the goals noted above, you deserve to give yourself a pat on the back. It is a significant, potentially life-changing accomplishment. It is also your new baseline for the next phase of the *process* of fitness. We have noted at different points in this book that fitness is like breathing — you cannot hope to live a long, healthy life by taking just one breath. You must continue to breathe. Fitness is the same. Reaching a healthy and fit state represents your accomplishments at a point in time, and there is no permanence attached to your success. It is your responsibility to ensure that the beneficial state you worked and planned so hard to achieve in this moment continues into your future. A persistent devotion to the process of fitness — making the same positive choices repeatedly — is the core value that you must carry forward.

In a significant way, the pursuit of fitness is like the pursuit of virtue. Think about Shaquille O'Neal. He has been a dominating player in the NBA, and among his nicknames have been "The Big Continuity" and "The Big Legendary." But when he accepted the MVP award in 1999, he asked to be called "The Big Aristotle." He said, "I want to be known as The Big Aristotle because Aristotle once said that excellence is not a singular act, it's a habit — you are what you repeatedly do."

Shaq knew what he was talking about. Excellence certainly is a habit. You *are* what you repeatedly *do*. Shaq even knew that Aristotle, the Greek philosopher, said that virtue is a state of character gained by repeatedly performing good actions. Repetition is the key to excellence, whether we are pursuing fitness or virtue — or both.

Look For Good, Fresh Information

The nature of scientific inquiry is that there is always a new question to answer and data emerging that requires critical assessment to see where it fits, if at all, in your fitness strategy. And, to be sure, in our chaotic and sometimes highly unhelpful fitness marketplace, there is also a thriving industry that produces a lot of junk ideas, products, and services. We encourage you to be open to new information, but to also be very skeptical, cautious consumers. We have tried to ground our advice in the best that current science can offer. This does not mean that present-day knowledge is cast in stone. We cannot know today when a future study will alter one of the recommendations in this book, but it will almost certainly happen. Indeed, any reader of this book can subscribe to Vik's *free* online exercise and nutrition newsletter, which he emails to readers in PDF format once every calendar quarter. To subscribe, send an email to: faithandfitness-subscribe@galileohealth.net. Make sure that your spam filters are set to allow you to receive emails with PDF attachments from galileohealth.net. The newsletters come out in January, April, July, and October and typically contain 8 to 10 pages of summaries of important studies, as well as feature interviews and commentary.

When you hear a claim about a product, service, or idea, remember the old adage that "if it sounds too good to be true, it probably is." The only magic bullets for fitness and good nutrition are your ability and willingness to learn, work, change, and then learn, work, and change some more. You can use this checklist to conduct your own mini-assessment of any fitness or nutrition related product or service:

- Am I being asked to buy something? How much does it cost?
- If yes, what is it and how does it fit into my exercise and nutrition plan? Does it make sense? How might it help or hinder my efforts to reach specific goals?
- Does the product or service ask me to deviate substantially from the scientifically grounded and evidence-based plan

outlined in this book? If it does, then the product should offer compelling evidence for doing so.

- What scientific evidence does the seller have to support any claims made? Most specifically, have they published, or do they cite, any studies in respected scientific or medical journals?[181] This is the gold standard for scientific evidence.
- If the product is a food or a supplement, does it carry a claim that it was approved by the Food and Drug Administration? Remember that the supplements industry is largely unregulated and can make virtually any unsupported claim without a shred of evidence of any kind. The scientific reality is that, for the vast majority of people, supplements — except for an inexpensive, store-brand USP-certified vitamins — are virtually unnecessary for good health.
- If there are no readily accessible published studies, has the product, idea, or service been critiqued by reputable independent publications, such as *Consumer Reports*, and major news media outlets such as *The Wall Street Journal* or *The Washington Post*, both of which have very useful health sections?
- What are the product's medical implications? Might it complicate a medical condition or interact with a drug that you use? In most cases, the best source of information on potential drug interactions is a licensed pharmacist or a pharmacist at your local college of pharmacy.

This is not to say that we do not believe in novel and interesting advances in exercise and nutrition. For example, innovative technologies have produced dramatic changes in equipment design and construction in sports as diverse as running, tennis, and cycling, just to name a few. The new equipment often makes it easier to participate, can relieve discomfort, and can help propel you toward excellence. These are good and useful changes, and, if you are a devotee of a particular activity, we encourage you to remain attuned to technological innovation in your endeavor, as well as evidence-based training techniques from qualified coaches. There is, however, a dramatic difference between technologies that improve activity performance and things that simply distract you from necessary steps by trying to seduce you into false belief and take your money in the process. Slow weight lifting, bizarre high-fat diets, or supplement-dependent diets are three things that immediately come to mind.

Forgive Yourself Your Lapses

Remember that neither you nor this process is perfect. As human beings, we may well be created in God's image, but he has clearly left us with considerable room for improvement. Perhaps that is God's way of testing our abilities to be creative, thoughtful problem solvers who can analyze, strategize, and implement. But, he has also given us the power of forgiveness, and it is nowhere more important than in any process of self-improvement, because on that journey you will invariably encounter difficulties and setbacks, some self-imposed through miscalculation, and others driven by external events over which you can exert little control.

If you have followed this process faithfully, you know by now that you have the tools to overcome lapses, and these tools do not include despair, self-flagellation, anger, or frustration, whether self-directed or outward-directed. Instead, your tools for recovery from error and subsequent growth are honest introspection, analysis, and the conscious, willful pursuit of better choices.

When lapses in your progress happen, they will bother you, and, frankly, they should. If you gloss over them without any reflection, we would gladly wager that you will repeat them. However, your setbacks should not become an obsession — your only obsession throughout the process of faith and fitness should be a commitment to continuous learning and improvement. Taking the time to break down and analyze mistakes and adversities is critical to learning lessons about how and why they happened, as well as your reactions to them, which are often the only component of the process that you can really control. This helps to put events in their proper context, and relieves you of endless self-doubt and a sense of failure; then you pick up where you left off, with new knowledge under your belt about how to do things better when similar circumstances arise in the future.

Remember that Jesus came not to condemn us, but to save us — his typical response to people who fail is to offer forgiveness and then say, "Go, and sin no more" (John 8:11). Whether the problem is a missed workout, a week of poor nutritional choices, or falling for a too-good-to-be-true sales scheme, there is virtually no error of omission or commission from which you cannot recover. Children learn early on in life that after you fall it is important to get up, brush yourself off, and get back in the game. You must take the same approach here.

Exercise Your Creativity

For everyone devoted to faith and fitness, the daily completion of your appointed rounds in both spheres is often challenging. Children, jobs, spouses, traffic, illnesses, and countless other things can conspire to overturn even the best workout and diet plan. In this world, a perfect storm is not a meteorological event, but a confluence of circumstances that take you far afield from where you really want to go. What to do? Think small and think in opposites:

- *Think small.* Long workouts are like long meals; they are complicated to plan and often challenging to complete. In many cases, they are not feasible. When you cannot get the long run or walk you want in, for example, shift your strategy to opt for smaller, but slightly more intense runs or walks. Even though you will complete a shorter workout, you will burn calories at a slightly higher rate than during a less intense effort, and you will maintain your fitness level. You can use the same strategy for your strength work. A small, quick, intense workout may not meet all your long-term performance goals, but it will give you the satisfaction of knowing that you successfully circumvented one or more obstacles and got your workout in.

  Take a similar approach on nutrition. Eating multiple small meals will probably help you reduce your overall calorie consumption, prevent between-meal hunger and, consequently, help you manage your weight. To help control portions, use a plate that is smaller in diameter than a traditional dinner plate. And, remember to downsize portions by sharing meals (particularly meals eaten out) with friends and family members. Downshift and downsize your relationship with food — particularly how much you need to eat to feel emotional, not physical, satisfaction — from obsession to appreciation. Food is fuel and a tool for success, but it is not who you are. Of all the Seven Deadly Sins, the one that most people of faith have the biggest problem with is gluttony. Sadly, many Christians in America today are, as former Arkansas Governor Mike Huckabee writes, digging their graves with their cutlery!

- *Think in opposites.* Hurt your leg and can't run? Make sure you continue to do your upper body strength work while you heal, to stay in a healthy exercise routine, albeit an abbreviated one. Strained a shoulder muscle and can't lift this week? Get out and walk as much and as vigorously as you can. Comfortable with the flat route that you are used to walking? It's time to find some hills; likewise, if you are used to hills, find as flat a route as you can and just see how fast you can go after having used all those hills to build a powerhouse cardiovascular system.

  Used to planning meals around meat? Make meat a treat (if it stays on your table at all) and plan your meals around fruits, vegetables, heart healthy fats, and whole grains, the nutrients that our culture typically relegates to side dish status. Never eat breakfast and can't figure out why your daily diet plan falls apart around 10:00 a.m.? Time to learn how to make a good old-fashioned bowl of oatmeal with walnuts, low-fat milk or soy milk, and a bit of honey every day. Then, combined with eating sensible, small meals throughout the day (getting a mix of fruits, vegetables, whole grains, and lean protein), you will be less inclined to overeat at dinner and in the evening.

Don't let travel plans interfere with your exercise and nutrition plan, either. Most hotels, motels, and inns today have gyms (some

238

very elaborate) and many have arrangements with local commercial gyms that allow guests to exercise at little or no cost. Call ahead and ask. In addition, many hotels, particularly in urban areas, can help you identify nearby parks, walking and jogging paths, and other recreational opportunities. And, just as when you are at home, build your exercise into your work or leisure day. Consider packing one or two exercise tubes or bands in your luggage, as they take up virtually no space and weigh next to nothing. Last but not least, make creative use of the airport if you are flying.

Recently, while Vik was waiting for a connection in Newark, he noticed that the same woman passed him on the concourse several times within a half hour or so. It then dawned on him that she was doing laps. After finishing his coffee, Vik arose, grabbed his carry-on bag and briefcase, and he, too, did several laps of the concourse, taking about 30 to 40 minutes. It may not have been a 2-hour bike ride, but with two bags in tow, it was a noticeable effort and it also taught Vik to pack lighter.

Remember Your Future

Faith and fitness are not idle pursuits with indeterminate endpoints. When you make choices about exercise, diet, and moral behavior, remember that you are helping to determine your future, in both spiritual and health terms. Two of the things that immoral behavior and poor health decision-making have in common are that their impacts are cumulative and often insidious. You may disregard an occasional excess at the dinner table, but excess at more meals than not will undoubtedly eventually harm you. Likewise, when you cause pain to another person with your actions or gratuitously destroy part of God's creation, you have not only hurt another person or the earth, but degraded yourself in the process.

This is arguably one of the toughest lessons to learn in life — just ask any parent. Teaching a child to understand that his or her actions today — such as smoking, eating poorly, or not exercising — will have consequences at a distant time and place, in the form of heart disease, stroke, or cancer, is remarkably difficult. Absent the integrity, will, and knowledge to choose wisely, we increase the risk of eventually living a life filled with regret about decisions not made or made poorly. The harm is often too great to substantially undo when it comes time for your life's accounts to be reconciled, whether that reconciliation happens under the bright white lights of a hospital emergency department or before God.

The smarter strategy is to remember your future when you choose. Remember that God's vision for you does not include a lifetime tied to health care services and prescription drugs that you could conceivably do without. His vision for you does not include permanent enslavement to the latest pitches from fast food companies and soft drink manufacturers, not when his own creation supplies all the abundance necessary for a fit, health-filled life. Finally, remember that when you put your spiritual and health future first, you help to meet not only your needs but the needs of those who depend on you. We don't live our lives in isolation, and we all — friends, family, coworkers, fellow parishioners — have an interest in each other's survival, happiness, and potential.

Remember Why You Seek Strength

We close this book with a quote attributed to St. Francis de Sales: "There is nothing so strong as gentleness and nothing so gentle as true strength." We can think of no better bookend to the words with which we began this journey: We want you to be strong, as strong as you can possibly be.

Our vision of strength is that it is a tool for achievement and purpose. Spiritual and physical strength are two of the most empowering forces we can imagine. When you have taken yourself from unfit to fit, from spiritually unfulfilled to overflowing, from medically at-risk to medically robust, you make yourself into a change agent for a world that needs people who better themselves and then work for the benefit of the world around them.

It is clear to us that the very last thing Jesus wants is a group of inactive, sedentary disciples. In fact, some of Christ's strongest condemnations are directed toward those who sit and talk rather than stand and serve. In the gospel according to Matthew, Jesus denounces the scribes and Pharisees who *sit* on Moses' seat; they "Love to have the place of honor at banquets," he observes, "and the best *seats* in the synagogues" (Matthew 23:6). The scribes and

240

Pharisees would have fit in among the executives of Standard Oil in the late 1880s. These were men who met every day for lunch with John D. Rockefeller, at the top of a tower in lower Manhattan with a commanding view of New York City. Dressed to the nines in formal attire, they sat around the so-called "long table" to dine on delicacies and babble about business.

Or no, better yet: These religious leaders of Jesus' day would have savored the satisfaction of sitting in J.P. Morgan's personal library, adjoining his midtown Manhattan mansion. The library sported bronze doors from Italy, walls of crimson damask from Rome's Chigi Palace, a ceiling taken from a 16th-century palace, and original art by Botticelli and Michelangelo. Walking out of J. P. Morgan's library, they would surely "be greeted with respect in the marketplaces" (v. 7)![182]

To all who feel tempted to take such seats, Jesus cries out, "Don't sit there!" Disciples of Christ are not to sit and become sedentary, they are to stand and use their strength to be active ... as servants. "The greatest among you will be your servant," says Jesus, (v. 11), standing to identify human needs and make an active effort to bring comfort, healing, and hope. The question for followers of Jesus in every time and place is this: Are we standing up and using our strength to serve others, or sitting down and focusing on ourselves?

The great irony of Christian life is that we will feel good about ourselves only if we stand to serve others. In the upside-down logic of the kingdom of God, the humble one is always exalted and the servant is always the greatest. So if we are going to feel good about ourselves, we're going to have to get out of our seats and ...

- take a stand for the ill, the dying, and the depressed. Are we strong enough to get on our feet and visit people in hospitals, hospices, and nursing homes?
- take a stand for single parents struggling to survive. Are we strong enough to provide them with an occasional evening of babysitting, so that they can get out and shop or run errands?

- take a stand for young people who are facing so many dangers and temptations. Are we strong enough to advise a youth group or chaperone a summer mission trip?
- take a stand for the earth. Are we strong enough to reduce, reuse, and recycle the materials we use in our daily lives, take action to reclaim a local stream or volunteer at an animal shelter?
- take a stand for the homeless. We can do this by following the example of Amber Coffman, a teenager in the City of Baltimore. Every Sunday at precisely 2 p.m., she arrives at city hall with her mother and a small team of volunteers. They lug trunk-size bins to a spot on the sidewalk, and then begin to hand out cold ham-and-cheese sandwiches to unkempt men and women in thick layers of clothing. Who is Amber Coffman? She's an aspiring teen beauty queen and committed feeder of the down and out. This is her "calling," she says — ministering to the homeless with the sandwiches she makes in the cramped living room of her apartment in suburban Glen Burnie. She considers this "God's work," and so should we: giving destitute children of God a sandwich and a smile. Are we strong enough to do what Jesus asks: to give food to the hungry and drink to the thirsty?[183]

Christ calls you to stand and get to work, to identify human needs and then use your strength to bring comfort, healing, and hope — the possibilities are limited only by your vision. Are you ready to reach out to a friend or coworker who is lonely or confused? Are you willing to invite a friend to church, to tutor a child, to take a meal to a shut-in, or to mentor a teenage mom? The discipleship directives of Jesus are to stand, not sit; to use strength for service, not self-aggrandizement or the satisfaction of superfluous "needs"; to lift the burdens of others and the earth instead of engaging in further oppression or destruction; and to find greatness through servitude, and to experience exaltation through humility.

We all know that kindness, compassion, mercy, justice, and love are among the hallmarks of a Christian life. To this list, we

242

hope you will add physical dynamism and strength, because it does not take much inspection of our world to see that there is an awful lot to do, and it will take strong people to do the heavy lifting. From at-risk children to adults who need help learning to read, from abandoned creatures to parts of the environment that desperately need our attention, there are many people, places, and things that need the ministrations of physically, intellectually, and spiritually strong people who are unbowed by weakness and driven by a conviction that there are higher causes and purposes in life that are worth fulfilling.

We hope that your newfound physical vitality will inspire you to lead others down the path to better health through knowledge, improved choices, and a desire to maximize their God-given potential. The ultimate way to thank God for what he has given you — the ability to learn how to live a better, healthier, more fulfilled life — is to turn around and help someone else accomplish that same goal. Look around your family, workplace, and circle of friends and we are confident you will find someone who wants to learn, change, grow, and improve but has been waiting for just the right teacher to come along. As the great Indian leader, Mahatma Gandhi, once said, "We are the change we wish to see in the world."

The Spiritual Power Of Remembrance

As we conclude our reflections on this final commandment, "Thou Shalt Remember," we need to say a word about the biblical understanding of remembrance, because it has a lot to teach us about the ongoing process of faith and fitness. In the Bible, you see, remembrance does not only look backward — it also looks to the present and the future. Remembrance is a creative and hopeful activity, one that has an important role to play in transformation and transition.

When the people of the Bible engage in remembrance, they are not simply recalling the past. They are actually drawing the past into the present and using important memories to teach them what to carry into the future. In Deuteronomy 26:1-11, Moses is speaking to the people of Israel in the wilderness, giving them instructions about how they are to live in the promised land. As Moses

243

remembers the past, he leaps ahead to the time when the Israelites will be in the land that the Lord has promised them, but he also jumps back to the period in which they were living as slaves in Egypt. The point of all this leaping is to help the Israelites get a good strong grip on the fundamentals of their faith. This is the same kind of exercise that we should be engaged in as we remember the "Ten Commandments of Faith and Fitness."

"When you have come into the land," predicts Moses, jumping ahead, "you shall take some of the first of all the fruit of the ground," and you shall put it in a basket and take it to the priest as an offering. The worshiper will then say to the priest, "Today I declare to the Lord your God that I have come into the land that the Lord swore to our ancestors to give us" (Deuteronomy 26:3).

Moses looks ahead with confidence, believing that God will surely lead his people into the promised land. All he asks the Israelites to do is give thanks and to show their appreciation with a gift of firstfruits. Not leftovers, you understand, not table scraps, not disposable income; not what remains in the checkbook after every other bill has been paid. Firstfruits — the good stuff — the cream of the crop — a gift of thanksgiving that comes right off the top.

This idea of "firstfruits" is an important one for us to remember as we look to the future in an active and ongoing process of faith and fitness. This means giving God time for Sunday worship and daily prayer, and also giving yourself time for regular exercise all through the week. Remember how in Commandment One we encouraged you to make appointments with yourself for three periods of exercise that each last 30 minutes? That's a way of giving your exercise program your firstfruits, not your leftovers.

After presenting the firstfruits, the worshiper in Deuteronomy is to tell a little story, and it is in this story that he leaps back many years to the greatest crisis in the history of God's people. He jumps back years, decades, generations, and he tells the tale, "A wandering Aramean was my ancestor; he went down into Egypt and lived there as an alien, few in number, and there he became a great nation, mighty and populous" (Deuteronomy 26:5). It is in this story that the people of God discover the things in life that are really worth preserving, in any time and place.

"When the Egyptians treated us harshly and afflicted us," recalls the worshiper, "by imposing hard labor on us, we cried to the Lord, the God of our ancestors; the Lord heard our voice and saw our affliction, our toil, and our oppression. The Lord brought us out of Egypt with a mighty hand and an outstretched arm, with a terrifying display of power, and with signs and wonders; and he brought us to this place and gave us this land, a land flowing with milk and honey" (Deuteronomy 26:6-9).

There you have it: The things worth hanging on to in every time, every place, every generation. The Lord hears our voice. He sees our affliction. He brings us out of captivity with a mighty hand. He gives us a new and better land to live in. These are great spiritual truths that are worth remembering and carrying with us into the future, because they shape a healthy and life-giving relationship with the Lord.

That's the spiritual side of the equation, but what about the physical side? What are the fitness truths that are worth remembering and preserving? We are convinced that you will find The Fitness Trinity — strength training, endurance exercise, and good nutrition — to be a foundational truth for your ongoing fitness routine. In addition, you will continue to benefit from raising the bar, practicing periodization, taking time to rest, and reflecting on your progress. In their own way, each of these "Ten Commandments of Faith and Fitness" is worth remembering and preserving in a life-long process of good nutrition and healthy physical activity.

Where our spiritual truths and physical truths come together is in the biblical idea that God is always working to bring us out of captivity, and to give us a new and better land to live in. This does not mean that we are going to move to a new place: a new country, a new state, a new community, a new job, a new health club, or a new church. It means that the Lord wants to lead us to a new and better land right where we are. It means that God is working for our personal transformation, as well as our transition to a better style of life. It means that the Lord frees us from captivity to fads and quick fixes, and shows us how to appreciate the value of solid theology and serious science. It means that our home and community — the place we live right now — becomes a fertile environment for steady growth and improvement in both spiritual and physical health. It means that our daily routines actually change the quality of our lives, so that we discover that we are now living in a promised land of faith and fitness.

By practicing our ten commandments, week by week and month by month, you will discover that God is with you, working to liberate you from anything that is keeping you from fullness of health. Through personal transformation and transition, you will find that the Lord is improving your strength, endurance, and nutrition, giving you a level of vitality that enables you to serve both him and your neighbor with energy and enthusiasm. Remember that God wants to bring you out of captivity "with a mighty hand and an outstretched arm, with a terrifying display of power," and he desires to bring you to "a land flowing with milk and honey" (Deuteronomy 26:6-9). This picture of liberation is not just a memory of the ancient past, but it can actually be a pattern for your present and your future. May you make it a reality in your own life, as you journey forward in an ongoing process of faith and fitness, moving ever closer to the fullness of life that God desires for you. We wish you godspeed in this good and important work.

Your Action Steps From Commandment Ten

1. Identify a lapse in your fitness program and forgive yourself for it.

2. Make creative use of an upcoming trip by devising an on-the-fly fitness strategy.

3. Take a stand for a person in need, or a troubled part of God's creation.

4. Remember the fitness truths that are worth preserving, from The Fitness Trinity to regular sabbath-keeping.

Epilogue

So that you will have easy access to the major recommendations of this book, turn the page and "take two tablets" ...

I — Thou shalt be knowledgeable

II — Thou shalt be self-aware

III — Thou shalt endure

IV — Thou shalt be strong

V — Thou shalt eat from the garden ... (of Eden, that is)

VI — **Thou shalt raise the bar**

VII — **Thou shalt periodize**

VIII — **Thou shalt rest**

IX — **Thou shalt reflect**

X — **Thou shalt remember**

Exercise And Nutrition
Note Pages

You may copy the following pages and put them in a three-ring binder, creating an annual exercise and diet diary for yourself. You should be able to fill out each day's record in just a couple of minutes. The first column on the first page is completed for you, to show you the standards to aim for. You can use empty squares in each column to make notes to yourself.

	Sunday	Monday	Tuesday	Wednesday	Thursday	Friday	Saturday
My weekly exercise and nutrition record					Week of:_____		
Your endurance activity							
Activity							
Duration (minutes)							
How hard was it (RPE of 1 to 11)							
Your strength activity							
Muscles worked today							
Duration (minutes)							
Sets per muscle group							
Average reps per set							
RPE (1 to 11)							
Nutrition							
Did you eat...							
5 to 9 servings of fruit or vegetables							
Whole grain carbohydrates							
Products made with white flour or high in sugar							
Red meat or deep-fried foods							
Skinless chicken or turkey							
Heart-healthy (plant-based) fats or nuts							
Seafood							
Did you also...							
Take a multivitamin							
Drink a little alcohol							
Stay within your desired daily calorie range							
Facts about you							
Your bodyweight							
Your waistline							
Your BMI							

My weekly exercise and nutrition record					Week of:_____			
	Sunday	Monday	Tuesday	Wednesday	Thursday	Friday	Saturday	
Your endurance activity								
Activity	Walk							
Duration (minutes)	45							
How hard was it (RPE of 1 to 11)	5							
Your strength activity								
Muscles worked today		Upper body						
Duration (minutes)		25						
Sets per muscle group		3						
Average reps per set		8						
RPE (1 to 11)		4						
Nutrition								
Did you eat...								
5 to 9 servings of fruit or vegetables*	Yes							
Whole grain carbohydrates	Yes							
Products made with white flour or high in sugar	No							
Red meat or deep-fried foods	No							
Skinless chicken or turkey	Yes							
Heart-healthy (plant-based) fats or nuts	Yes							
Seafood	Yes							
Did you also...								
Take a multivitamin	Yes							
Drink a little alcohol	Yes							
Stay within your desired daily calorie range	Yes							
Facts about you								
Your bodyweight	150							
Your waistline	32							
Your BMI	24.5							

* People are often confused by what constitutes a serving. A great website for sorting this information out is www.fruitsandveggiesmatter.gov.

Endnotes

Commandment One

1. For people who need to lose weight and keep it off, you likely will need to have a long-term goal of exercising for up to 60 minutes most or all days of the week. However, for many people this is an unrealistic goal at the outset and trying to do too much too fast may not only discourage you, it may lead to illness or injury. It is particularly important for people who are new to exercise or returning to it after an extended layoff to proceed slowly and in small increments, thus maximizing the likelihood that you will stick to newly learned habits.

2. Stone, W.J. and Klein, D.A. "Long term exercisers: what can we learn from them?" *ACSM's Health & Fitness Journal.* March/April 2004. 8:2; 11-14.

3. Greenspan, Stanley I., M.D. *The Challenging Child* (Reading, Massachusetts: Addison-Wesley Publishing Co., 1995). 125.

4. Tutu, Desmond. *An African Prayer Book* (New York: Doubleday, 1995). 78.

5. Frederick Buechner, "Prayer," *Wishful Thinking: A Seeker's ABC* (San Francisco: HarperSanFrancisco, [1973], 1993). 87.

Commandment Two

6. Tsai, A.G. and Wadden, T.A. "Systematic review: an evaluation of the major commercial weight loss programs in the U.S." *Annals of Internal Medicine.* January 4, 2005. 142:7; 56-66.

7. Hayter, T.L., et al. "Effects of electrical muscle stimulation on oxygen consumption." *J. of Strength and Cond. Res.* February 2005. 19:1; 98-101.

8. Sternlicht, E., et al. "Electomyograhpical analysis and comparison of selected abdominal training devices with a traditional crunch." *J. of Strength and Cond. Res.* February 2005. 19:1; 157-162.

9. White, S.B., et al. "Effect of continuous passive motion exercise as an alternative form of training." *J. of Strength and Cond. Res.* August 2005. 19:3; 635-639.

10. Richardson, C.R., et al. "Physical activity and mortality across cardiovascular disease risk groups." *Medicine & Science in Sports & Exercise.* November 2004. 36:11; 1923-1929.

11. Sullivan, D., et al. "Effects of muscle strength training and testosterone in frail elderly males." *Medicine & Science in Sports & Exercise.* October 2005. 37:10; 1664-1672.

12. Winters-Stone, K.M. and Snow, C.S. "Musculoskeletal response to exercise is greatest in women with low initial values." *Medicine & Science in Sports & Exercise.* October 2003. 35:10; 1691-1696.

13. Levinger, I., et al. "The effect of resistance training on left ventricular function and structure of patients with congestive heart failure." *Int'l J. of Cardiology.* 105:2005; 159-163.

14. Bartholomew, J.B. "Effects of acute exercise on mood and well-being in patients with major depressive disorder." *Medicine & Science in Sports & Exercise.* December 2005. 37:12; 2032-2037.

15. Pokan, R., et al. "Effect of high-volume and intensity endurance training in heart transplant recipients." *Medicine & Science in Sports & Exercise.* December 2004. 36:12; 2011-2016.

16. Galvão, D.A. and Newton, R.U. "Review of exercise intervention studies in cancer patients." *J. of Clinical Oncology.* February 1, 2005. 23:4; 899-909.

17. Cheema, B.S.B. and Gaul, C.A. "Full-body exercise training improves fitness and quality of life in survivors of breast cancer." *J. of Strength and Cond. Res.* February 2006. 20:1; 14-21.

18. Spencer, E.H., et al. "Predictors of nutrition counseling behaviors and attitudes in US medical students." *American J. of Clinical Nutrition.* September 2006. 84:3; 655-661.

19. Washington, R.L., et al. "Strength Training by Children and Adolescents." *Pediatrics*. June 2001. 107:6; 1470-1472.

20. Kohrt, W.M., et al. "Physical activity and bone health." A Position Stand of the American College of Sports Medicine. *Medicine & Science in Sports & Exercise*. November 2004. 1985-1996.

21. Kraemer, W.J., et al. "Progression Models in Resistance Training for Healthy Adults." A Position Stand of the American College of Sports Medicine. *Medicine & Science in Sports & Exercise*. February 1, 2002. 364-380.

22. Wilson, M., et al. "Exercise strategies for the individual with chronic obstructive pulmonary disease." *Strength and Conditioning Journal*. June 2004. 26:3; 58-63.

23. Seals, D. "Habitual exercise and the age-associated decline in large artery compliance." *Exercise and Sports Sciences Reviews*. April 2003. 31:2; 68-72.

24. Albright, A., et al. "Exercise and type 2 diabetes." A Position Stand of the American College of Sports Medicine. *Medicine & Science in Sports & Exercise*. July 2001. 1345-1360.

25. Pescatello, L.S., et al. "Exercise and hypertension." A Position Stand of the American College of Sports Medicine. *Medicine & Science in Sports & Exercise*. March 1, 2004. 533-553.

26. Wong, S.L., et al. "Cardiorespiratory fitness is associated with lower abdominal fat independent of body mass index." *Medicine & Science in Sports & Exercise*. February 2004. 36:2; 286-291.

27. Williams, P.T. and Pate, R.R. "Cross-sectional relationships of exercise and age to adiposity in 60,617 male runners." *Medicine & Science in Sports & Exercise*. August 2005. 37:8; 1329-1337.

28. Williams, P.T. "Maintaining vigorous activity attenuates 7-yr weight gain in 8,340 runners." *Medicine & Science in Sports & Exercise*. May 2007. 39:5; 801-809.

29. Jensen, M.K., et al. "Intakes of whole grains, bran, and germ and the risk of coronary heart disease." *Am. J. of Clinical Nutrition*. December 2004. 80:6; 1492-1499.

30. Willett, Walter. *Eat, drink, and be healthy* (New York: Free Press, 2005).

31. USP stands for Unites States Pharmacopeia. The USP is a not-for-profit organization in Rockville, Maryland, that sets ingredient standards for drug and supplement makers. When a product label says USP it means that the ingredients meet specific quality, purity, and dissolution standards. An unfortunate number of vitamins in the marketplace do not say USP on the label, which means that those manufacturers cannot certify the purity or dissolvability of their products.

32. Salmon, Jacqueline L. "Calling the Flock To God, Away From the Fridge: N.Va. Pastor Joins Ranks Of Faithful Eyeing Scales." *The Washington Post*. January 22, 2007. A1.

33. Mitchell, T.L., et al. "Effects of cardiorespiratory fitness on healthcare utilization." *Medicine & Science in Sports & Exercise*. December 2004. 36:12; 2088-2092.

34. Source for PAR-Q information: *The ACSM's Guidelines for Exercise Testing and Prescription*, Seventh Edition. Lippincott Williams & Wilkins. 2006.

35. The ACSM defines a positive family history of heart disease as a heart attack, coronary artery bypass or angioplasty, or sudden death before age 55 of a father or other male, first degree relative (brother, son, etc.) or before age 65 in a mother or other first degree female relative.

36. A maximal fitness test is one in which the person undergoing the test works to a very high level of intensity, and continues until exhaustion. In a submaximal test, the person undergoing the test works according to a predetermined workload pattern, which varies during the test. Most people can complete submaximal exercise testing on a treadmill, stationary exercise cycle, step bench, or on a track, and come away with a very useful estimate of their fitness and work

capacity. Maximal exercise testing is generally reserved for clinical situations, such as cardiac stress testing done by a cardiologist, research purposes, or to assess the fitness of highly fit competitive athletes. You can also do a field test of cardiovascular capacity, such as a timed walk or run.

37. A good example of the need for caution pertains to use of metformin by diabetics. Metformin is a very commonly used oral antiglycemic that helps diabetics manage their blood sugar. One of its side effects is a very serious condition called lactic acidosis, which can lead to kidney or liver damage and even death. Lactic acidosis is also a potential side effect of intense exercise. The implications, then, for a fitness professional are that a diabetic on metformin should be taught to exercise at low to moderate intensities that will not provoke lactic acidosis.

38. Henricks, M. "Would-Be Fitness Trainers Need Clients Way More Than Muscles." *The Wall Street Journal*. August 30, 2005. B6.

39. Albert, C.A. "Triggering of sudden death from cardiac causes by vigorous exertion." *New England Journal of Medicine*. November 9, 2000.

40. Levin, Jeff. *God, Faith, and Health: Exploring the Spirituality-Healing Connection* (New York: John Wiley & Sons, 2001).

41. Wessel, David. "Sad Little Rich Country." *The Washington Monthly*. November 2003. 51-53.

Commandment Three
42. American Heart Association Heart Disease and Stroke Statistics — 2005 Update. Dallas, Texas.

43. Levin, B.D., et al. "The cardiovascular evaluation of women athletes." *Medicine & Science in Sports & Exercise*. August 2005. 37:8; 1431-1446.

44. Conroy, M.B., et al. "Past physical activity, current physical activity, and risk of coronary heart disease." *Medicine & Science in Sports & Exercise*. August 2005. 37:8; 1251-1256.

45. Slentz, C.A., et al. "Modest exercise prevents the progressive disease associated with physical inactivity." *Exercise and Sports Sciences Reviews.* January 2007. 35:1; 19-23.

46. Kaminsky, L.A., senior editor. *ACSM's Resource manual for guidelines for exercise testing and prescription.* American College of Sports Medicine Fifth Edition. Lippincott Williams & Wilkins. 2006. Chapter 5.

47. Lichtenstein, A., et al. "Diet and lifestyle recommendations revision 2006." A scientific statement from the American Heart Association Nutrition Committee. *Circulation.* June 2006. 114. (Published online.)

48. Kaminsky, L.A., at 97.

49. Kraus, W.E., et al. "Effects of the amount and intensity of exercise on plasma lipoproteins." *New England J. of Medicine.* November 7, 2002. 347:19; 1483-1492.

50. Wood, P.D., et al. "Changes in plasma lipids and lipoproteins in overweight men during weight loss through dieting as compared with exercise." *New England J. of Medicine.* November 3, 1988. 319:18; 1173-1179.

51. Kaminsky, L.A., at 97.

52. Seals, D. "Habitual exercise and the age-associated decline in large artery compliance." *Exercise and Sports Sciences Reviews.* April 2003. 31:2; 68-72.

53. Maeda, S., et al. "Aortic stiffness and aerobic exercise: mechanistic insight from microarray analysis." *Medicine & Science in Sports & Exercise.* October 2005. 37:10; 1710-1716.

54. Buchheir, M., et al. "Heart rate variability and intensity of habitual physical activity in middle-aged persons." *Medicine & Science in Sports & Exercise.* September 2005. 37:9; 1530-1534.

55. Carnethon, M.R., et al. "A longitudinal study of physical activity and heart-rate recovery: CARDIA, 1987-1993." *Medicine & Science in Sports & Exercise.* April 2005. 37:4; 606-612.

56. Huang, G., et al. "Resting heart rate changes after endurance training in older adults: a meta analysis." *Medicine & Science in Sports & Exercise.* August 2005. 37:8; 1381-1386.

57. Garet, M., et al. "Relationship between daily physical activity and ANS activity in patients with CHF." *Medicine & Science in Sports & Exercise.* August 2005. 37:8; 1257-1263.

58. Arbab-Zadeh, A., et al. "Effect of aging and physical activity on left ventricular compliance." *Circulation.* September 28, 2004. 110; 1805-1811.

59. Huang, G., et al. "Resting heart rate changes after endurance training in older adults: a meta analysis." *Medicine & Science in Sports & Exercise.* August 2005. 37:8; 1381-1386.

60. Williams, P.T. and Pate, R.R. "Cross-sectional relationships of exercise and age to adiposity in 60,617 male runners." *Medicine & Science in Sports & Exercise.* August 2005. 37:8; 1329-1337.

61. It is not entirely clear why people move less as they age. The unanswered question about aging and physical activity is: Do age-related neuromuscular and hormonal changes slow people down and prompt them to move less or do people make a conscious decision to be less active, which, in turn, accelerates the aging process and contributes to a downward spiral of chronic disease and disability? As of today, no one knows the answer for sure. But, you can mitigate your risk through a rigorous endurance exercise program built around activities that you enjoy doing.

62. Hu, F., et al. "Adiposity as compared with physical activity in predicting mortality among women." *New England J. of Medicine.* December 23, 2004. 351:26; 2694-2703.

261

63. van Dam, R., et al. "The relationship between overweight in adolescence and premature death in women." *Annals of Internal Medicine.* July 18, 2006. 145:2; 91-97.

64. Ekeland, U., et al. "Physical activity energy expenditure predicts change in body composition." *Amer. J. of Clinical Nutrition.* May 2005. 81:5; 964-969.

65. Jouven, X., et al. "Heart-rate profile during exercise as a predictor of sudden death." *New England J. of Medicine.* May 12, 2005. 352:19; 1951-1958.

66. Reaven, G. "The metabolic syndrome: is this diagnosis necessary?" *Am. J. of Clinical Nutrition.* June 2006. 83:6; 1237-1247.

67. Grundy, S. "Does a diagnosis of metabolic syndrome have value in clinical practice?" *Am. J. of Clinical Nutrition.* June 2006. 83:6; 1248-1251.

68. Katzmarzyk, P.T., et al. "Targeting the metabolic syndrome with exercise: evidence from the HERITAGE family study." *Medicine & Science in Sports & Exercise.* October 2003. 35:10; 1703-1709.

69. See generally, *Medicine & Science in Sports & Exercise,* November 2003.

70. Herrero, F., et al. "Is cardiorespiratory fitness related to quality of life in survivors of breast cancer?" *J. of Strength and Cond. Res.* August 2006. 20:3; 535-540.

71. Kriska, A. "Can a physically active lifestyle prevent type 2 diabetes?" *Exercise and Sport Sciences Reviews.* July 2003. 31:3; 132-137.

72. Kaminsky, L.A. at 471 et seq.

73. Ryan, A.S. "Insulin resistance with aging: effects of diet and exercise." *Sports Medicine.* November 2000. 30:5; 327-46.

74. Ferrara, C., et al. "Metabolic effects of the addition of resistive to aerobic exercise in older men." *Int'l J. of Sports Nutrition and Exercise Metabolism.* February 2004. 14:1; 73-80.

75. Blumenthal, J.A., et al. "Exercise, depression, and mortality after myocardial infarction in the ENRICHD Trial." *Medicine & Science in Sports & Exercise.* May 2004. 36:5; 746-755.

76. Kaminsky, L.A. at 186-187.

77. Bartholomew, J.B., et al. "Effects of acute exercise on mood and well-being in patients with major depressive disorder." *Medicine & Science in Sports & Exercise.* December 2005. 37:12; 2032-2037.

78. Kohrt, W.M., et al. "Physical activity and bone health." A Position Stand of the American College of Sports Medicine. *Medicine & Science in Sports & Exercise.* November 2004. 36:11; 1985-1996.

79. Laurin, D., et al. "Physical activity and risk of cognitive impairment and dementia in elderly persons." *Archives of Neurology.* March 2001. 58:3; 498-504.

80. Adlard, P., et al. "Voluntary exercise decreases amyloid load in a transgenic model of Alzheimer's disease." *J. of Neuroscience.* April 2005. 25:17; 4217-4221.

81. Larson, E.B., et al. "Exercise is associated with reduced risk for incident dementia among persons 65 years of age and older." *Annals of Internal Medicine.* January 17, 2006. 144:2; 74-81.

82. Griffin, T. and Guilak, F. "The role of mechanical loading in the onset and progression of osteoarthritis." *Exercise and Sports Sciences Reviews.* October 2005. 33:4; 195-200.

83. Quinn, T.J., et al. "Two short, daily activity bouts vs. one long bout." *J. of Strength and Cond. Res.* February 2006. 20:1; 130-135.

84. Persinger, R., et al. "Consistency of the talk test for exercise prescription." *Medicine & Science in Sports & Exercise.* September 2004. 36:9; 1632-1636.

85. Sporer, B. & Wenger, H.A. "Effects of aerobic exercise on strength performance following various recovery periods." *J. Strength and Conditioning Research.* November 2003. 17:4; 638-644.

86. Jakicic, J. and Otto, A. "Physical activity considerations for the treatment and prevention of obesity." *Am. J. of Clinical Nutrition Supplement: Science-based solutions to obesity.* July 2005. 82:1(S); 226S-229S.

87. Dietary reference intakes for energy, carbohydrates, fiber, fat, protein, and amino acids. The Institute of Medicine. National Academies Press. 2002.

88. Baer, J.D., et al. "The Literacy of America's College Students." The Pew Charitable Trusts and the American Institute for Research. Washington DC. January 2006.

89. *ACSM's Guidelines for Exercise Testing and Prescription*, Seventh Edition. Lippincott Williams Wilkins. 2006. 77.

90. Unfortunately, this is a very fractured professional environment. There are no widely accepted, uniform academic training or certification standards for personal trainers, fitness coaches, and the like. Virtually anyone can call himself or herself a personal trainer because there is no standard definition of what that is. You should interview potential exercise professionals thoroughly before agreeing to work with anyone. Look for people with *at least* a bachelor's degree in exercise science, physical education, or a directly related health field (such as physical therapy or athletic training), and the most rigorous possible certification as an exercise professional. Ideally, you want someone who has completed an intensive certification training program, as well as a written and practical exam and who must take continuing education classes to maintain his or her certification. We suggest that you look for individuals with strong education or those who completed meaningful measures of professional preparation and knowledge, not take-home exams, open-book tests, or mailed in videotapes of themselves to secure their certification. You should especially avoid anyone who was certified without enduring any kind of testing process. Also ask the person to affirm that they carry malpractice insurance and that they have taken training in first aid and cardiopulmonary resuscitation (CPR).

91. Wing, R. and Phelan, S. "Long-term weight loss maintenance." *Am. J. of Clinical Nutrition Supplement: Science-based solutions to obesity.* July 2005. 82:1(S); 222S-225S.

92. Wing, R., et al. "A self-regulation program for the maintenance of weight loss." *New England J. of Medicine.* October 12, 2006. 355:15; 1563-1570.

93. For example, if your theoretical maximum heart rate is 165 and your heart rate at the end of the walk was 100 beats per minute, then you completed the walk at 60% of your MHR. A more fit person might finish the walk at 120 beats per minute or 72% (and would take less time), while a less fit person might complete the walk at only 90 beats per minute or 55% of maximum (and take more time to walk the mile).

94. Tyson, Peter. "A Tree's Secret to Living Long." *NOVA Online.* November 2001. www.pbs.org/wgbh/nova/methuselah/long.html

Commandment Four

95. Humphries, B., et al. Muscular fitness (Chapter 13) in the American College of Sports Medicine's *Resource Manual for Guidelines for Exercise Testing and Prescription.* American College of Sports Medicine. 2006. 207.

96. Ades, P.A., et al. "Resistance training on physical performance in disabled older female cardiac patients." *Medicine & Science in Sports & Exercise.* August 2003. 35:8; 1265-1270.

97. Ferrara, C., et al. "Metabolic effects of the addition of resistive to aerobic exercise in older men." *Int'l J. of Sports Nutrition and Exercise Metabolism.* February 2004. 14:1; 73-80.

98. Ketelhut, R.G., et al. "Regular exercise as an effective approach in antihypertensive therapy." *Medicine and Science in Sports and Exercise.* January 2004. 36:1; 4-8.

99. Jurca, R., et al. "Associations of muscle strength and aerobic fitness with metabolic syndrome in men." *Medicine & Science in Sports & Exercise.* August 2004. 36:8; 1301-1307.

100. Jurca, R., et al. "Association of muscular strength with incidence of metabolic syndrome in men." *Medicine & Science in Sports & Exercise.* November 2005. 37:11; 1849-1855.

101. Cheema, B.S.B. and Gaul, C.A. "Full-body exercise training improves fitness and quality of life in survivors of breast cancer." *J. of Strength and Cond. Res.* February 2006. 20:1; 14-21.

102. Galvão, D.A. and Newton, R.U. "Review of exercise intervention studies in cancer patients." *J. of Clinical Oncology.* February 1, 2005. 23:4; 899-909.

103. Willardson, J. and Tudor-Locke, C. "Survival of the strongest: a brief review examining the association between muscular fitness and mortality." *Strength and Conditioning Journal.* June 2005. 27:3; 80-84.

104. Wolfe, R.R. "The underappreciated role of muscle in health and disease." *Am. J. of Clinical Nutrition.* September 2006. 84:3; 475-482.

105. Galvão, D.A., et al. "Resistance training and reduction of treatment side effects in prostate cancer patients." *Medicine & Science in Sports & Exercise.* December 2006. 38:12; 2045-2052.

106. Anton, M., et al. "Age-related declines in anaerobic muscular performance: weightlifting and powerlifting." *Medicine & Science in Sports & Exercise.* January 2004. 36:1; 143-147.

107. Muscles account for about 70% of your body weight and 30% of the energy you burn at rest (fat consumes about 5% of the energy you burn at rest, and your organs account for the remaining 65%); when you are physically active, this balance shifts, and your muscles use about 60% to 65% of the energy that you burn. Your muscles are also the engine that drives all other physical activity ... let your muscles break down and weaken and you have greatly diminished your quality of life because you will be able to do less and less of the things that matter to you. See for example, "Aging muscle," by Nair, K.S., in the *American Journal of Clinical Nutrition.* May 2005. 81:5; 953-963.

108. Fiatarone, M.A., et al. "Exercise training and nutritional supplementation for physical frailty in very elderly people." *New England J. of Medicine*. June 23, 1994. 330:25; 1769-1775.

109. Kalapotharakos, A.I., et al. "Effects of a heavy and a moderate resistance training on functional performance in older adults." *J. of Strength and Cond. Res.* August 2005. 19:3; 652-657.

110. Sullivan, D.H., et al. "Effects of muscle strength training and testosterone in frail elderly males." *Medicine & Science in Sports & Exercise*. October 2005. 37:10; 1664-1672.

111. Washington, R.L., et al. *Pediatrics*. June 2001. 107:6; 1470-1472.

112. Vehrs, P.R. "Strength Training in Children and Teens: Dispelling Misconceptions — Part One and Part Two." *ACSM's Health & Fitness Journal*. July/August 2005. 9:4; 8-12 and 13-18.

113. Clay, C.C., et al. "The metabolic cost of hatha yoga." *J. of Strength and Cond. Res.* August 2005. 19:3; 604-610.

114. Spiide, S. and Porcari, J.P. "Can Pilates do it all?" *ACE Fitness Matters*. November/December 2005. 10-11.

115. During our preparation of this book, Vik received a mail solicitation from the Bottom Line Personal newsletter, which contained a box on the purported benefits of slow weight lifting. The box incorrectly claims that conventional strength training is injurious and that slow lifting is proven effective at both building muscle and burning fat. Done properly, conventional strength training is both safe and effective. Further, on February 20, 2007, the *Washington Post* Health Section also carried a box, titled "The Moving Crew," written by Post restaurant reviewer, Eve Ziebart, extolling the virtues of slow weight lifting. She cited no expert opinion or studies to support her advocacy for this unsubstantiated training technique, noting instead that "some personal trainers recommend a 10 count up and a 10 count down."

116. See for example: Greer, B. "The effectiveness of low velocity (superslow) resistance training." *Strength and Conditioning Journal*. April 2005. 27:2; 32-37; Sakamoto, A. and Sinclair, P.J. "Effect of movement velocity on the relationship between training load and the number of repetitions of the bench press." *J. of Strength and Cond. Res.* August 2006. 20:3; 523-527; and, Hatfield, D., et al. "The impact of velocity of movement on performance factors in resistance exercise." *J. of Strength and Cond. Res.* November 2006. 20:4; 760-766.

117. *ACSM's Guidelines for exercise testing and prescription*, Seventh Edition. Whaley, M.H., senior editor. Lippincott Williams & Wilkins, 2005.

118. For more information on muscular strength and endurance testing, we recommend that readers look at in the *Health Fitness Instructor's Handbook* (Howley, E.T. and Franks, B.D., 2003, Human Kinetics Press) and the *American College of Sports Medicine's Guidelines for Exercise Testing and Prescription*, Seventh Edition (Whaley, M.H., senior editor, 2005, Lippincott Williams & Wilkins), from which this information is adapted.

119. Peterson, M.D., et al. "Applications of the dose-response for muscular strength development." *J. of Strength and Cond. Res.* November 2005. 19:4; 950-958.

120. Kalapotharakos, V., et al. "Effects of heavy and moderate resistance training." *J. of Strength and Cond. Res.* August 2005. 19:3; 652-657.

121. Holviala, J.H.S., et al. "Effects of strength training on muscle strength characteristics, functional capabilities, and balance in middle aged and older women." *J. of Strength and Cond. Res.* May 2006. 20:2; 336-344.

122. Sullivan, D.H., et al. "Effects of muscle strength training and testosterone in frail elderly males." *Medicine & Science in Sports & Exercise*. October 2005. 37:10; 1664-1672.

123. Gotshalk, L.A., et al. "Cardiovascular responses to a high-volume continuous circuit resistance training program." *J. of Strength and Cond Res.* November 2004. 18:4; 760-764.

124. Cameron, David. "Artificial Muscles Gain Strength." *Wired* magazine. February 15, 2002. www.techreview.com/articles/cameron021502.asp.

Commandment Five

125. Olshansky, S.J., et al. "A potential decline in life expectancy in the United States in the 21st Century." *New England J. of Medicine.* March 17, 2005. 352:11; 1138-1145.

126. Wadden, T.A. and Tsai, A.G. "Systematic review: an evaluation of major commercial loss programs in the United States." *Annals of Internal Medicine.* January 4, 2005. 142:1; 56-66.

127. Redman, L.M., et al. "Effect of calorie restriction with or without exercise on body composition and fat distribution." *J. of Clinical Endocrinology & Metabolism.* Published ahead of print, January 2, 2007.

128. National Heart, Lung, and Blood Institute. "Clinical guidelines on the identification, evaluation, and treatment of overweight and obesity in adults: The Evidence Report." *Obesity Research.* 1998. 6 (Supplement): 51S-210S.

129. Another crude way to estimate your resting metabolism is to simply multiply your body weight times 10. (For example, a 150-pound person has an estimated resting metabolism of 1,500 calories by this method.) You can take an average of the two calculations to estimate your resting metabolism.

130. To demonstrate the impact of body weight on caloric requirements, consider that if our 150 pound man weighed 300 pounds, he would burn exactly double the number of calories in the 3-mile walk. The less of you that there is to move through time and space, the less energy required to do so. This is one reason that weight loss is difficult, especially as you make progress. As you approach your goal, you need to either be more restrictive about what you eat or exercise more or at a greater intensity to maintain a daily calorie deficit.

131. "Pump iron to stop middle-aged spread." The Associated Press. March 3, 2006. Downloaded from MSNBC.com on March 4, 2006.

132. Wolfe, R.R. "The underappreciated role of muscle in health and disease." *Am. J. of Clinical Nutrition.* September 2006. 84:3; 475-482.

133. Hunter, G., and Byrne, N. "Physical activity and muscle function, but not resting energy expenditure impact on weight gain." *J. of Strength and Conditioning Res.* February 2005. 19:1; 225-230.

134. We recommend the 2005 paperback edition of this book, widely available for about $15.00.

135. Some "nutrition experts" rail against frozen or canned vegetables, encouraging people to always buy only fresh. This really misses the point. In a country where the overwhelming majority of people under-consume fruits and vegetables, saying that only fresh has nutritional value really makes the perfect the enemy of the good. If you choose canned fruit, opt for fruits canned in juice or light syrup and drain the syrup before you eat. Likewise, with canned vegetables, opt for low-sodium varieties. You can always season to taste, but add salt with care.

136. To avoid food-borne illnesses, please pay close attention to FDA guidelines and warnings on whether the prepackaged, washed items should be washed again or cooked before consumption.

137. More important nutritional imagery that can help you manage your portions: a serving of protein in the form of meat, such as chicken breast, is about the size of a deck of cards (or the palm of your hand); a serving of ice cream is 1/4 cup or a scoop about the size of a tennis ball; and, a serving of bread is one slice. Until you get the hang of judging the difference between these standardized serving sizes and what you actually put on your plate (called a portion), we encourage you to, whenever possible, weigh and measure your food. Many people, when they start to do this, shock themselves with their portion sizes and come to realize, quite quickly, where all the extra calories in their diet come from ... portions that are disproportionately large for their health and fitness needs.

138. Lairon, D., et al. "Dietary fiber intake and risk factors for cardio-vascular disease." *Amer. J. of Clinical Nutrition*. December 2005. 82:6; 1185-1194.

139. Sahyoun, N.R., et al. "Whole grain intake is inversely associated with the metabolic syndrome and mortality in older adults." *Am. J. of Clinical Nutrition*. January 2006. 83:1; 124-131.

140. Jensen, M.K., et al. "Intakes of whole grains, bran, and germ and the risk of coronary heart disease." *Am. J. of Clinical Nutrition*. December 2004. 80:6; 1492-1499.

141. Wu, H., et al. "Dietary fiber and progression of atherosclerosis: the Los Angeles Atherosclerosis Study." *Am J of Clinical Nutrition*. December 2003. 78:6; 1085-1091.

142. Pitsavos, C., et al. "Adherence to the Mediterranean diet is associated with total antioxidant capacity in healthy adults." *Am. J. of Clinical Nutrition*. September 2005. 82:3; 694-699.

143. Beware, however, that a manufacturer can claim 0 on the label as long as the product has less than 0.5 gm of trans fat per serving. If you tend to numerous servings of packaged foods each day, you could actually accumulate 1 or 2 grams of trans fat daily because of this loophole in the labeling requirement.

144. We exclude red meat from this list, because we want you to dramatically cut red meat intake to get saturated fats and cholesterol out of your diet. The long-term benefit of avoiding red meat, and seeking out alternative sources of protein, will likely pay benefits by helping to reduce your risk of heart disease. In general, studies of the benefits of the Mediterranean diet show that people who eat this way consume very little red meat. Thus, we believe, that if you opt to eat red meat, which you do not need for good health, do so no more than 2 or 3 times monthly. Further, because they are often loaded with saturated fat, cholesterol, and sodium, processed meats, such as lunch meats and hot dogs, have no place at all in a healthy diet, except as a very occasional treat.

145. Weigle, D.S. "A high-protein diet induces sustained reductions in appetite, ad libitum caloric intake, and body weight." *Am. J. of Clinical Nutrition.* July 2005. 85:1; 41-48; and, Astrup, A. "The satiating power of protein — a key to obesity prevention?" *Am. J. of Clinical Nutrition.* July 2005. 85:1; 1-2 (accompanying editorial).

146. Hu, F.B. "Protein, body weight, and cardiovascular health. Science-based solutions to obesity." *American J. of Clinical Nutrition* (Supplement). July 2005. 82:1(S); 242S-247S.

147. See, for example, Mastaloudis, A., et al. "Antioxidants did not prevent muscle damage in response to an ultramarathon run." *Medicine & Science in Sports & Exercise.* January 2006. 38:1; 72-80 and, Payne, J. "A bad year for supplements." *The Washington Post* (Health Section). June 20, 2006.

148. Varady, K., et al. "Plant sterols and endurance training combine to favorably alter plasma lipid profiles in previously sedentary hypercholesterolemic adults after 8 weeks." *Am. J. of Clinical Nutrition.* November 2004. 80:5; 1159-1166.

149. Behall, K.M. "Diets containing barley significantly reduce lipids in mildly hypercholesterolemic men and women." *Amer. J. of Clinical Nutrition.* November 2004. 80:5; 1185-1193.

150. Huang, H., et al. "The efficacy and safety of multivitamin and mineral supplement use to prevent cancer and chronic disease in adults." *Annals of Internal Medicine.* September 5, 2006. 145:5; 372-385.

151. See Multivitamin/mineral supplements and chronic disease prevention. NIH State-of-the-Science Conference. Proceedings published in the *American Journal of Clinical Nutrition.* January 2007 Supplement. 85:1; 215S-327S.

152. Remember also the difference between a serving and a portion. A serving is the standardized amount of food that the food label information is based upon. A portion is what you put on your plate. Americans eat large portions, often many servings of a particular food, which has contributed substantially to the obesity crisis.

153. Giugliano, D., et al. "The effects of diet on inflammation." *J. of the American College of Cardiology*. August 15, 2006. 48:4; 677-685.

154. Polk, Peggy. "First the Reformation, Then the Indigestion?" *Religion News Service*, November 18, 2000.

155. Buechner, Frederick. *Wishful Thinking: A Seeker's ABC* (San Francisco: HarperSanFrancisco, 1993). 2.

Commandment Six

156. Napolitano, M., et al. "Principles of health behavior change." Chapter 39 in American College of Sports Medicine's *Resource Manual for Guidelines for Exercise Testing and Prescription* (Fifth Edition; L. Kaminsky, senior editor). Lippincott Williams & Wilkins. 2006.

157. Collins, Jim. "Leadership Lessons of a Rock Climber." *Fast Company*. December 2003. 105-110.

Commandment Seven

158. Ebben, W., et al. "Strength and conditioning practices of major league baseball strength and conditioning coaches." *J. of Strength and Cond. Res*. August 2005. 19:3; 538-546.

159. Simenz, C., et al. "Strength and conditioning practice of National Basketball Association strength and conditioning coaches." *J. of Strength and Cond. Res*. August 2005. 19:3; 495-504.

160. For our purposes, we will assume that he is generally healthy, takes no prescription medicines that might affect his exercise performance, and is only slightly overweight, at 165 pounds on a 5'8" frame. This gives him a body mass index (BMI) of 25.1. He would like to lose 5 pounds and build stronger muscles. The weight loss will give him a normal BMI. For our purposes, we assume that he has exercised regularly for 2 or more years, but would now like to advance his program to get more out of it.

161. Martel, Jay. "Hot Strategy: Milking It." *Rolling Stone*. September 14, 2000. 120.

162. Ganio, M.S., et al. "Fluid ingestion attenuates the decline in VO_2peak associated with cardiovascular drift." *Medicine & Science in Sports & Exercise.* May 2006. 38:5; 901-909.

163. Esteve-Lanao, J., et al. "How do endurance runners actually train? Relationship with competition performance." *Medicine & Science in Sports & Exercise.* March 2005. 37:3; 496-504.

164. Foster, C., et al. "Regulation of energy expenditure during prolong athletic competition." *Medicine & Science in Sports & Exercise.* April 2005. 37:4; 670-675.

165. Lucia, A., et al. "Tour de France versus Vuelta a Espana: which is harder?" *Medicine & Science in Sports & Exercise.* May 2003. 35:5; 872-878.

166. Nair, K.S. "Aging muscle." *Am. J. of Clinical Nutrition.* May 2005. 81:5; 953-963.

167. Jurca, R., et al. "Association of muscular strength with incidence of metabolic syndrome in men." *Medicine & Science in Sports & Exercise.* November 2005. 37:11; 1849-1855.

Commandment Eight
168. Brown, D., et al. "Associations between physical activity dose and health-related quality of life." *Medicine & Science in Sports & Exercise.* May 2004. 36:5; 890-896.

169. Ogawa, K., et al. "A single bout of exercise influences natural killer cells in elderly women." *J. of Strength and Cond. Res.* February 2005. 19:1; 45-50.

170. Phillips, A.C., et al. "Stress and exercise: getting the balance right for aging immunity." *Exercise and Sports Sciences Reviews.* January 2007. 35:1; 35-39.

171. Nieman, D. and Courneya, K. "Immunological conditions." Chapter 38 in ACSM's *Resource Manual for Guidelines for Exercise Testing and Prescription.* Fifth Edition. Kaminsky, L., Senior Editor. Lippincott Williams & Wilkins. 2006.

172. Keteyian, S.J. and Brawner, C.A. "Cardiopulmonary adaptations to exercise." Chapter 22 in ACSM's *Resource Manual for Guidelines for Exercise Testing and Prescription*. Fifth Edition. Kaminsky, L., senior editor. Lippincott Williams & Wilkins. 2006.

Commandment Nine

173. Beunen, G.P., et al. "Adolescent correlates of adult physical activity: a 26-year follow-up." *Medicine & Science in Sports & Exercise*. November 2004. 36:11; 1930-1936.

174. Ekelund, U., et al. "Associations between physical activity and fat mass in adolescents in the Stockholm Weight Development Study." *Am. J. of Clinical Nutrition*. February 2005. 81:2; 355-360.

175. Gellman, Marc. "Worry. Don't Be Happy: What we think of as happiness is usually just pleasure. How to find real, lasting joy." *Newsweek* — MSNBC.com. October 5, 2006.

176. Reeves, M.J. and Rafferty, A.P. "Healthy lifestyle characteristics among adults in the United States, 2000." *Archives of Internal Medicine*. April 25, 2005. 165:8; 854-857.

177. Vasan, R., et al. "Relative importance of borderline and elevated levels of coronary heart disease risk factors." *Annals of Internal Medicine*. March 15, 2006. 142:5; 393-402.

178. Chiuve, S.E., et al. "Healthy lifestyle factors in the primary prevention of coronary heart disease among men: benefits among users and nonusers of lipid-lowering and antihypertensive medications." *Circulation*. Published online July 3, 2006.

179. Jurca, R., et al. "Association of muscular strength with incidence of metabolic syndrome in men." *Medicine & Science in Sports & Exercise*. November 2005. 37:11; 1849-1855.

180. We strongly encourage you to read the Executive Summary. It will give you a good primer on the importance of dealing with these issues, as well as good information about the available drug therapies, their effectiveness, and potential side effects.

Commandment Ten

181. A member of the bike racing team that Vik once coached approached him about the supposed value of a line of supplements, and, knowing his skepticism, indicated that this company was "different" and that it backed its health claims with scientific data. Well, not really. After perusing the company's website, Vik realized quickly that amongst the "published" studies that the company used to support its claims were papers that were more than a decade old, reports of animal studies (not randomized, controlled trials in humans), and studies published in obscure, highly questionable journals. Worse still, most of the studies were of such little utility that they were not cited by other researchers, which is one of the key ways of learning whether a piece of work really has credibility. Good scientific work gets used and cited repeatedly by other scientists because it breaks new conceptual ground. This is unfortunately a concept quite unfamiliar in the supplements field, where the concentration is on making money, not making a difference.

182. *Attaché* magazine. January 1999. 18.

183. Fountain, John W. "Fame, Hope & Charity." *The Washington Post* magazine. February 21, 1999. 7-8.

About The Authors

Henry Brinton is senior pastor of Fairfax Presbyterian Church in Fairfax, Virginia, and a staff writer for the *Homiletics* preaching journal. He is a frequent contributor to *USA TODAY* and *The Washington Post*, and author of the book, *Balancing Acts: Obligation, Liberation, And Contemporary Christian Conflicts* (CSS Publishing Company, 2006). He is a popular retreat and conference speaker on topics ranging from healing to social justice, and from Christian vocation to faith and fitness. Henry received his B.A. from Duke University and M.Div. from Yale Divinity School. A long-distance runner, he has completed one marathon a year since he turned forty in the year 2000. He is married to Nancy Freeborne, a physician assistant, and together they have two teenage children, Sarah and Sam.

Vikram Khanna, M.H.S., P.A., is an exercise coach, health educator, and CEO of Galileo Health Partners, LLC, of Ellicott City, Maryland. Vik is an active and involved parishioner at St. John's Episcopal Church in Ellicott City, Maryland. Vik is an Exercise Specialist®, certified by the American College of Sports Medicine; he also has a B.S. (cum laude) in physical education from SUNY Cortland (1979), is a physician assistant (B.S., with honors, Hahnemann University, 1982), and he earned his Master of Health Science from the Johns Hopkins University School of Hygiene and Public Health in 1984. A lifelong weight lifter, Vik is also an avid cyclist and runner. He is married to Teri Deutsch, an economist, and they have one son, Jaxon. Readers can subscribe for free to his quarterly online exercise science newsletter by sending an email to **faithandfitness-subscribe@galileohealth.net**. Make sure to set your spam filters to allow you to receive emails from this address with PDF attachments.